TRANSFORMERS

VOLUME 7

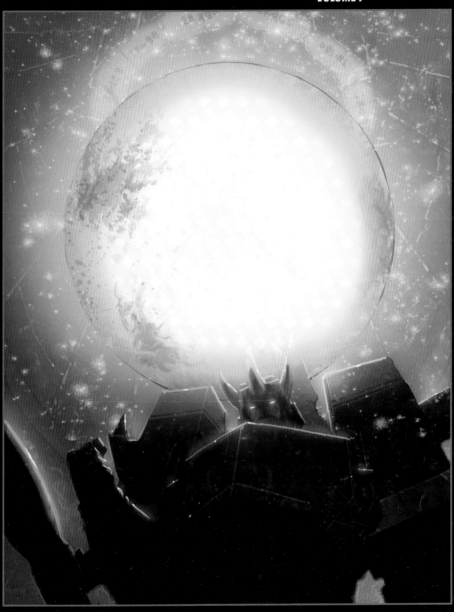

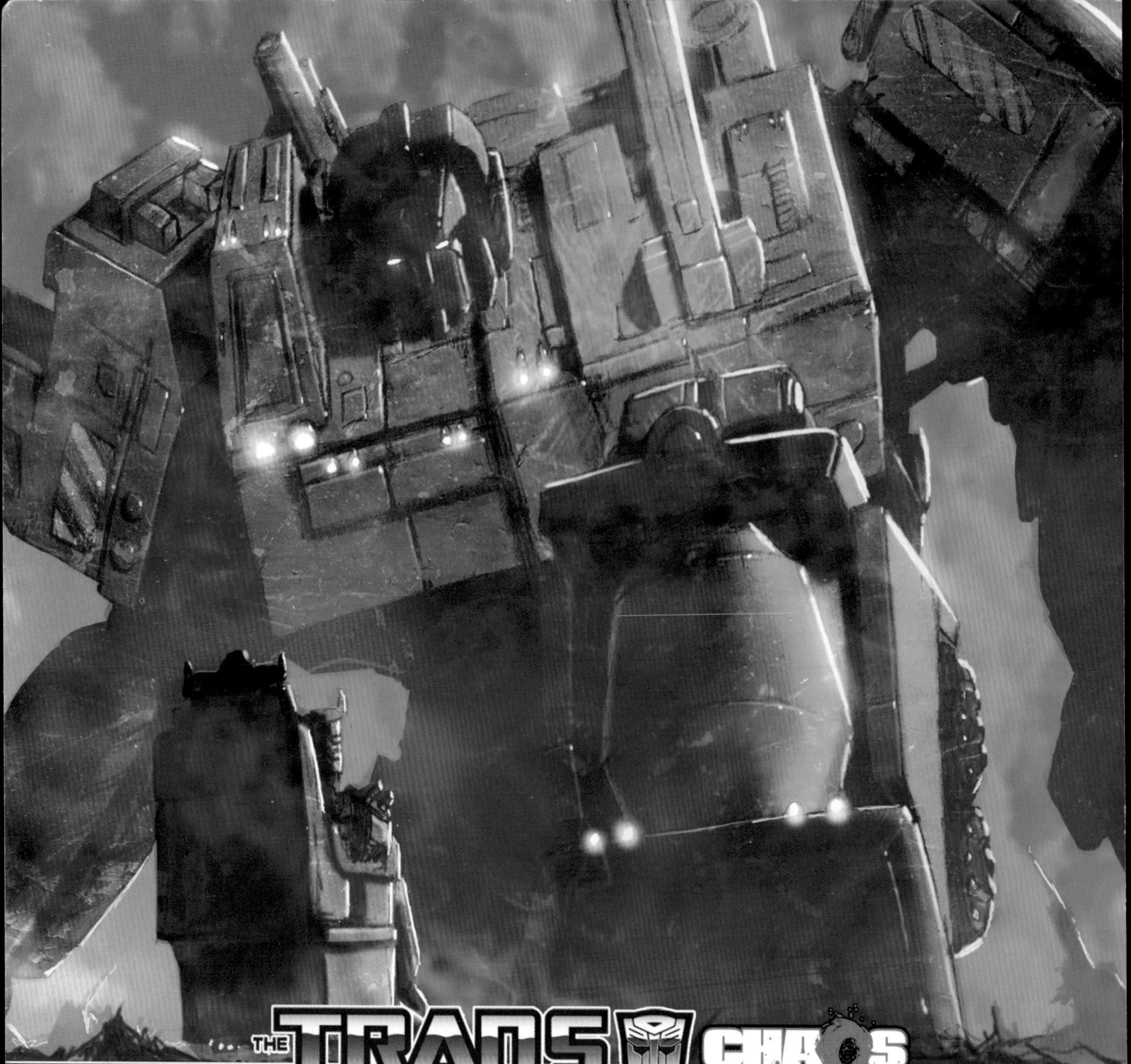

THE TRANSFORMERS CHAOS
VOLUME 7

Story by MIKE COSTA and JAMES ROBERTS
Script by MIKE COSTA
Art by LIVIO RAMONDELLI and CASEY COLLER (Issue #31)
Colors by LIVIO RAMONDELLI and JOANA LAFUENTE (Issue #31)
Letters by CHRIS MOWRY, NEIL UYETAKE, and SHAWN LEE
Series Edits by CARLOS GUZMAN and JOHN BARBER

Collection Edits by JUSTIN EISINGER and ALONZO SIMON
Collection Production by SHAWN LEE
Collection Cover by LIVIO RAMONDELLI

Special thanks to Hasbro's Aaron Archer, Rik Alvarez, Jerry Jivoin, Michael Verret, Ed Lane, Joe Furfaro, Jos Huxley and Michael Kelly for their invaluable assistance.

IDW founded by Ted Adams, Alex Garner, Kris Oprisko, and Robbie Robbins | International Rights Representative, Christine Meyer: christine@gfloystudio.com

ISBN: 978-1-61377-140-2

15 14 13 12 1 2 3 4

IDW® Licensed By: Hasbro

Ted Adams, CEO & Publisher
Greg Goldstein, President & COO
Robbie Robbins, EVP/Sr. Graphic Artist
Chris Ryall, Chief Creative Officer/Editor-in-Chief
Matthew Ruzicka, CPA, Chief Financial Officer
Alan Payne, VP of Sales

Originally published as THE TRANSFORMERS Issues #24, 26, 28, 30, and 31.

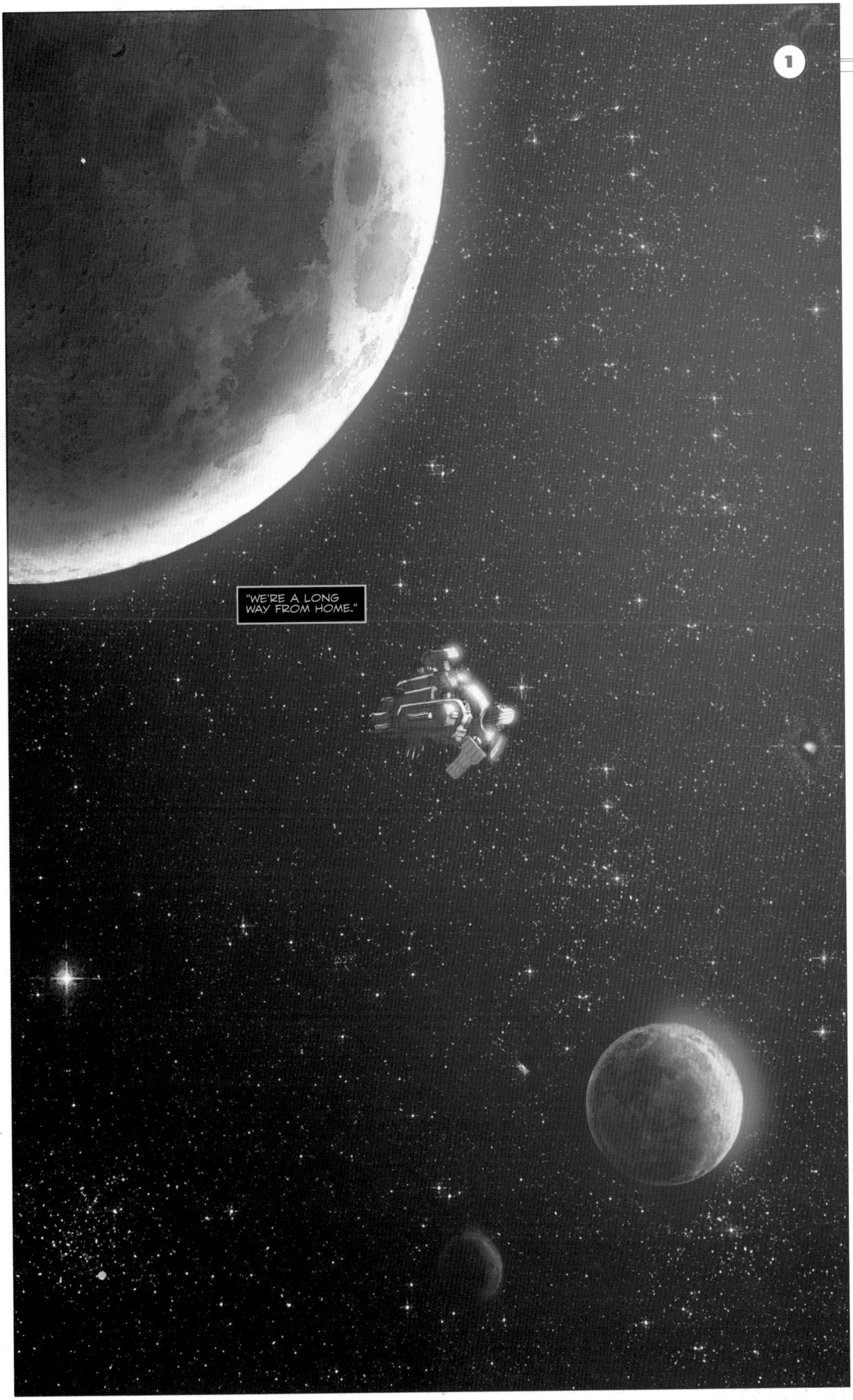
1
"WE'RE A LONG WAY FROM HOME."

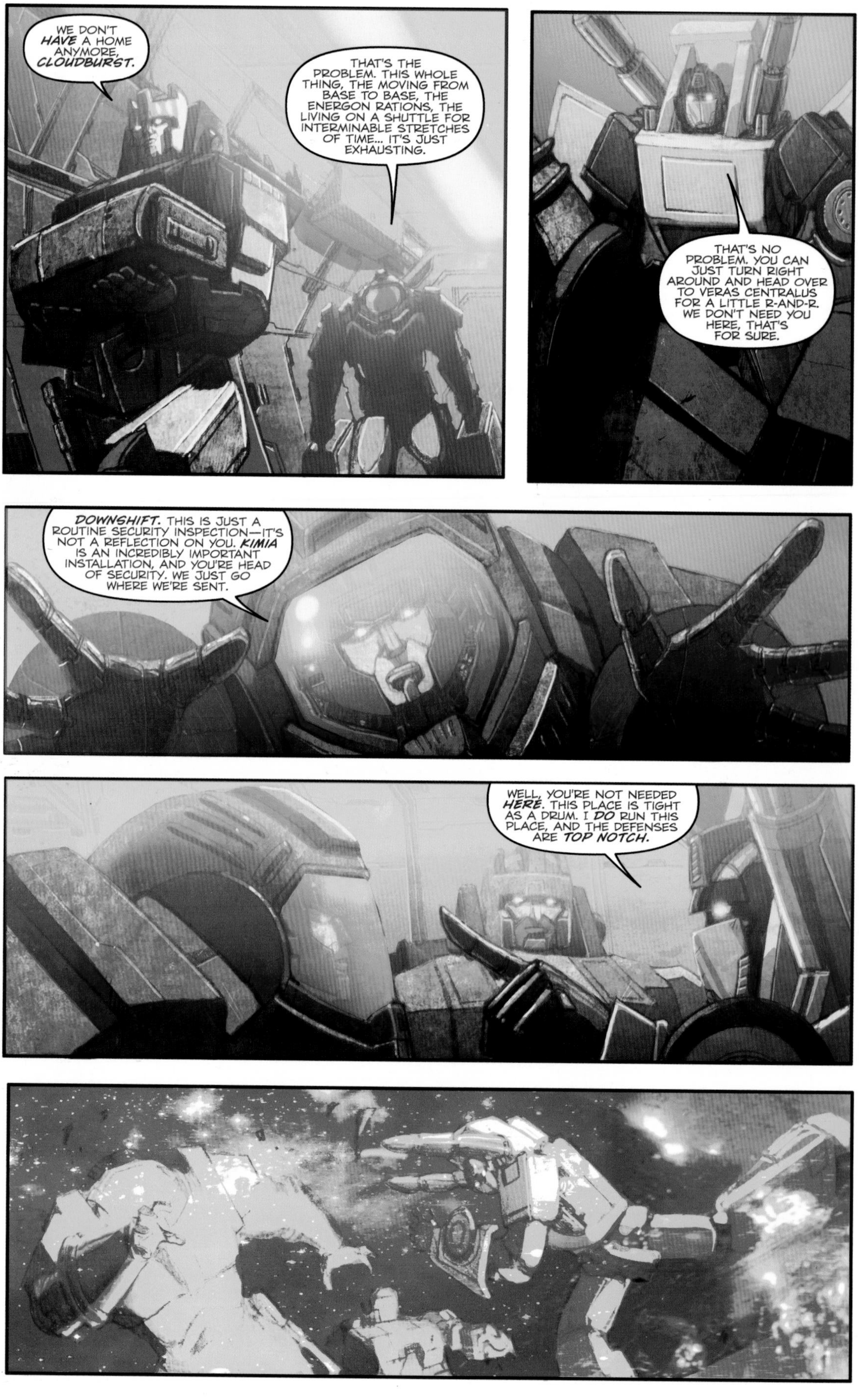

WE DON'T HAVE A HOME ANYMORE, CLOUDBURST.
THAT'S THE PROBLEM. THIS WHOLE THING, THE MOVING FROM BASE TO BASE, THE ENERGON RATIONS, THE LIVING ON A SHUTTLE FOR INTERMINABLE STRETCHES OF TIME... IT'S JUST EXHAUSTING.
THAT'S NO PROBLEM. YOU CAN JUST TURN RIGHT AROUND AND HEAD OVER TO VERAS CENTRALUS FOR A LITTLE R-AND-R. WE DON'T NEED YOU HERE, THAT'S FOR SURE.
DOWNSHIFT. THIS IS JUST A ROUTINE SECURITY INSPECTION—IT'S NOT A REFLECTION ON YOU. KIMIA IS AN INCREDIBLY IMPORTANT INSTALLATION, AND YOU'RE HEAD OF SECURITY. WE JUST GO WHERE WE'RE SENT.
WELL, YOU'RE NOT NEEDED HERE. THIS PLACE IS TIGHT AS A DRUM. I DO RUN THIS PLACE, AND THE DEFENSES ARE TOP NOTCH.

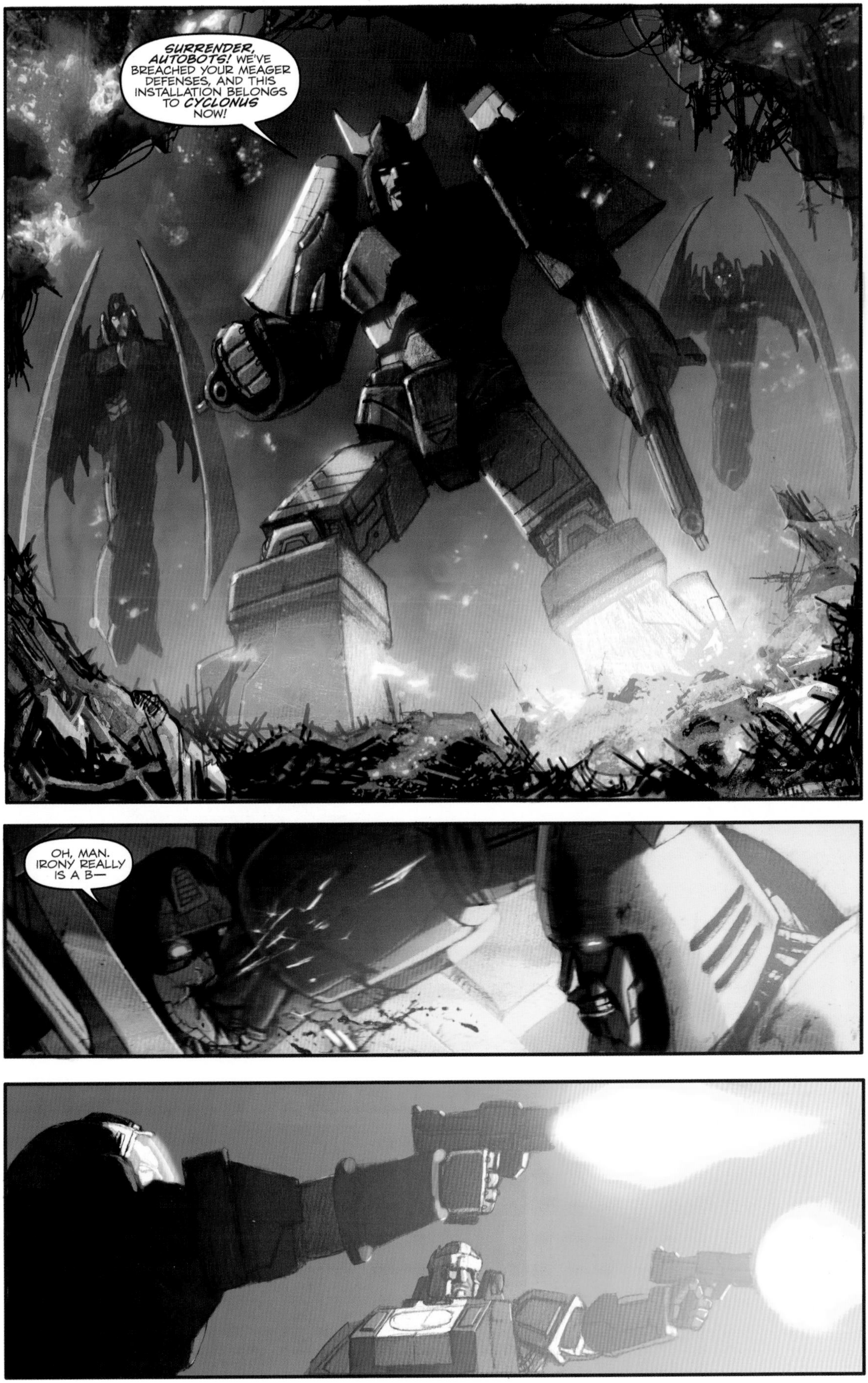
SURRENDER, AUTOBOTS! WE'VE BREACHED YOUR MEAGER DEFENSES, AND THIS INSTALLATION BELONGS TO CYCLONUS NOW!
OH, MAN. IRONY REALLY IS A B—

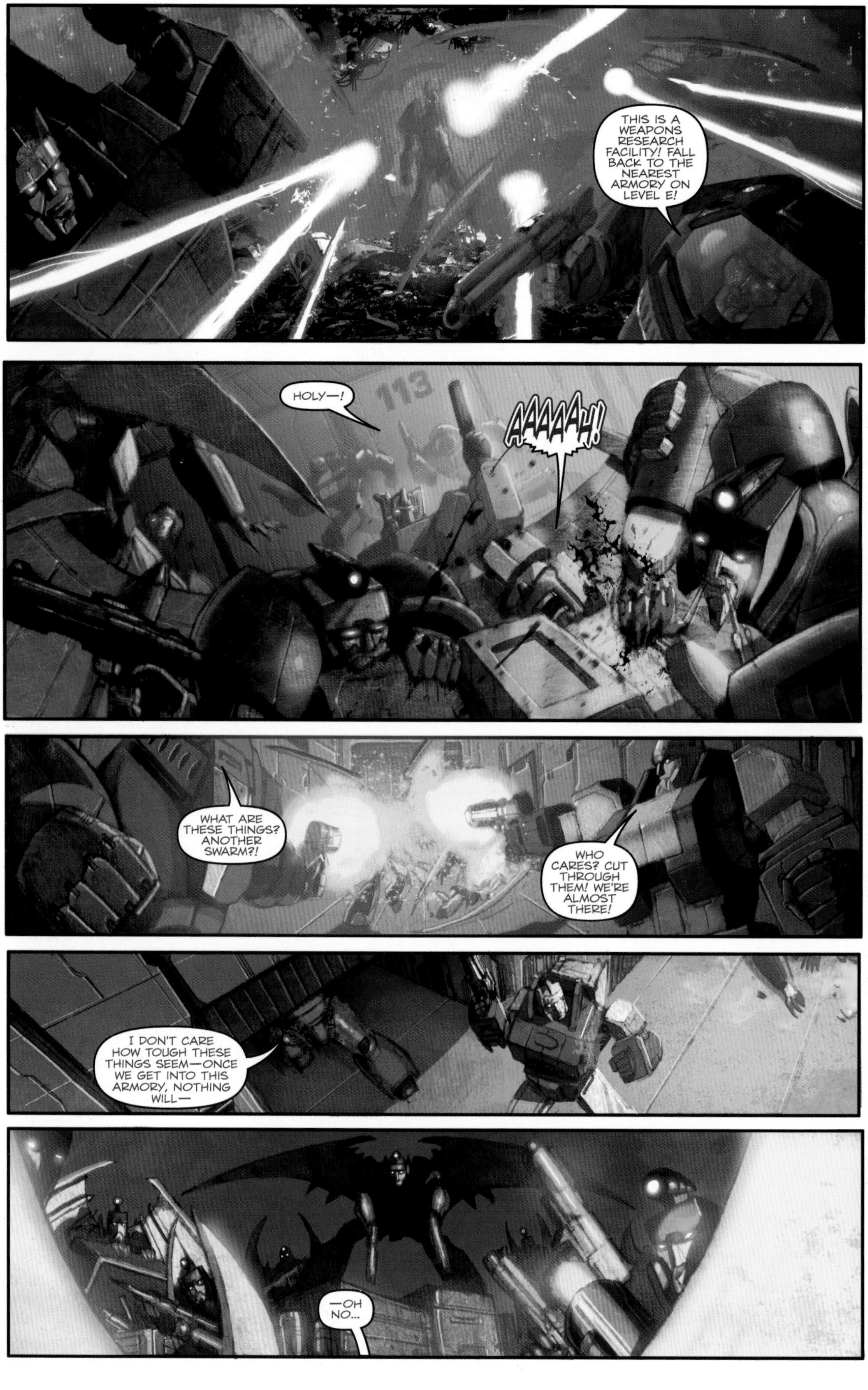
THIS IS A WEAPONS RESEARCH FACILITY! FALL BACK TO THE NEAREST ARMORY ON LEVEL E!
HOLY—!
AAAAAH!
WHAT ARE THESE THINGS? ANOTHER SWARM?!
WHO CARES? CUT THROUGH THEM! WE'RE ALMOST THERE!
I DON'T CARE HOW TOUGH THESE THINGS SEEM—ONCE WE GET INTO THIS ARMORY, NOTHING WILL—
—OH NO...

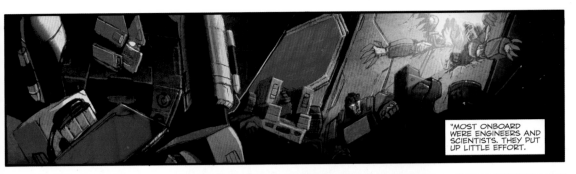

"MOST ONBOARD WERE ENGINEERS AND SCIENTISTS. THEY PUT UP LITTLE EFFORT.

"THE FEW SECURITY STAFF THAT WEREN'T CAUGHT ASLEEP COST US SOME NUMBERS... BUT WE HAVE THOSE TO SPARE.

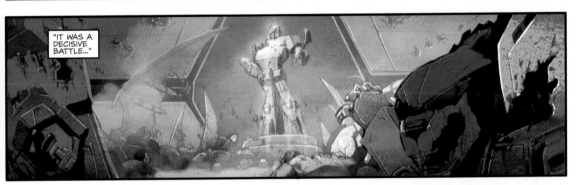

"IT WAS A DECISIVE BATTLE..."

...KIMIA IS *OURS.*

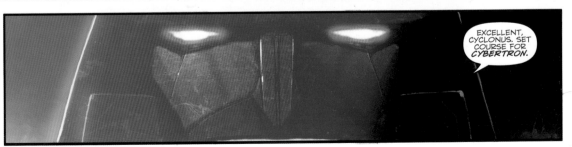

EXCELLENT, CYCLONUS. SET COURSE FOR *CYBERTRON.*

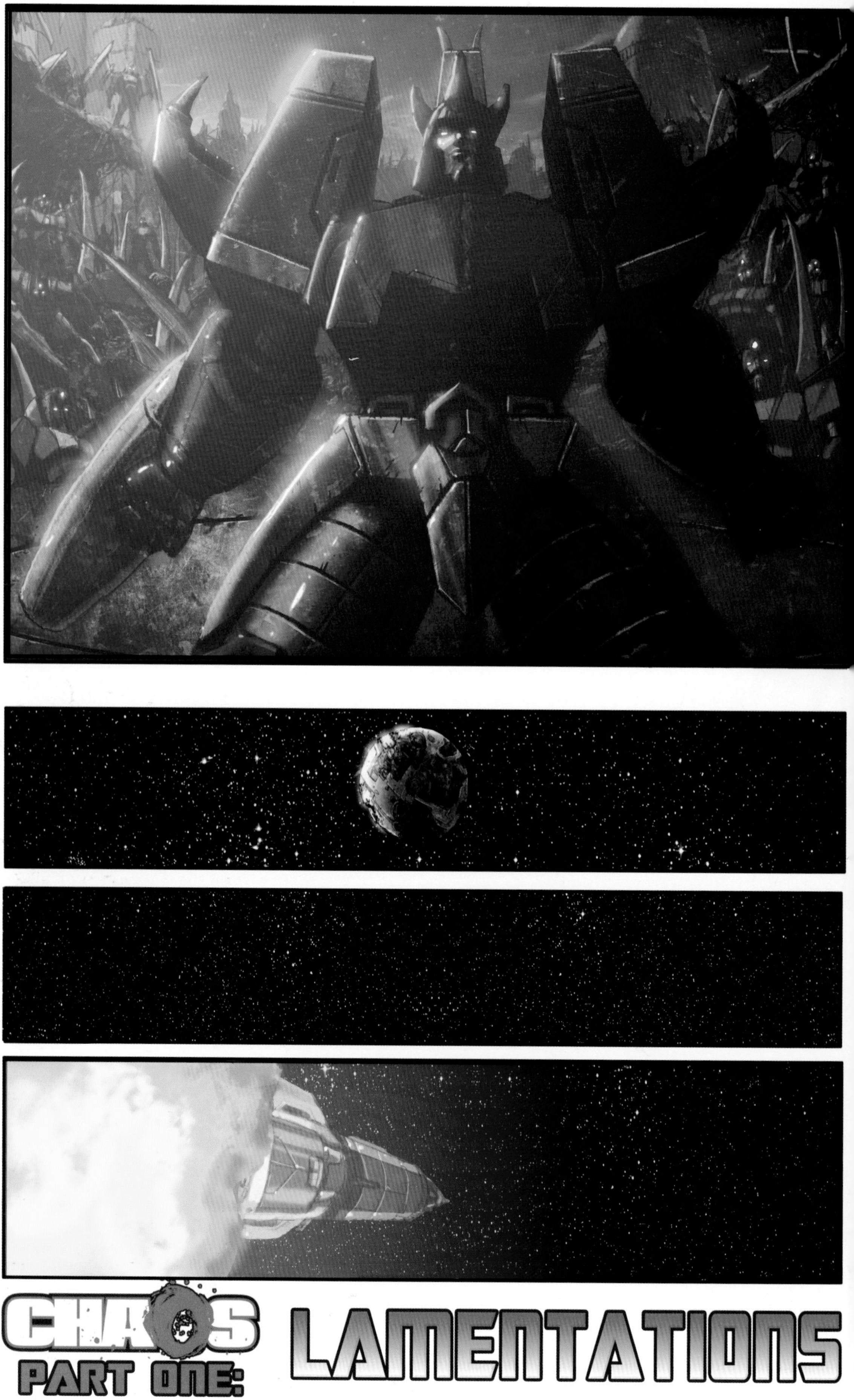

CHAOS PART ONE: LAMENTATIONS

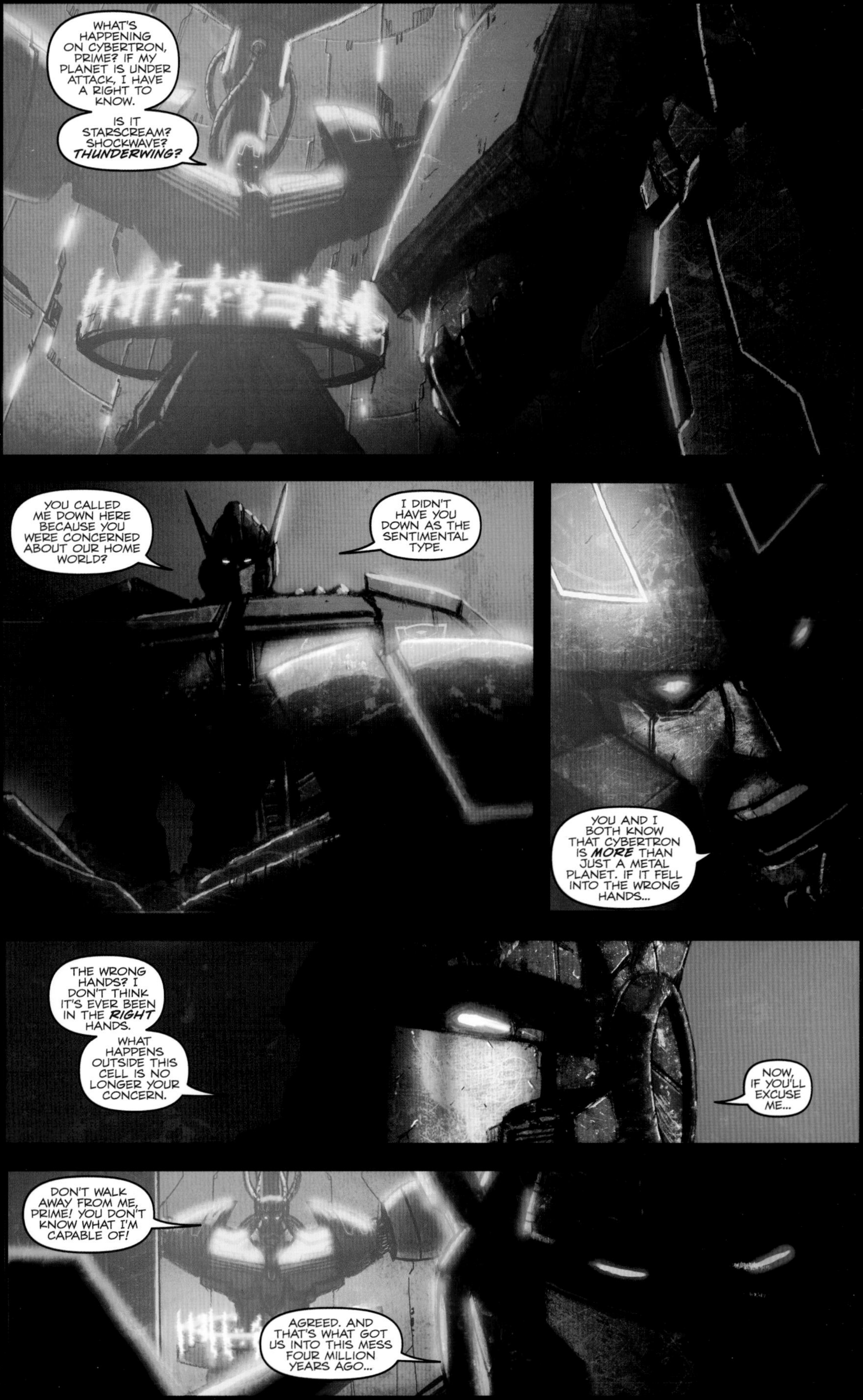
WHAT'S HAPPENING ON CYBERTRON, PRIME? IF MY PLANET IS UNDER ATTACK, I HAVE A RIGHT TO KNOW.
IS IT STARSCREAM? SHOCKWAVE? *THUNDERWING?*
YOU CALLED ME DOWN HERE BECAUSE YOU WERE CONCERNED ABOUT OUR HOME WORLD?
I DIDN'T HAVE YOU DOWN AS THE SENTIMENTAL TYPE.
YOU AND I BOTH KNOW THAT CYBERTRON IS *MORE* THAN JUST A METAL PLANET. IF IT FELL INTO THE WRONG HANDS...
THE WRONG HANDS? I DON'T THINK IT'S EVER BEEN IN THE *RIGHT* HANDS.
WHAT HAPPENS OUTSIDE THIS CELL IS NO LONGER YOUR CONCERN.
NOW, IF YOU'LL EXCUSE ME...
DON'T WALK AWAY FROM ME, PRIME! YOU DON'T KNOW WHAT I'M CAPABLE OF!
AGREED. AND THAT'S WHAT GOT US INTO THIS MESS FOUR MILLION YEARS AGO...

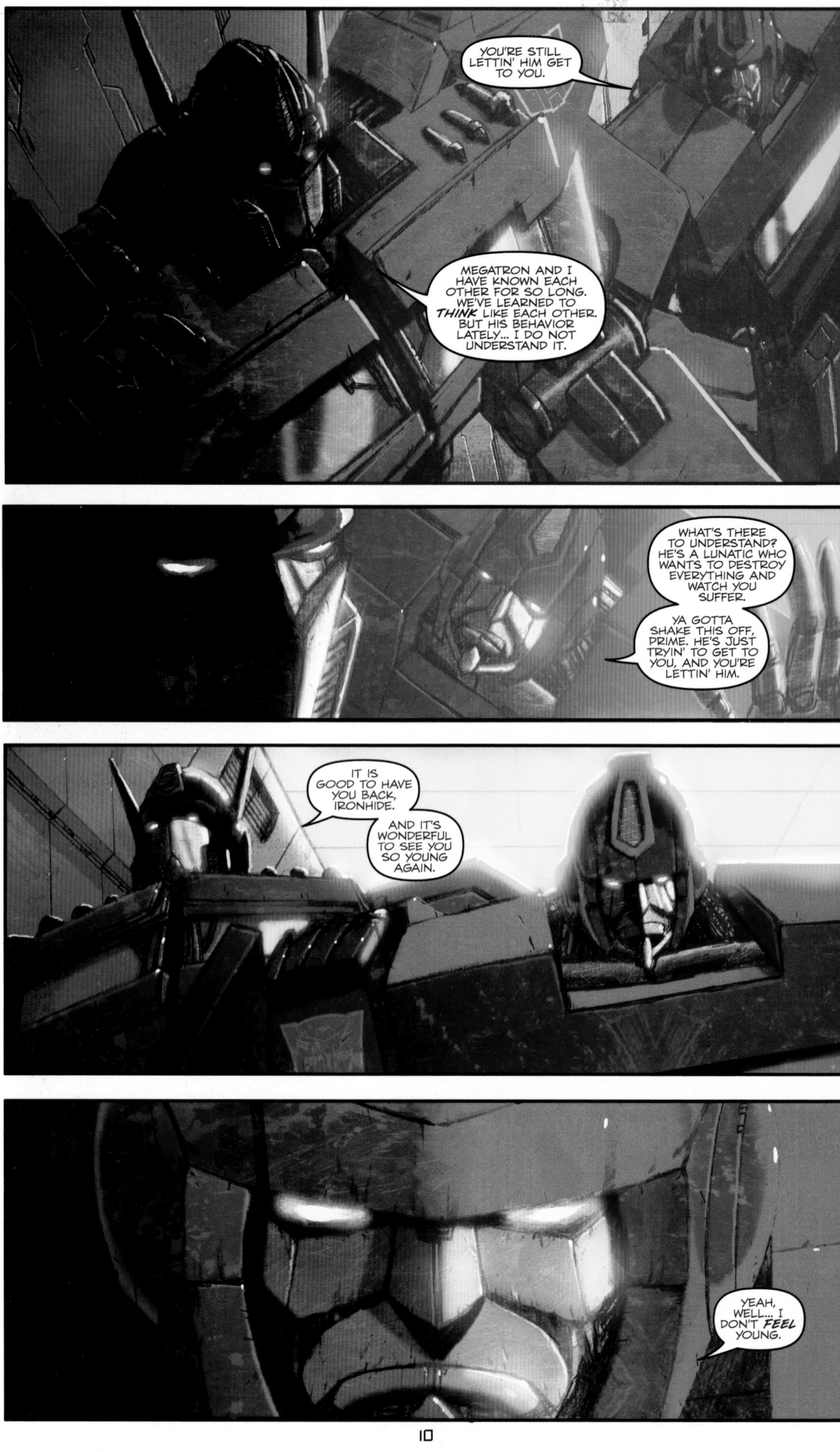
YOU'RE STILL LETTIN' HIM GET TO YOU.
MEGATRON AND I HAVE KNOWN EACH OTHER FOR SO LONG. WE'VE LEARNED TO *THINK* LIKE EACH OTHER. BUT HIS BEHAVIOR LATELY... I DO NOT UNDERSTAND IT.
WHAT'S THERE TO UNDERSTAND? HE'S A LUNATIC WHO WANTS TO DESTROY EVERYTHING AND WATCH YOU SUFFER.
YA GOTTA SHAKE THIS OFF, PRIME. HE'S JUST TRYIN' TO GET TO YOU, AND YOU'RE LETTIN' HIM.
IT IS GOOD TO HAVE YOU BACK, IRONHIDE.
AND IT'S WONDERFUL TO SEE YOU SO YOUNG AGAIN.
YEAH, WELL... I DON'T *FEEL* YOUNG.

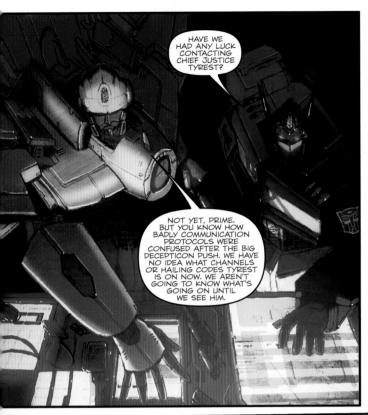

HAVE WE HAD ANY LUCK CONTACTING CHIEF JUSTICE TYREST?

NOT YET, PRIME. BUT YOU KNOW HOW BADLY COMMUNICATION PROTOCOLS WERE CONFUSED AFTER THE BIG DECEPTICON PUSH. WE HAVE NO IDEA WHAT CHANNELS OR HAILING CODES TYREST IS ON NOW. WE AREN'T GOING TO KNOW WHAT'S GOING ON UNTIL WE SEE HIM.

KEEP TRYING.

...SO THEN, YOU KNOW, I SLUGGED HIM.

HA HA HA! YOU'RE LYING! NO WAY THAT HAPPENED!

HEY, WELL, MAYBE I GOT A LITTLE TOO HOT UNDER THE CHASSIS BUT... WHADDAYA WANT? GUY WAS MAKING FUNNA ME.

HA HA HA!

INSANE!

YEAH. THAT WAS REALLY SOMETHING.

YOU GUYS SHOULD HAVE HEARD THE CRAZY THINGS HE WAS BABBLING WHEN HE WAS PATCHING ME UP. HE WAS SAYIN—

UH HUH.

SO, IRONHIDE. HOW CAN YOU BE *SURE* IT WAS ALPHA TRION? I MEAN... HOW DO YOU KNOW IT WASN'T BLUDGEON IN DISGUISE OR SOMETHING?

ARE YOU SERIOUS? THAT'S THE *DUMBEST* THING I'VE EVER HEARD.

HA HA HA HA!

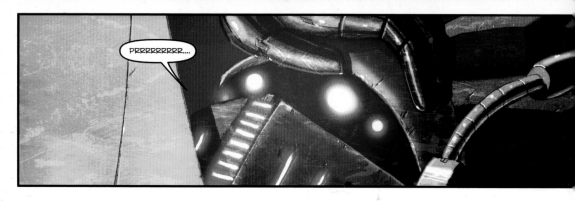

PRRRRRRRRR....

BEGGIN' YER PARDON, SIRS, BUT RODIMUS 'AS SENT ME TO SAY THAT WE'VE ARRIVED, AND 'EES GETTIN' A MESSAGE FROM THE SURFACE.

WHAT? I'VE BEEN MONITORING COMMUNICATIONS THIS WHOLE TIME. WE HAVEN'T RECEIVED ANYTHING.

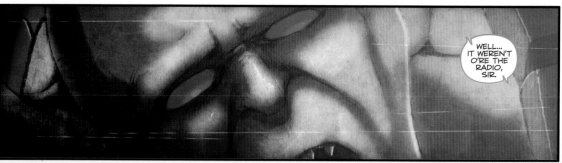

WELL... IT WEREN'T O'RE THE RADIO, SIR.

IT'S ACTUALLY PRETTY IMPRESSIVE.

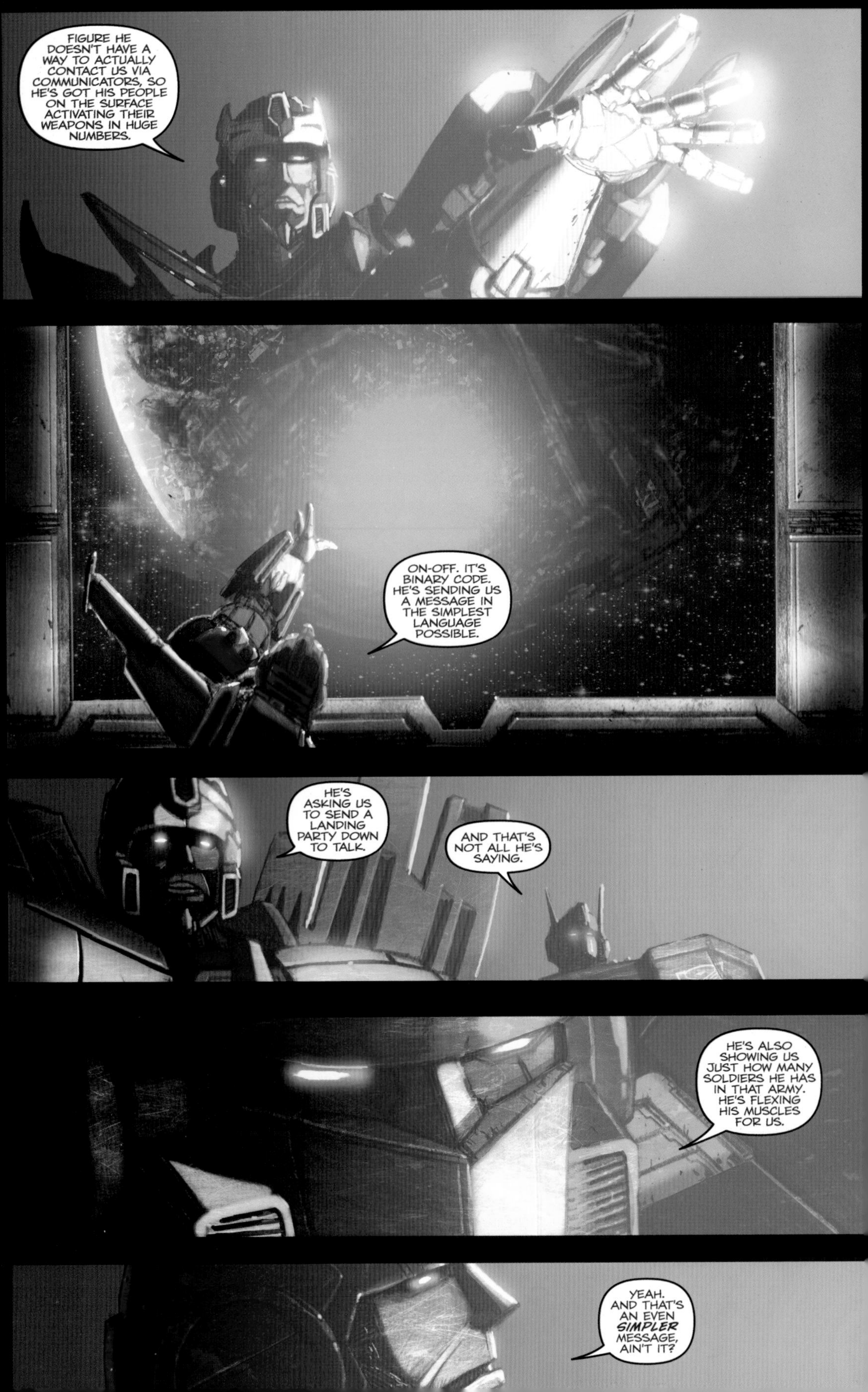
FIGURE HE DOESN'T HAVE A WAY TO ACTUALLY CONTACT US VIA COMMUNICATORS, SO HE'S GOT HIS PEOPLE ON THE SURFACE ACTIVATING THEIR WEAPONS IN HUGE NUMBERS.
ON-OFF. IT'S BINARY CODE. HE'S SENDING US A MESSAGE IN THE SIMPLEST LANGUAGE POSSIBLE.
HE'S ASKING US TO SEND A LANDING PARTY DOWN TO TALK.
AND THAT'S NOT ALL HE'S SAYING.
HE'S ALSO SHOWING US JUST HOW MANY SOLDIERS HE HAS IN THAT ARMY. HE'S FLEXING HIS MUSCLES FOR US.
YEAH. AND THAT'S AN EVEN *SIMPLER* MESSAGE, AIN'T IT?

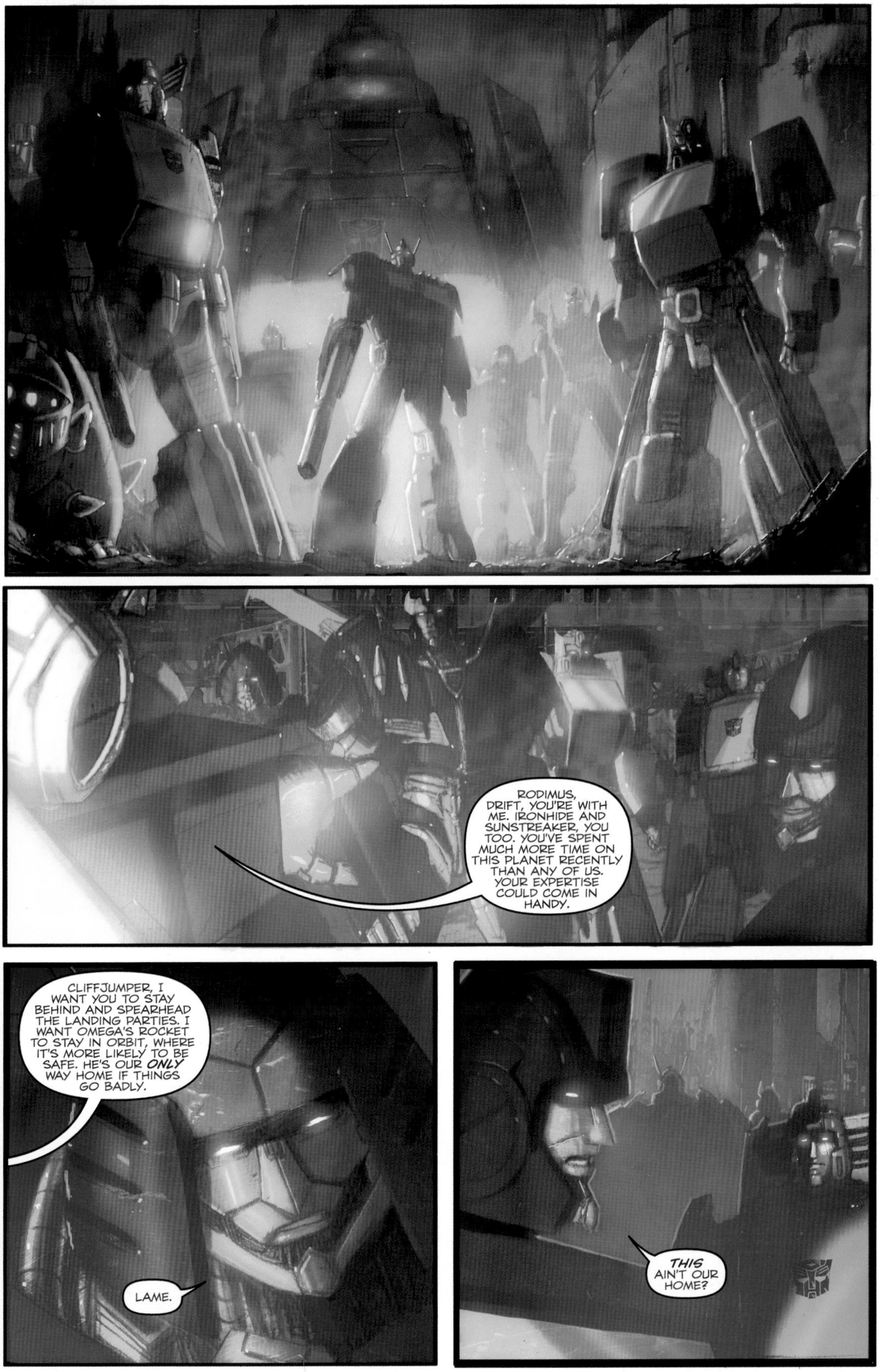
RODIMUS, DRIFT, YOU'RE WITH ME. IRONHIDE AND SUNSTREAKER, YOU TOO. YOU'VE SPENT MUCH MORE TIME ON THIS PLANET RECENTLY THAN ANY OF US. YOUR EXPERTISE COULD COME IN HANDY.
CLIFFJUMPER, I WANT YOU TO STAY BEHIND AND SPEARHEAD THE LANDING PARTIES. I WANT OMEGA'S ROCKET TO STAY IN ORBIT, WHERE IT'S MORE LIKELY TO BE SAFE. HE'S OUR ***ONLY*** WAY HOME IF THINGS GO BADLY.
LAME.
THIS AIN'T OUR HOME?

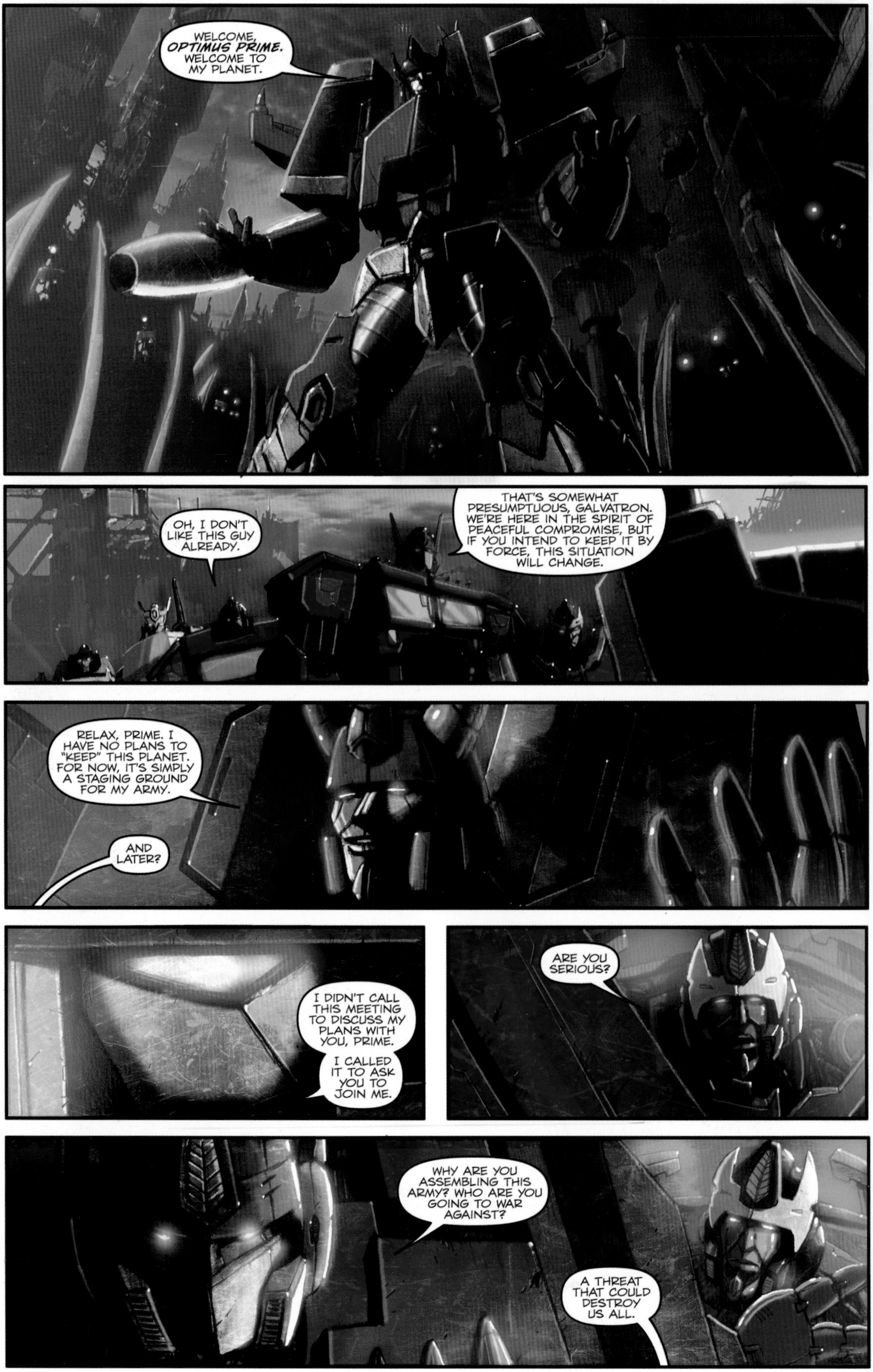
WELCOME, *OPTIMUS PRIME.* WELCOME TO MY PLANET.
OH, I DON'T LIKE THIS GUY ALREADY.
THAT'S SOMEWHAT PRESUMPTUOUS, GALVATRON. WE'RE HERE IN THE SPIRIT OF PEACEFUL COMPROMISE, BUT IF YOU INTEND TO KEEP IT BY FORCE, THIS SITUATION WILL CHANGE.
RELAX, PRIME. I HAVE NO PLANS TO "KEEP" THIS PLANET. FOR NOW, IT'S SIMPLY A STAGING GROUND FOR MY ARMY.
AND LATER?
I DIDN'T CALL THIS MEETING TO DISCUSS MY PLANS WITH YOU, PRIME.
I CALLED IT TO ASK YOU TO JOIN ME.
ARE YOU SERIOUS?
WHY ARE YOU ASSEMBLING THIS ARMY? WHO ARE YOU GOING TO WAR AGAINST?
A THREAT THAT COULD DESTROY US ALL.

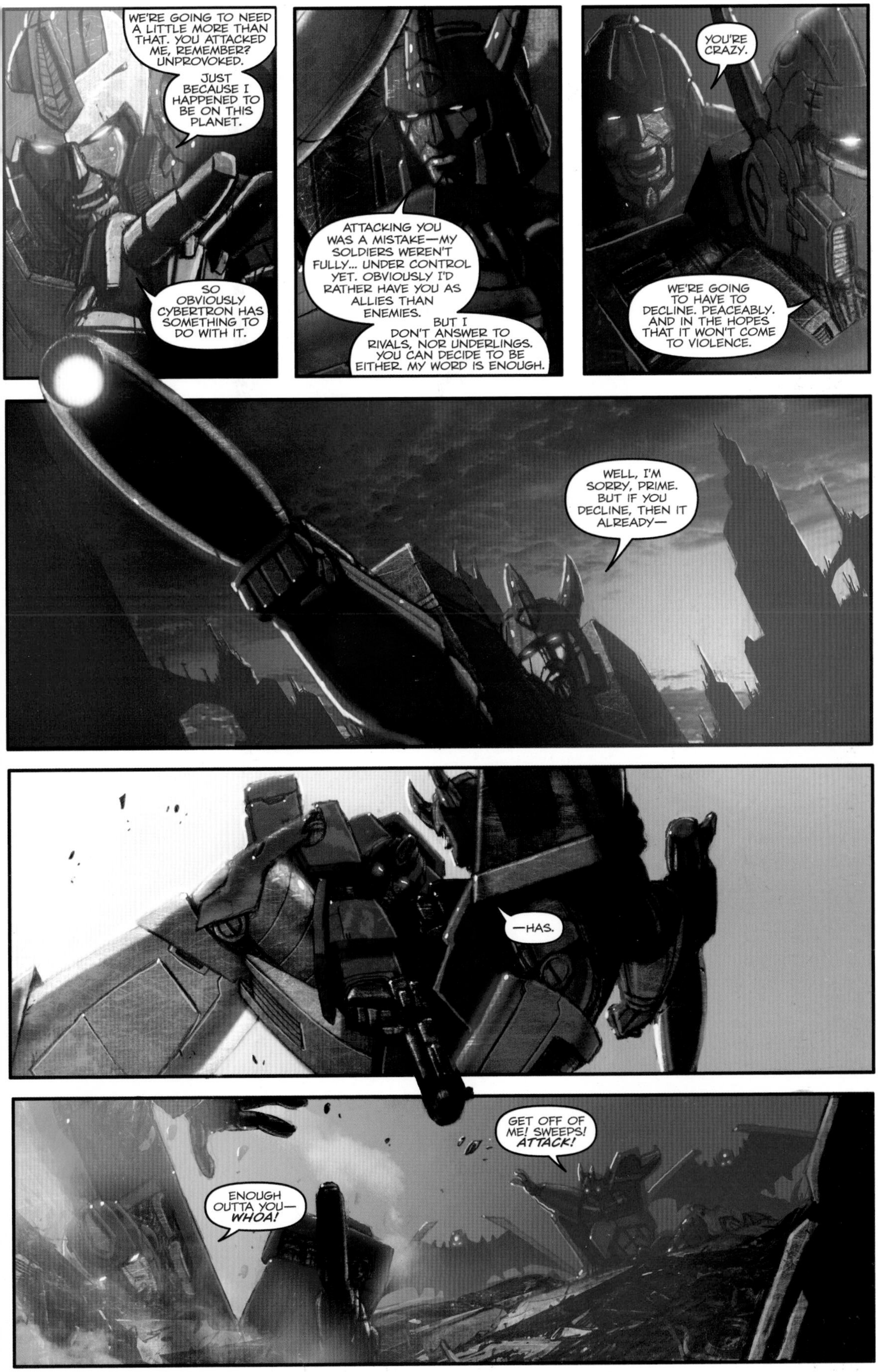
WE'RE GOING TO NEED A LITTLE MORE THAN THAT. YOU ATTACKED ME, REMEMBER? UNPROVOKED.
JUST BECAUSE I HAPPENED TO BE ON THIS PLANET.
SO OBVIOUSLY CYBERTRON HAS SOMETHING TO DO WITH IT.
ATTACKING YOU WAS A MISTAKE—MY SOLDIERS WEREN'T FULLY... UNDER CONTROL YET. OBVIOUSLY I'D RATHER HAVE YOU AS ALLIES THAN ENEMIES.
BUT I DON'T ANSWER TO RIVALS, NOR UNDERLINGS. YOU CAN DECIDE TO BE EITHER. MY WORD IS ENOUGH.
YOU'RE CRAZY.
WE'RE GOING TO HAVE TO DECLINE. PEACEABLY. AND IN THE HOPES THAT IT WON'T COME TO VIOLENCE.
WELL, I'M SORRY, PRIME. BUT IF YOU DECLINE, THEN IT ALREADY—
—HAS.
GET OFF OF ME! SWEEPS! *ATTACK!*
ENOUGH OUTTA YOU— *WHOA!*

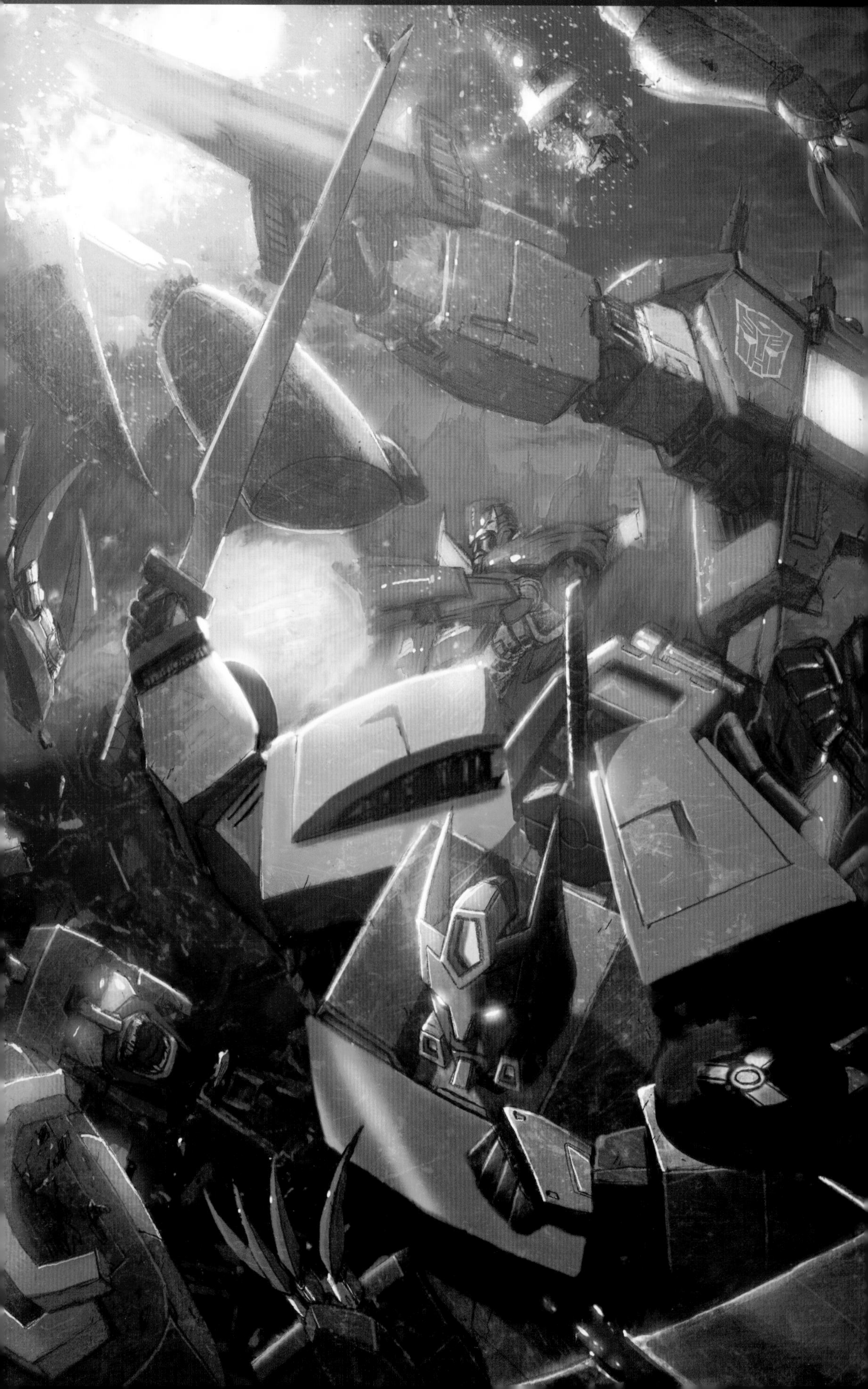

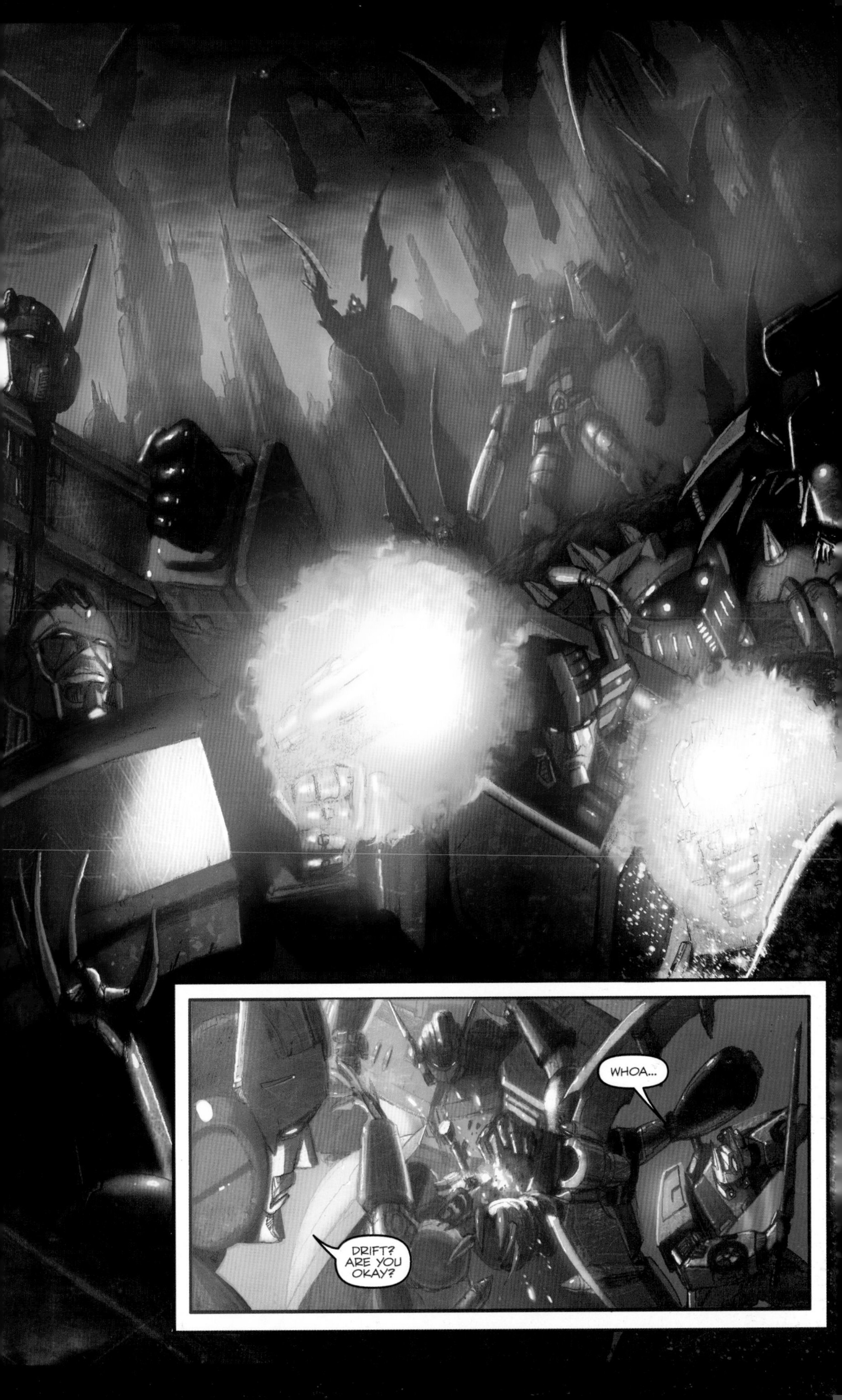
WHOA...
DRIFT? ARE YOU OKAY?

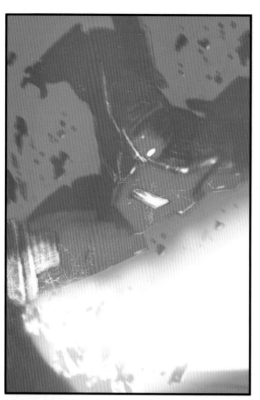

ARROGANT AUTOBOTS. YOU WILL *NOT* STOP ME. I HAVE AN *ARMY.*

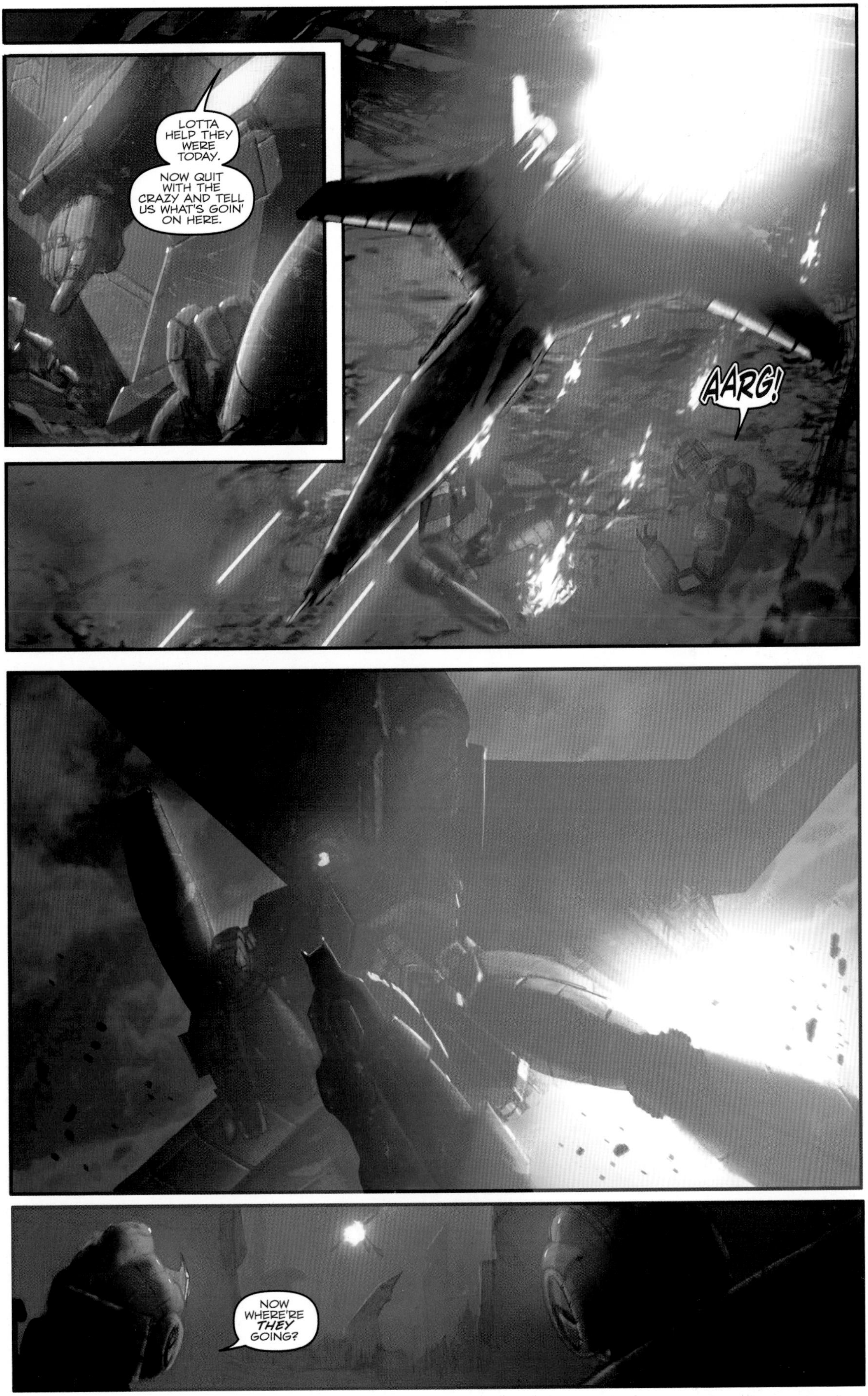

LOTTA HELP THEY WERE TODAY.
NOW QUIT WITH THE CRAZY AND TELL US WHAT'S GOIN' ON HERE.
AARG!
NOW WHERE'RE *THEY* GOING?

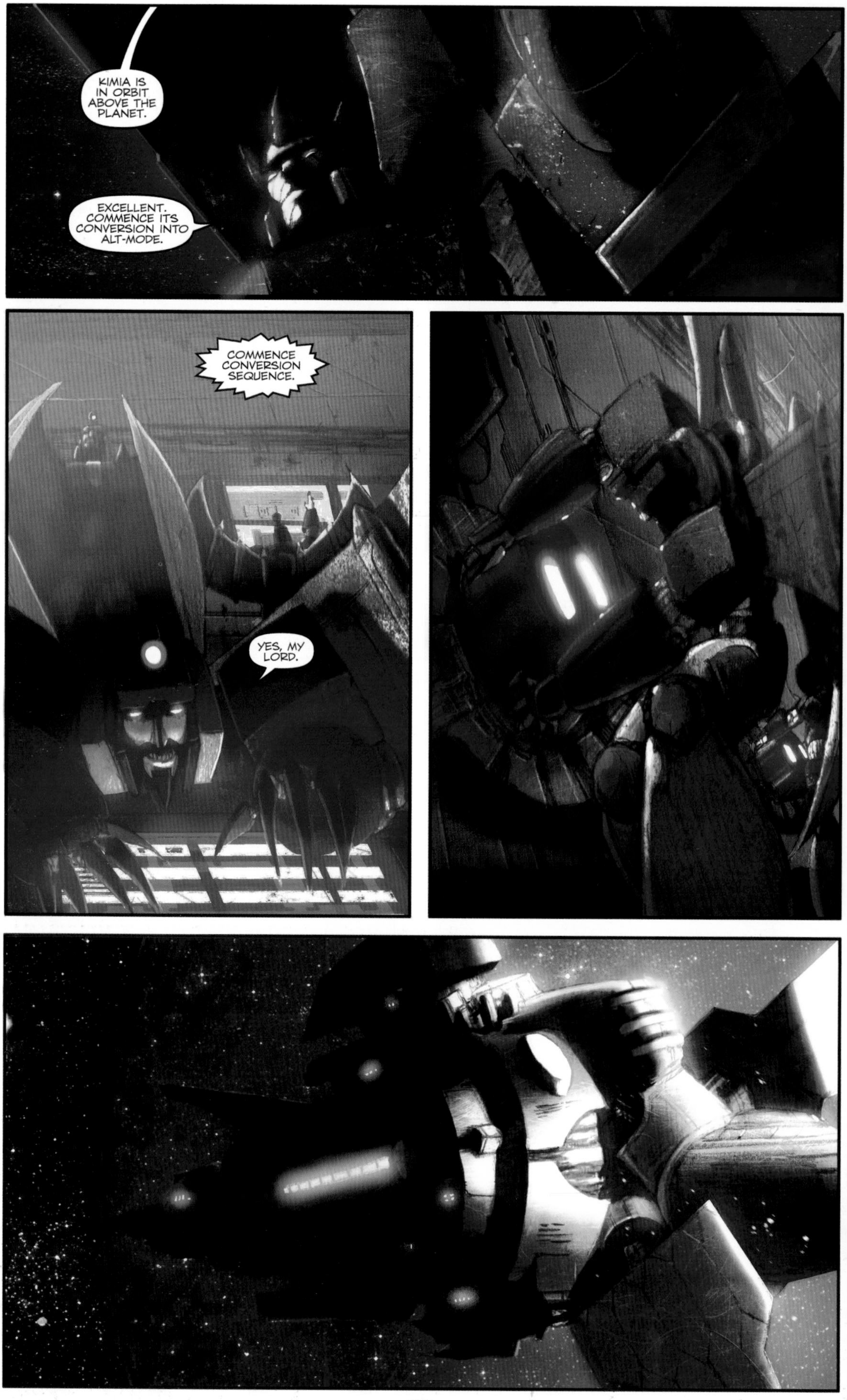

KIMIA IS IN ORBIT ABOVE THE PLANET.
EXCELLENT. COMMENCE ITS CONVERSION INTO ALT-MODE.
COMMENCE CONVERSION SEQUENCE.
YES, MY LORD.

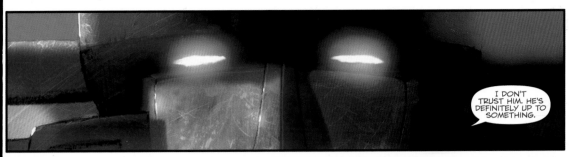

I DON'T TRUST HIM. HE'S DEFINITELY UP TO SOMETHING.

OH. WELL. *YOU* DON'T TRUST HIM. I GUESS YOU'D BE AN EXPERT ON THAT, HUH?

ENOUGH, CLIFFJUMPER. I WON'T HEAR ANYMORE OF THAT. SUNSTREAKER IS RIGHT. GALVATRON MAY ACT INSANE—HE MAY ACTUALLY *BE* INSANE—BUT HE IS VERY CUNNING.

HE OBVIOUSLY HAS SOME PLAN FOR THIS PLANET THAT HE DOESN'T WANT US TO KNOW ABOUT. HE MAY HAVE BEEN KEEPING IT EVEN FROM HIS OWN SOLDIERS.

WELL... WHY DO WE JUST *ASSUME* THAT?

WHAT DO YOU MEAN?

HE'S OBVIOUSLY ASSEMBLED AN ARMY FOR SOME REASON, AND IT'S JUST AS OBVIOUSLY NOT TO FIGHT US OR ANY OTHER AUTOBOTS, OR HE WOULDN'T HAVE ASKED US TO JOIN.

SO... WHAT IF HE'S TELLING THE TRUTH? MY INSTINCTS ARE TELLING ME TO TRUST HIM.

ARE YOU NUTS? THAT'S GALVATRON. HAVE YOU NOT BEEN PAYING A—EH?

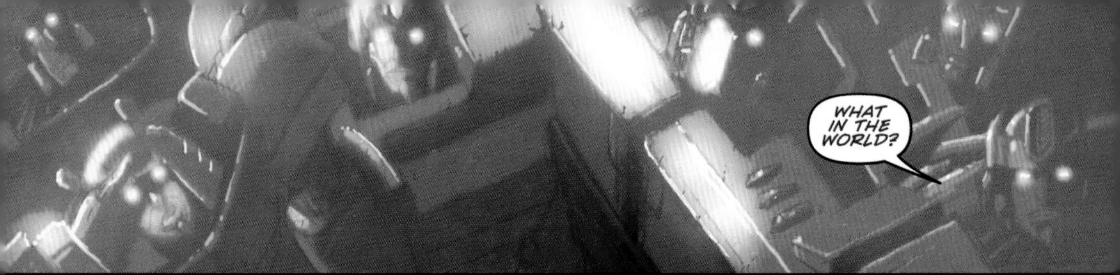
WHAT IN THE WORLD?

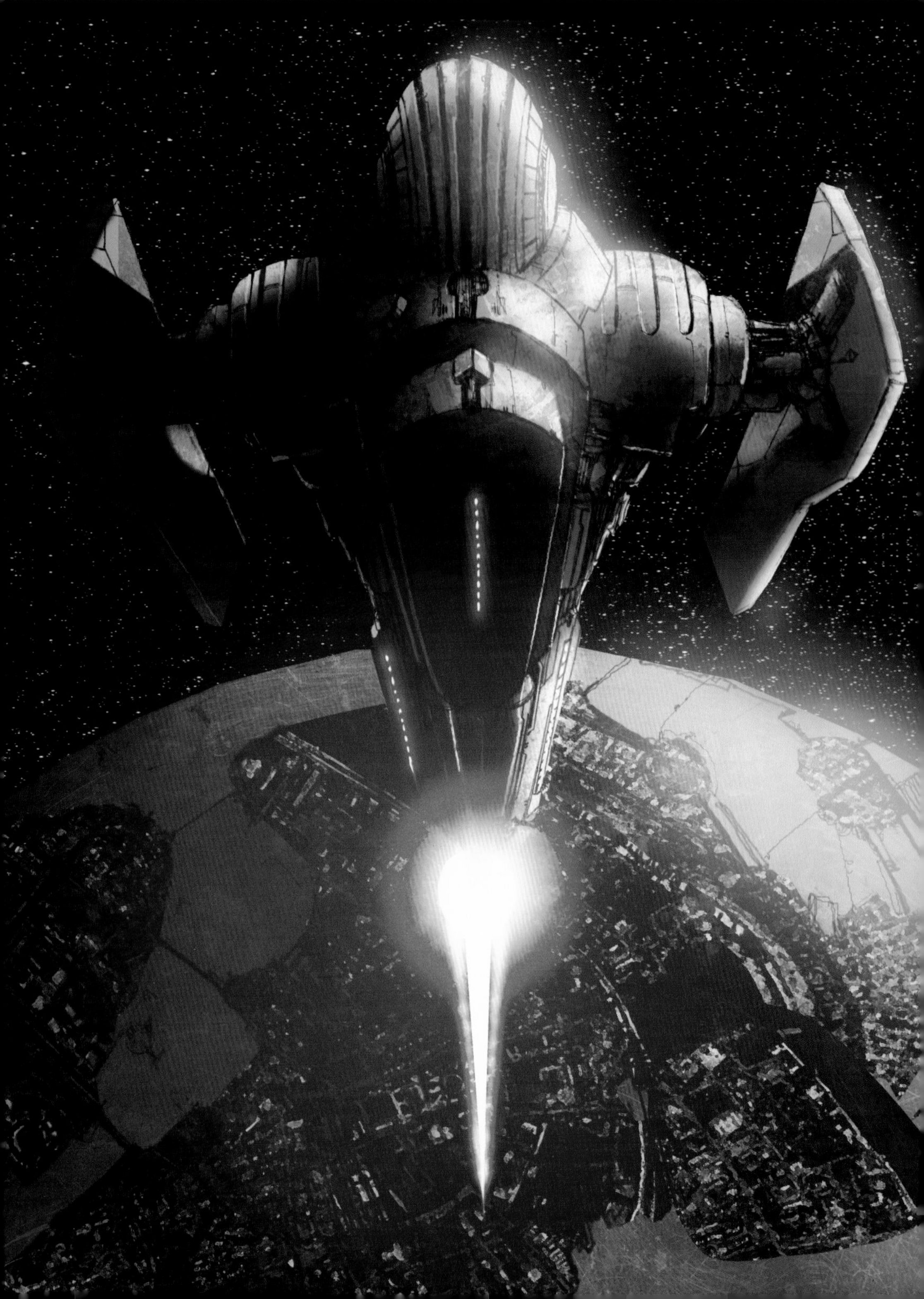

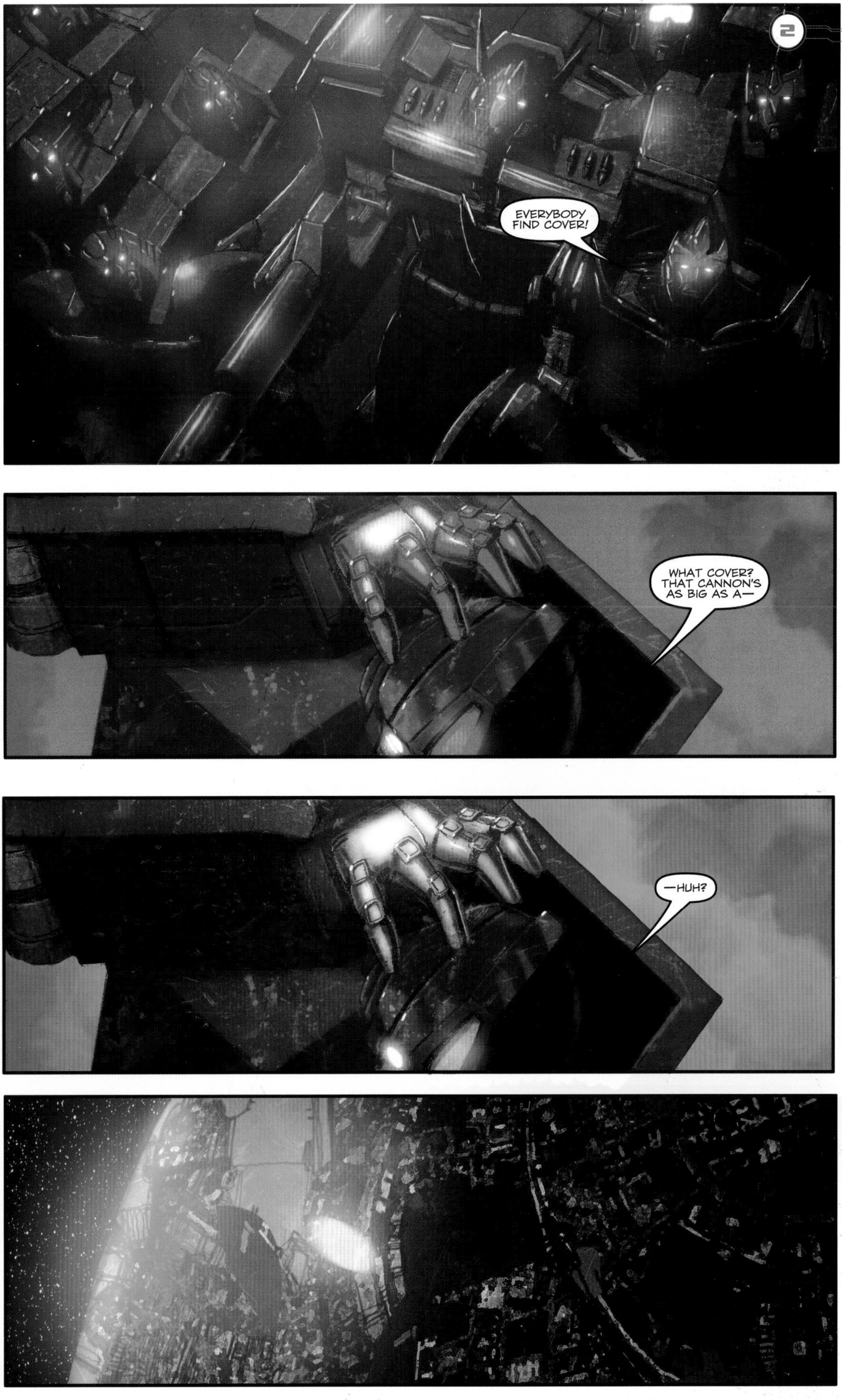
EVERYBODY FIND COVER!
WHAT COVER? THAT CANNON'S AS BIG AS A—
—HUH?

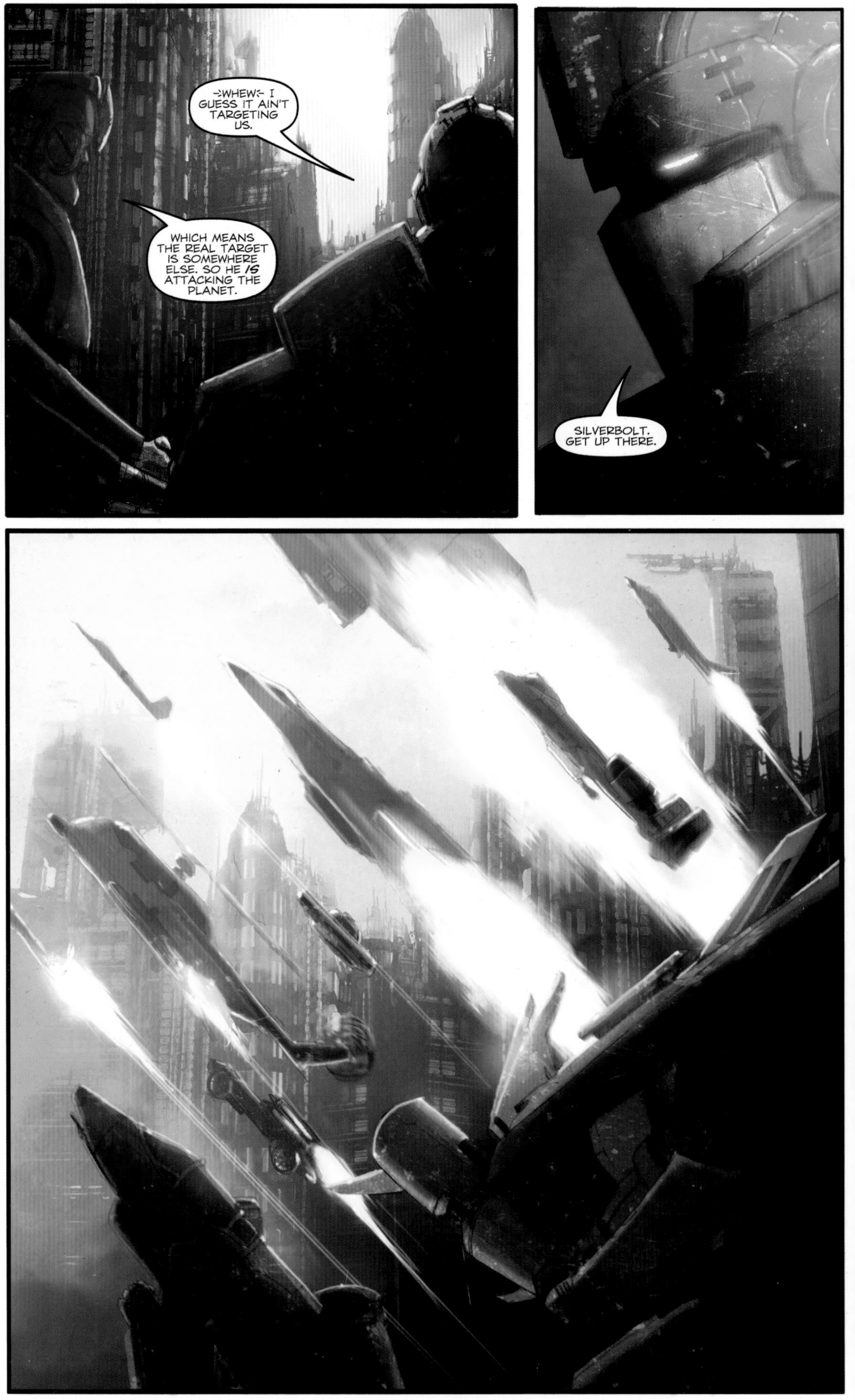
-WHEW- I GUESS IT AIN'T TARGETING US.
WHICH MEANS THE REAL TARGET IS SOMEWHERE ELSE. SO HE *IS* ATTACKING THE PLANET.
SILVERBOLT. GET UP THERE.

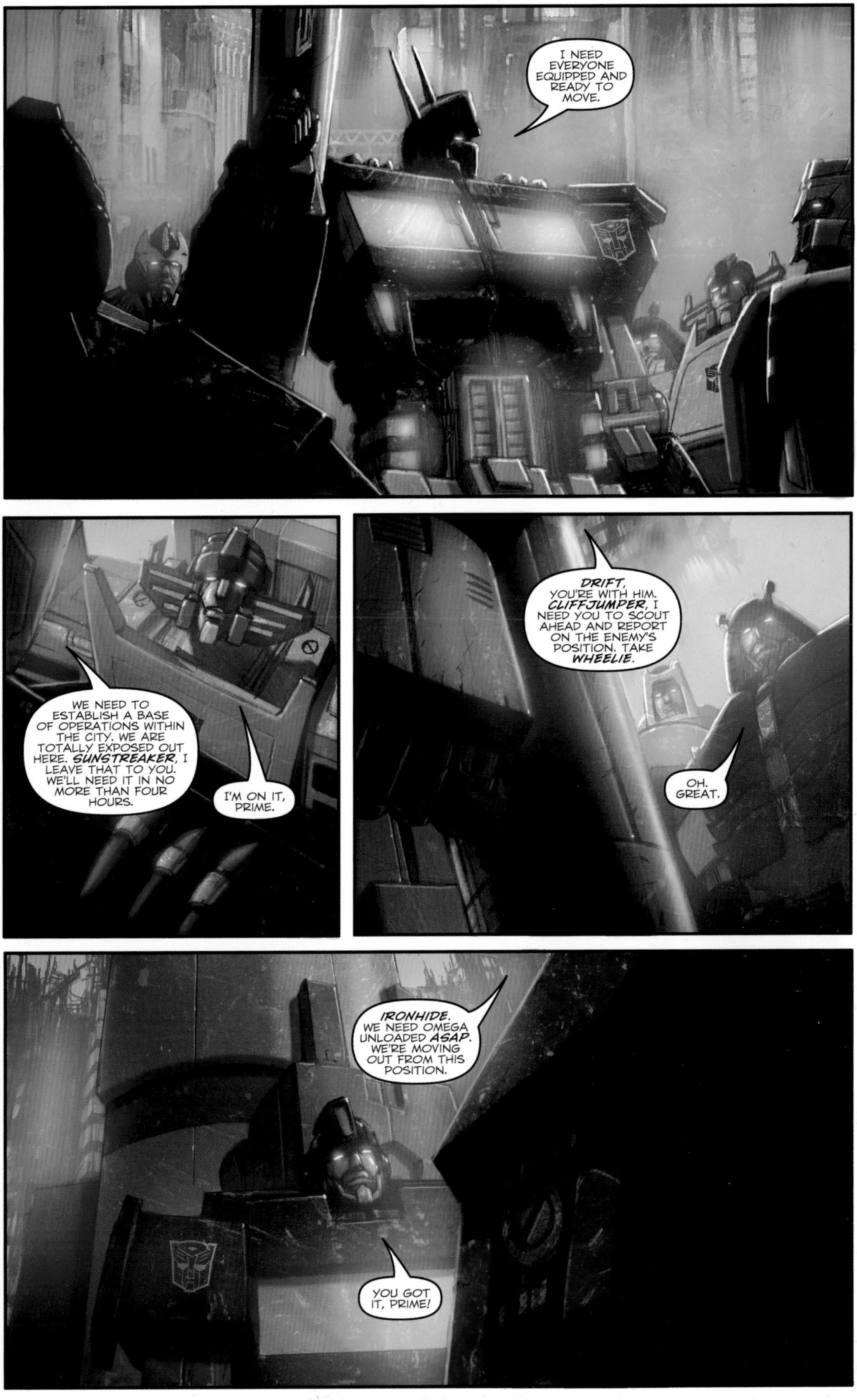
I NEED EVERYONE EQUIPPED AND READY TO MOVE.
WE NEED TO ESTABLISH A BASE OF OPERATIONS WITHIN THE CITY. WE ARE TOTALLY EXPOSED OUT HERE. *SUNSTREAKER*, I LEAVE THAT TO YOU. WE'LL NEED IT IN NO MORE THAN FOUR HOURS.
I'M ON IT, PRIME.
DRIFT, YOU'RE WITH HIM. *CLIFFJUMPER*, I NEED YOU TO SCOUT AHEAD AND REPORT ON THE ENEMY'S POSITION. TAKE *WHEELIE*.
OH. GREAT.
IRONHIDE. WE NEED OMEGA UNLOADED *ASAP*. WE'RE MOVING OUT FROM THIS POSITION.
YOU GOT IT, PRIME!

PRIME, I THINK I'D BE BEST UTILIZED IN ORBIT.

HOW SO?

WE'VE GOT A BATTLE WITH TWO FRONTS NOW. IT'D BE BETTER TO ESTABLISH A COMMAND POST FOR EACH OF THEM.

I'LL TAKE OMEGA UP WHEN YOU'RE FINISHED UNLOADING. I CAN OVERSEE THE ATTACK ON KIMIA AND ALSO GIVE YOU INTELLIGENCE ON GALVATRON'S MOVEMENTS THAT SILVERBOLT WON'T BE ABLE TO COLLECT IN THE MIDDLE OF AN ENGAGEMENT.

THAT'S GOOD THINKING. DO IT.

TRAILBREAKER, YOU'RE WITH ME.

WHY DO YOU NEED ME?

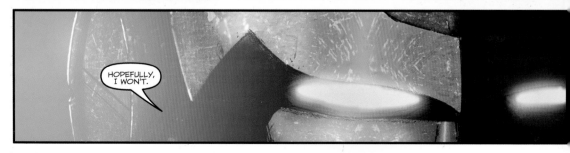

HOPEFULLY, I WON'T.

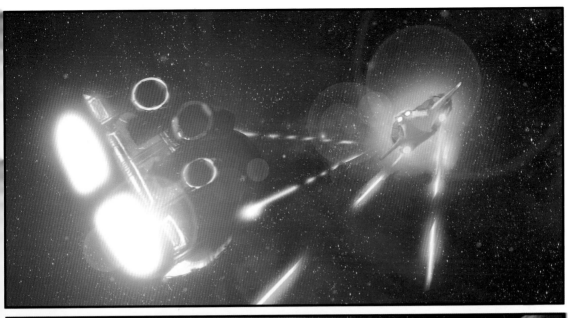

GREAT SHOOTING, SILVERBOLT. TRAILBREAKER AND I ARE GOING TO BE YOUR EYES UP HERE, SO YOU JUST FOCUS ON BLASTING DECEPTICONS OUT OF THE SKY.

GLAD TO HAVE YOU, RODIMUS.

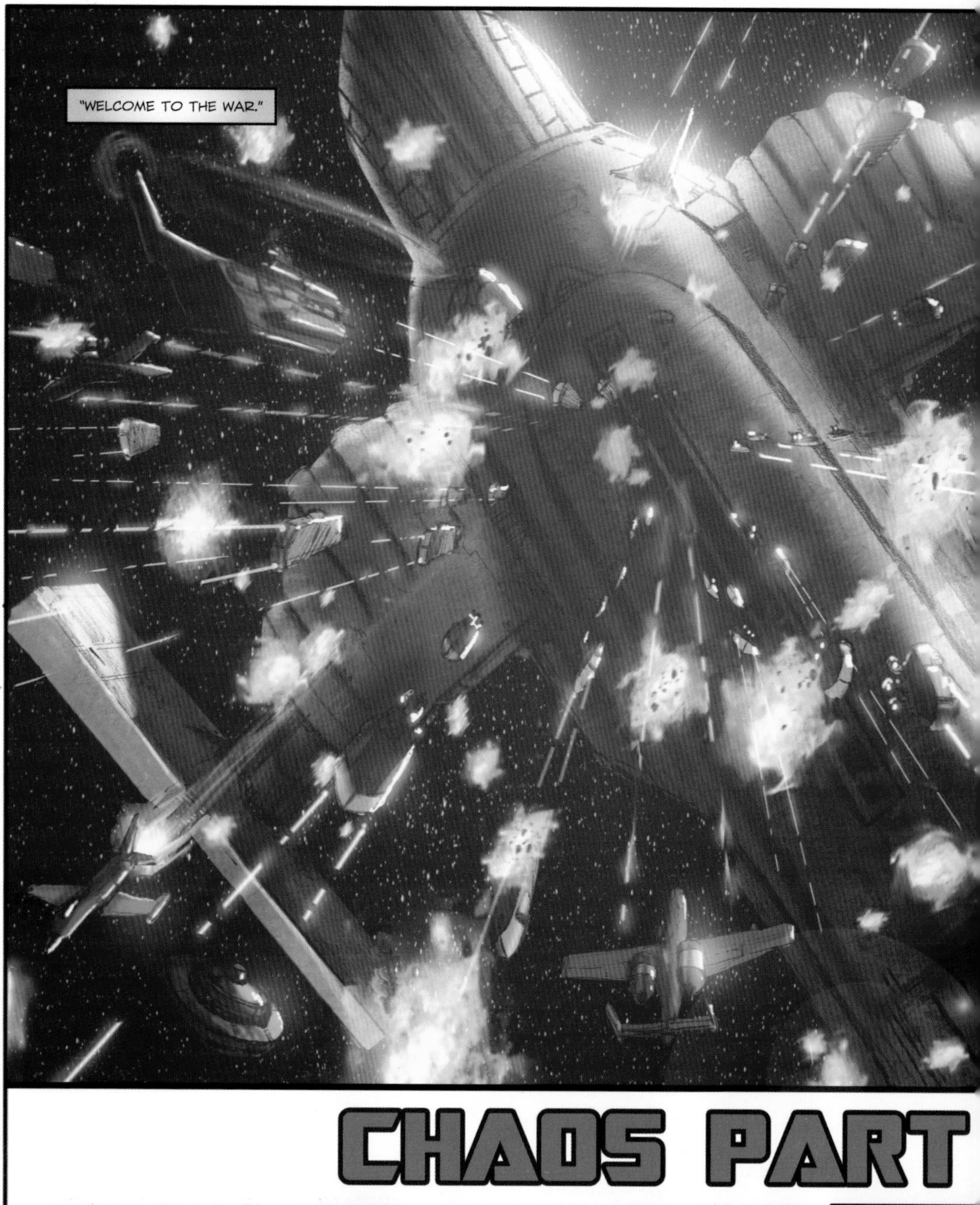
"WELCOME TO THE WAR."

CHAOS PART

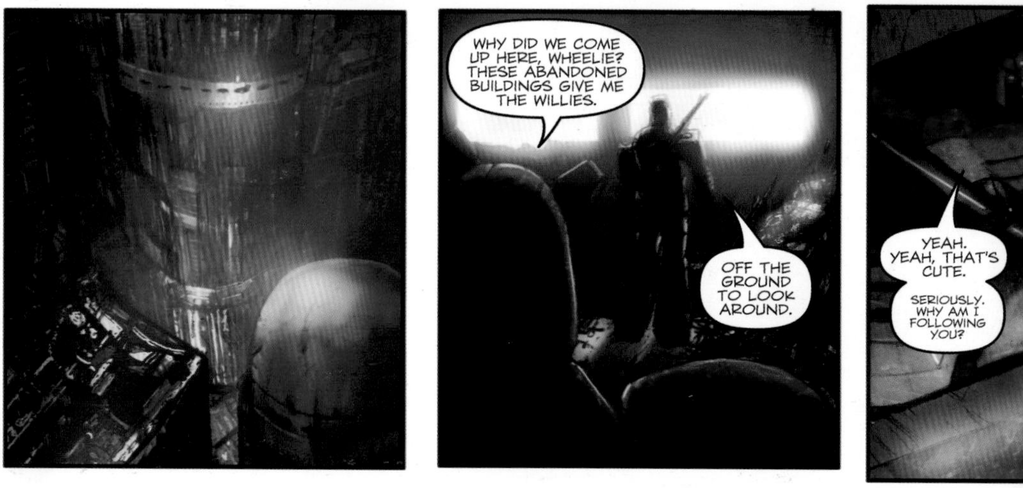
WHY DID WE COME UP HERE, WHEELIE? THESE ABANDONED BUILDINGS GIVE ME THE WILLIES.
OFF THE GROUND TO LOOK AROUND.
YEAH. YEAH, THAT'S CUTE.
SERIOUSLY. WHY AM I FOLLOWING YOU?

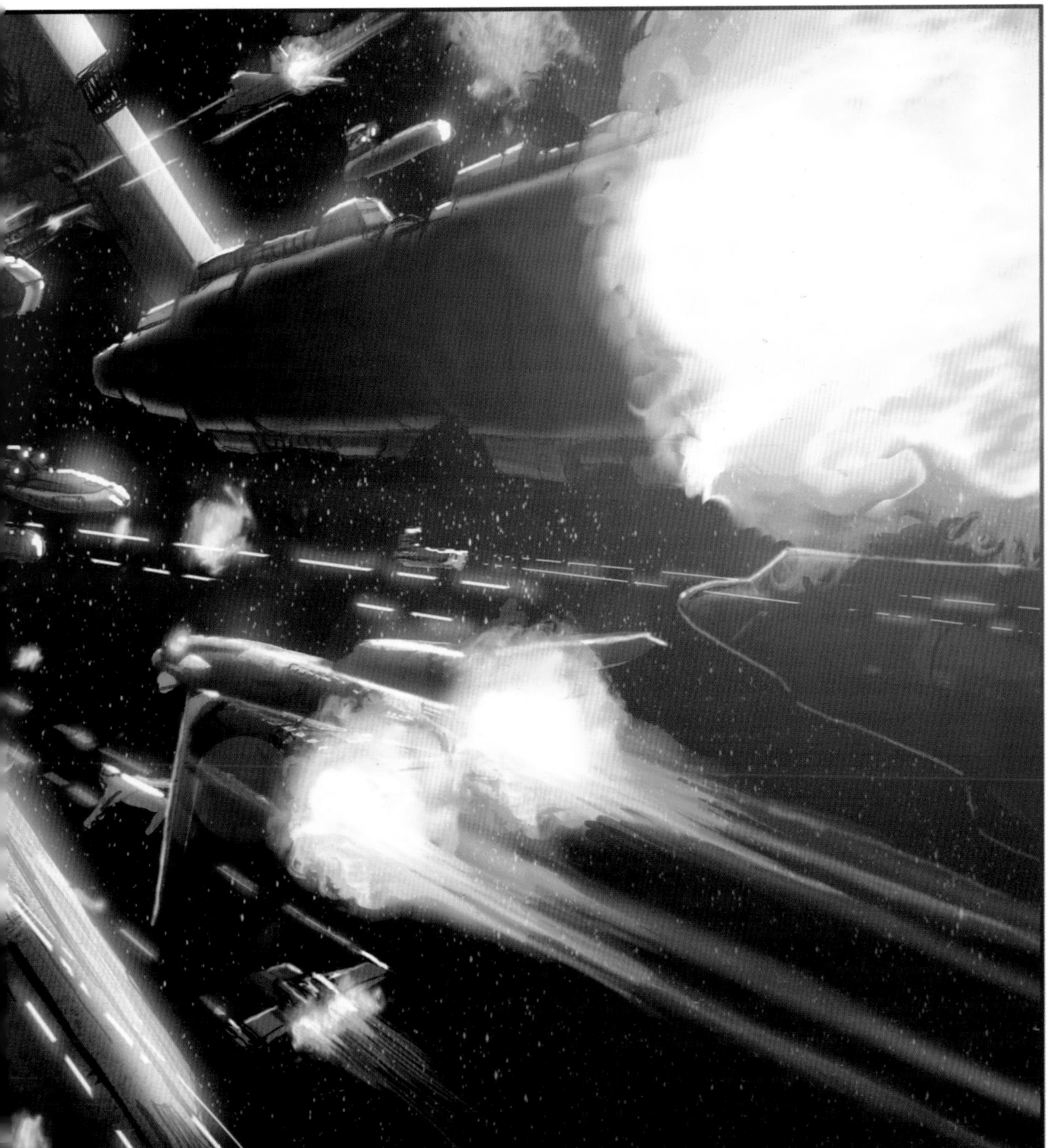

TWO: NUMBERS

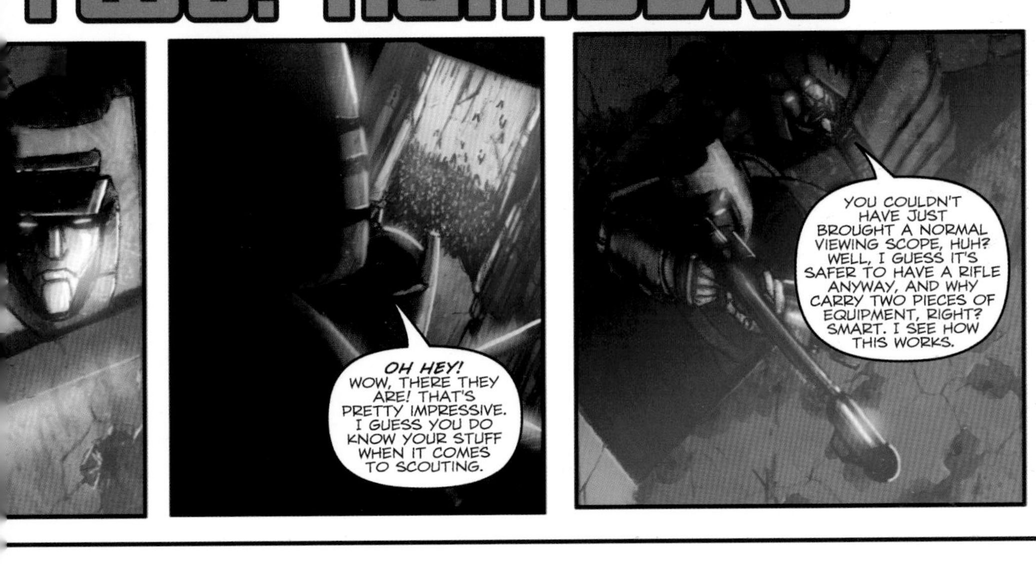
OH HEY! WOW, THERE THEY ARE! THAT'S PRETTY IMPRESSIVE. I GUESS YOU DO KNOW YOUR STUFF WHEN IT COMES TO SCOUTING.
YOU COULDN'T HAVE JUST BROUGHT A NORMAL VIEWING SCOPE, HUH? WELL, I GUESS IT'S SAFER TO HAVE A RIFLE ANYWAY, AND WHY CARRY TWO PIECES OF EQUIPMENT, RIGHT? SMART. I SEE HOW THIS WORKS.

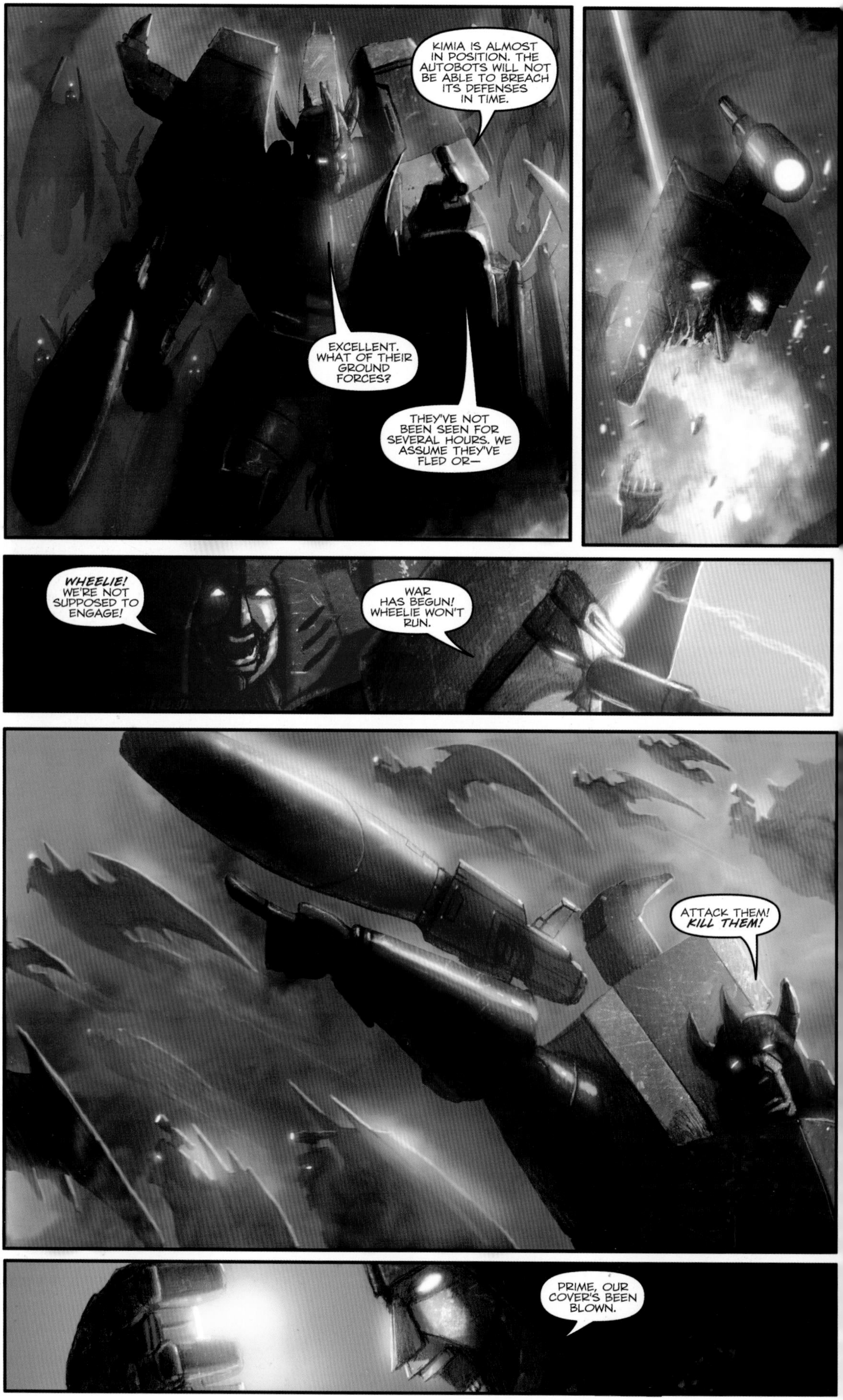
KIMIA IS ALMOST IN POSITION. THE AUTOBOTS WILL NOT BE ABLE TO BREACH ITS DEFENSES IN TIME.
EXCELLENT. WHAT OF THEIR GROUND FORCES?
THEY'VE NOT BEEN SEEN FOR SEVERAL HOURS. WE ASSUME THEY'VE FLED OR—
WHEELIE! WE'RE NOT SUPPOSED TO ENGAGE!
WAR HAS BEGUN! WHEELIE WON'T RUN.
ATTACK THEM! *KILL THEM!*
PRIME, OUR COVER'S BEEN BLOWN.

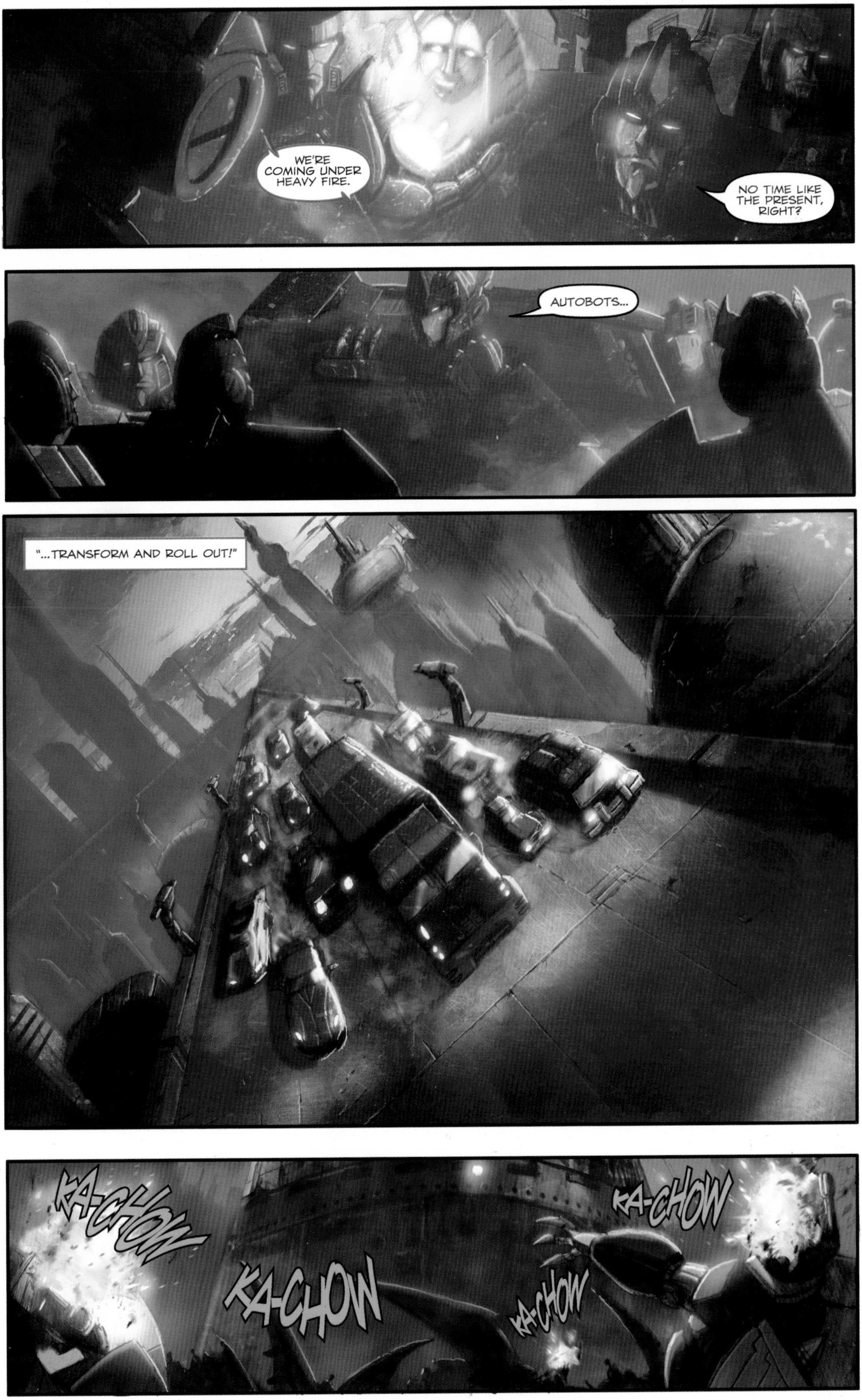
WE'RE COMING UNDER HEAVY FIRE.
NO TIME LIKE THE PRESENT, RIGHT?
AUTOBOTS...
"...TRANSFORM AND ROLL OUT!"
KA-CHOW
KA-CHOW
KA-CHOW
KA-CHOW

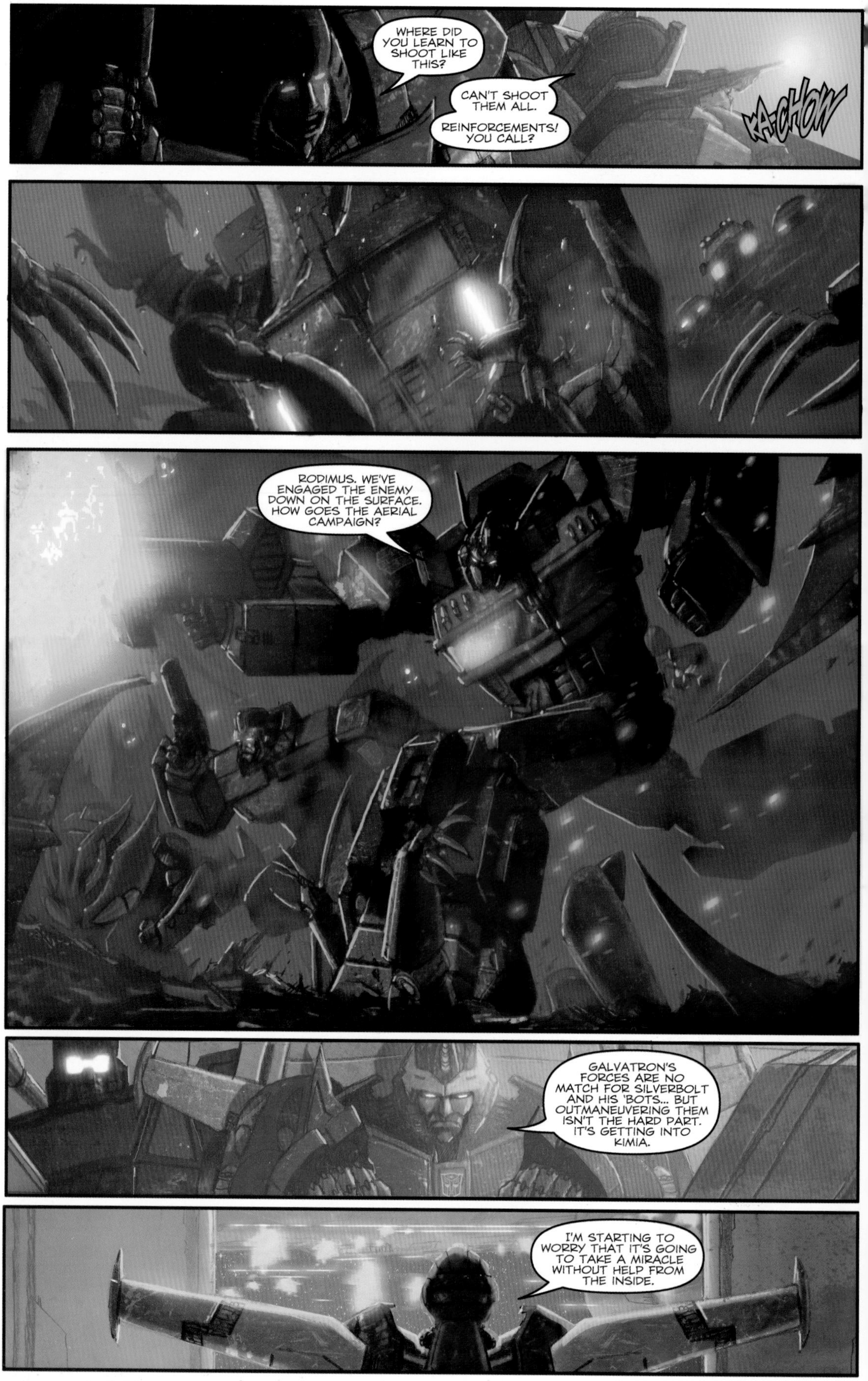
WHERE DID YOU LEARN TO SHOOT LIKE THIS?
CAN'T SHOOT THEM ALL.
REINFORCEMENTS! YOU CALL?
KA-CHOW
RODIMUS. WE'VE ENGAGED THE ENEMY DOWN ON THE SURFACE. HOW GOES THE AERIAL CAMPAIGN?
GALVATRON'S FORCES ARE NO MATCH FOR SILVERBOLT AND HIS 'BOTS... BUT OUTMANEUVERING THEM ISN'T THE HARD PART. IT'S GETTING INTO KIMIA.
I'M STARTING TO WORRY THAT IT'S GOING TO TAKE A MIRACLE WITHOUT HELP FROM THE INSIDE.

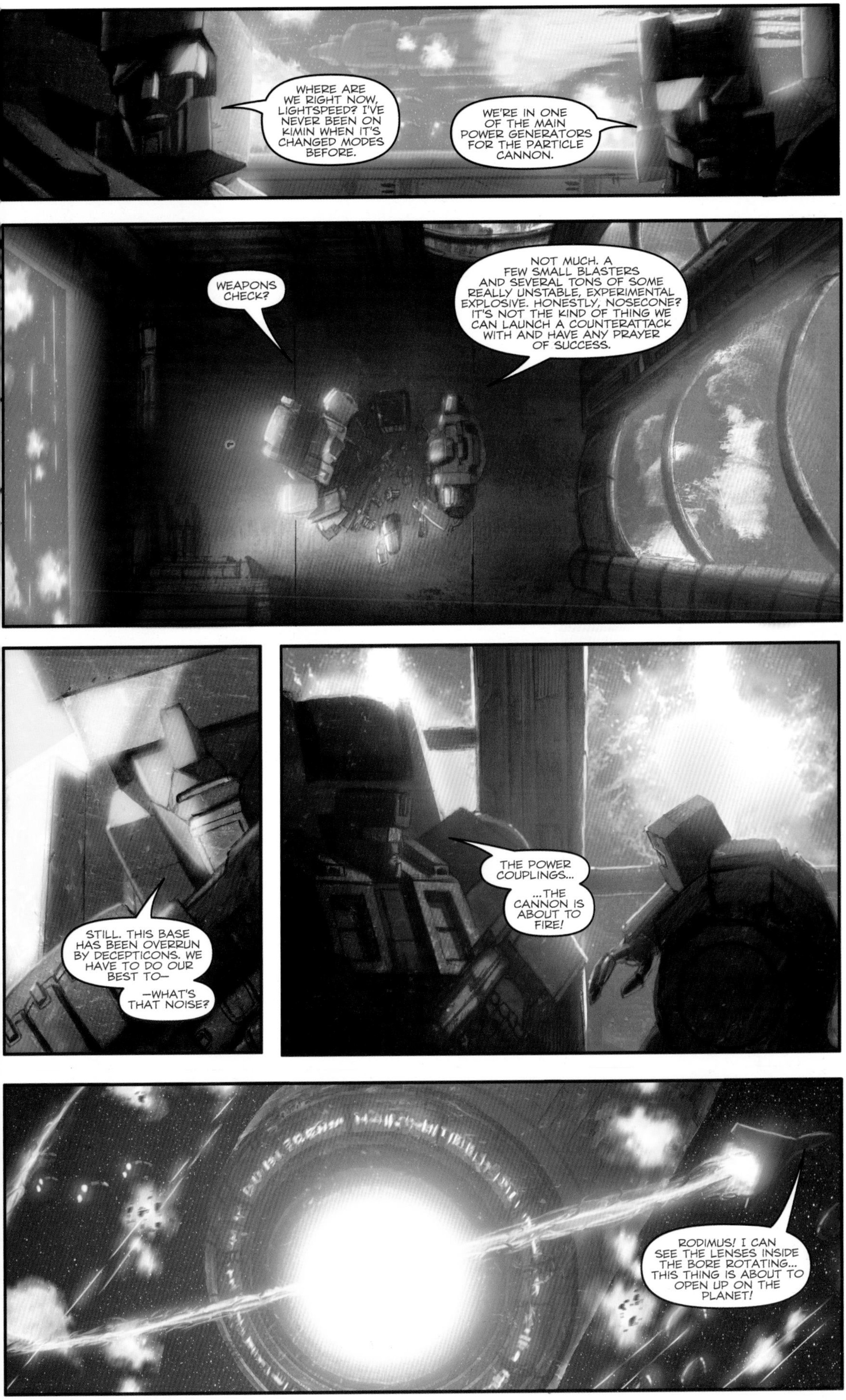

WHERE ARE WE RIGHT NOW, LIGHTSPEED? I'VE NEVER BEEN ON KIMIN WHEN IT'S CHANGED MODES BEFORE.
WE'RE IN ONE OF THE MAIN POWER GENERATORS FOR THE PARTICLE CANNON.
WEAPONS CHECK?
NOT MUCH. A FEW SMALL BLASTERS AND SEVERAL TONS OF SOME REALLY UNSTABLE, EXPERIMENTAL EXPLOSIVE. HONESTLY, NOSECONE? IT'S NOT THE KIND OF THING WE CAN LAUNCH A COUNTERATTACK WITH AND HAVE ANY PRAYER OF SUCCESS.
STILL. THIS BASE HAS BEEN OVERRUN BY DECEPTICONS. WE HAVE TO DO OUR BEST TO—
—WHAT'S THAT NOISE?
THE POWER COUPLINGS...
...THE CANNON IS ABOUT TO FIRE!
RODIMUS! I CAN SEE THE LENSES INSIDE THE BORE ROTATING... THIS THING IS ABOUT TO OPEN UP ON THE PLANET!

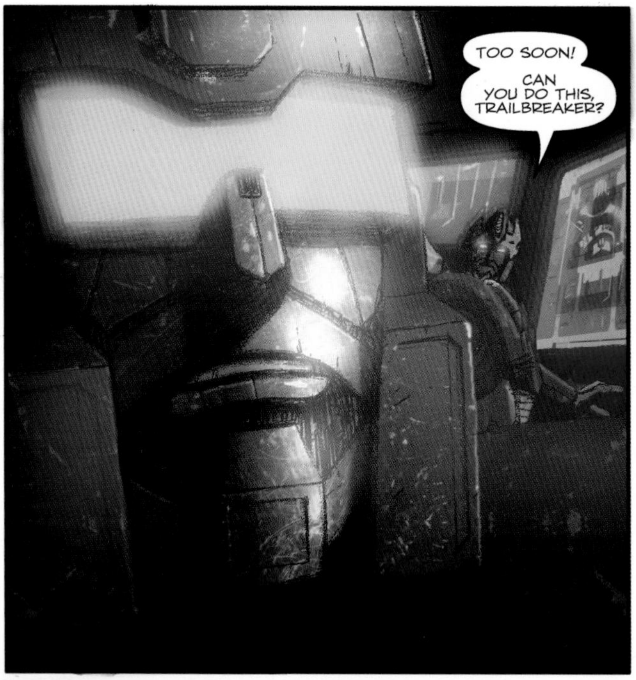
TOO SOON!
CAN YOU DO THIS, TRAILBREAKER?

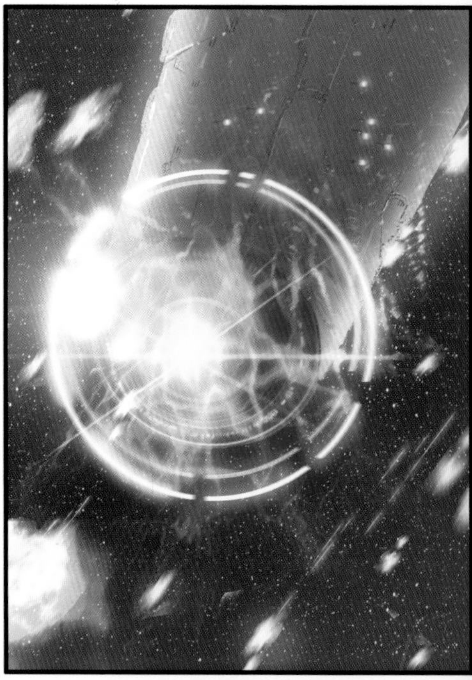

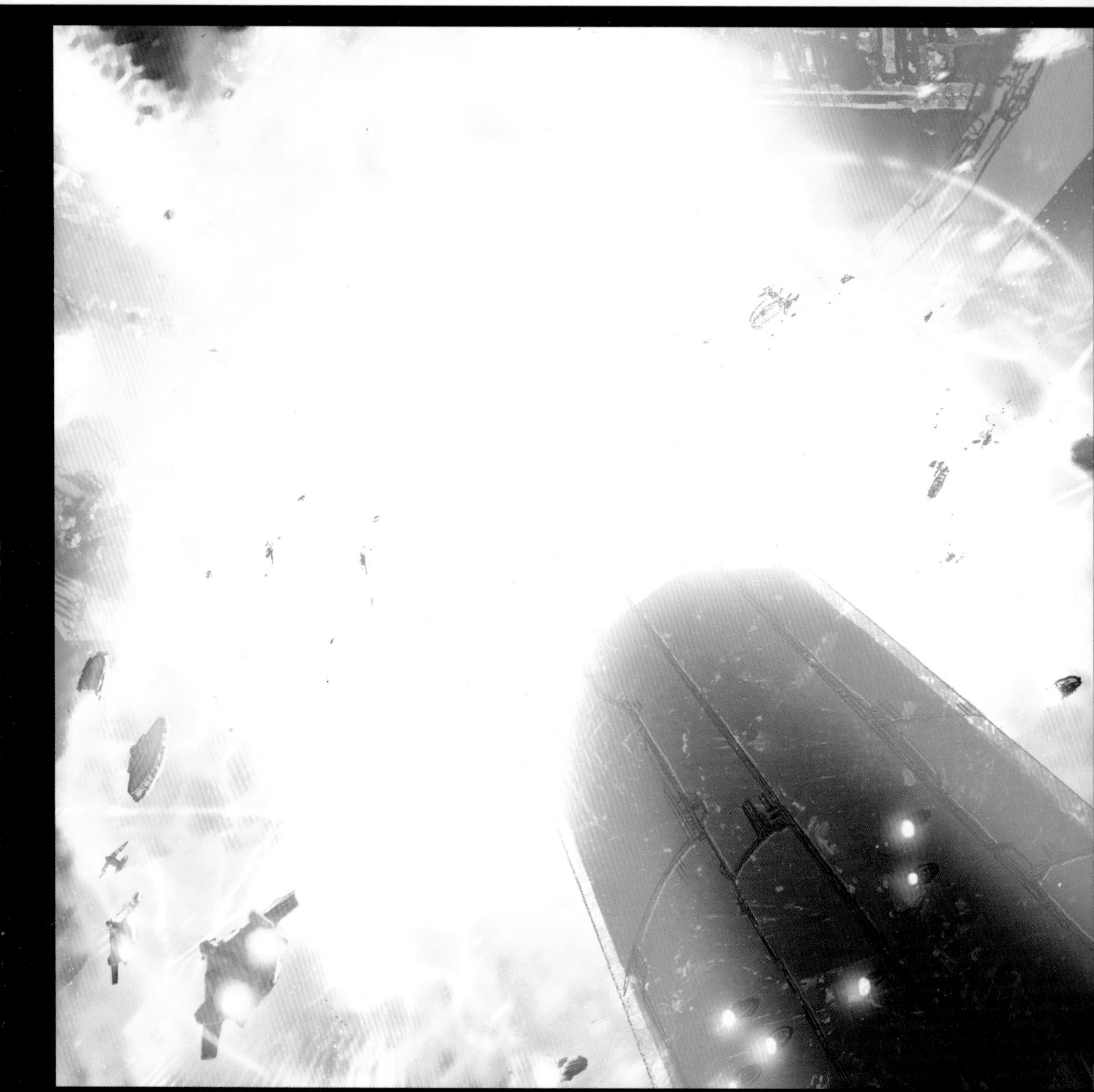

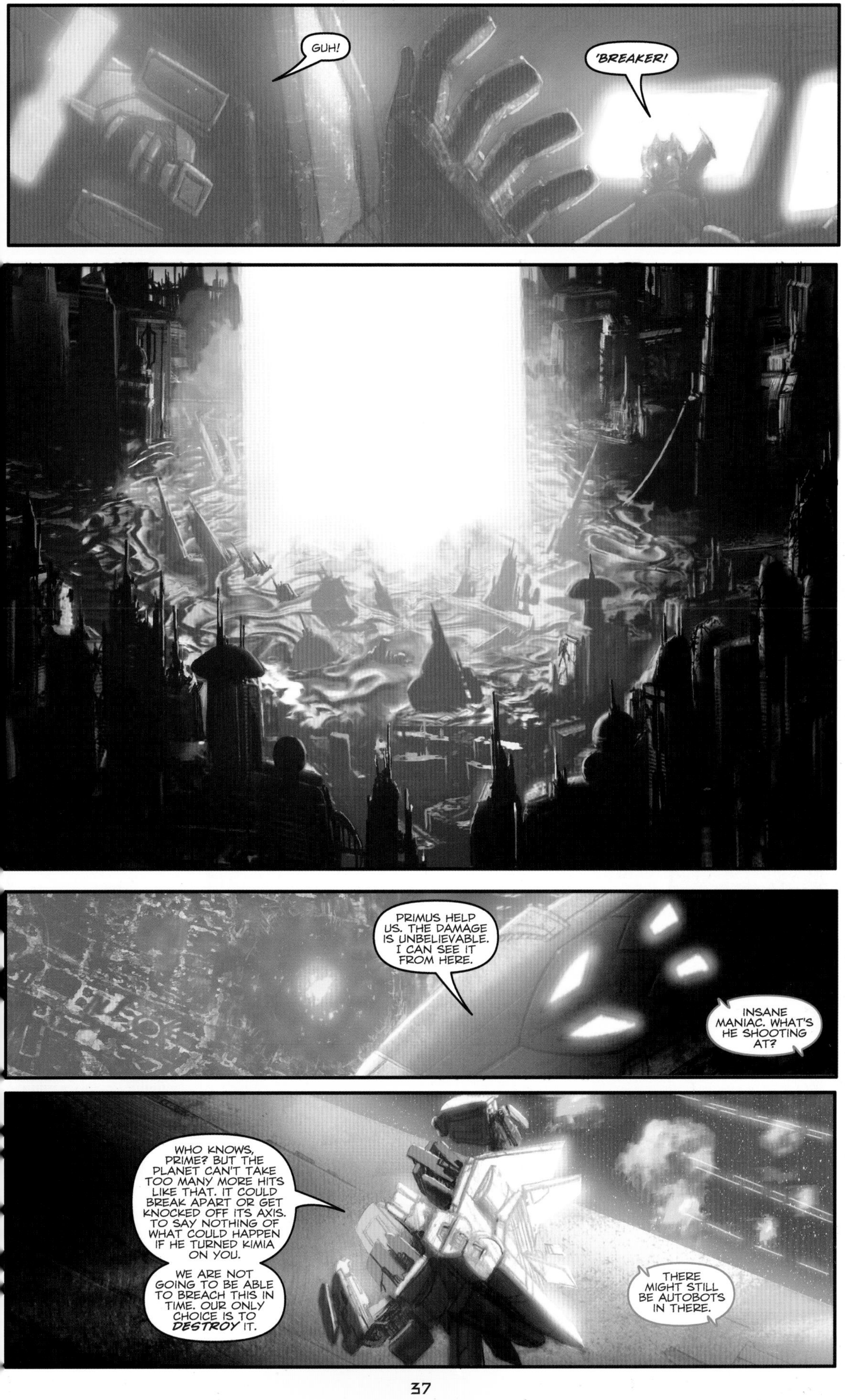
GUH!
'BREAKER!
PRIMUS HELP US. THE DAMAGE IS UNBELIEVABLE. I CAN SEE IT FROM HERE.
INSANE MANIAC. WHAT'S HE SHOOTING AT?
WHO KNOWS, PRIME? BUT THE PLANET CAN'T TAKE TOO MANY MORE HITS LIKE THAT. IT COULD BREAK APART OR GET KNOCKED OFF ITS AXIS. TO SAY NOTHING OF WHAT COULD HAPPEN IF HE TURNED KIMIA ON YOU.
WE ARE NOT GOING TO BE ABLE TO BREACH THIS IN TIME. OUR ONLY CHOICE IS TO DESTROY IT.
THERE MIGHT STILL BE AUTOBOTS IN THERE.

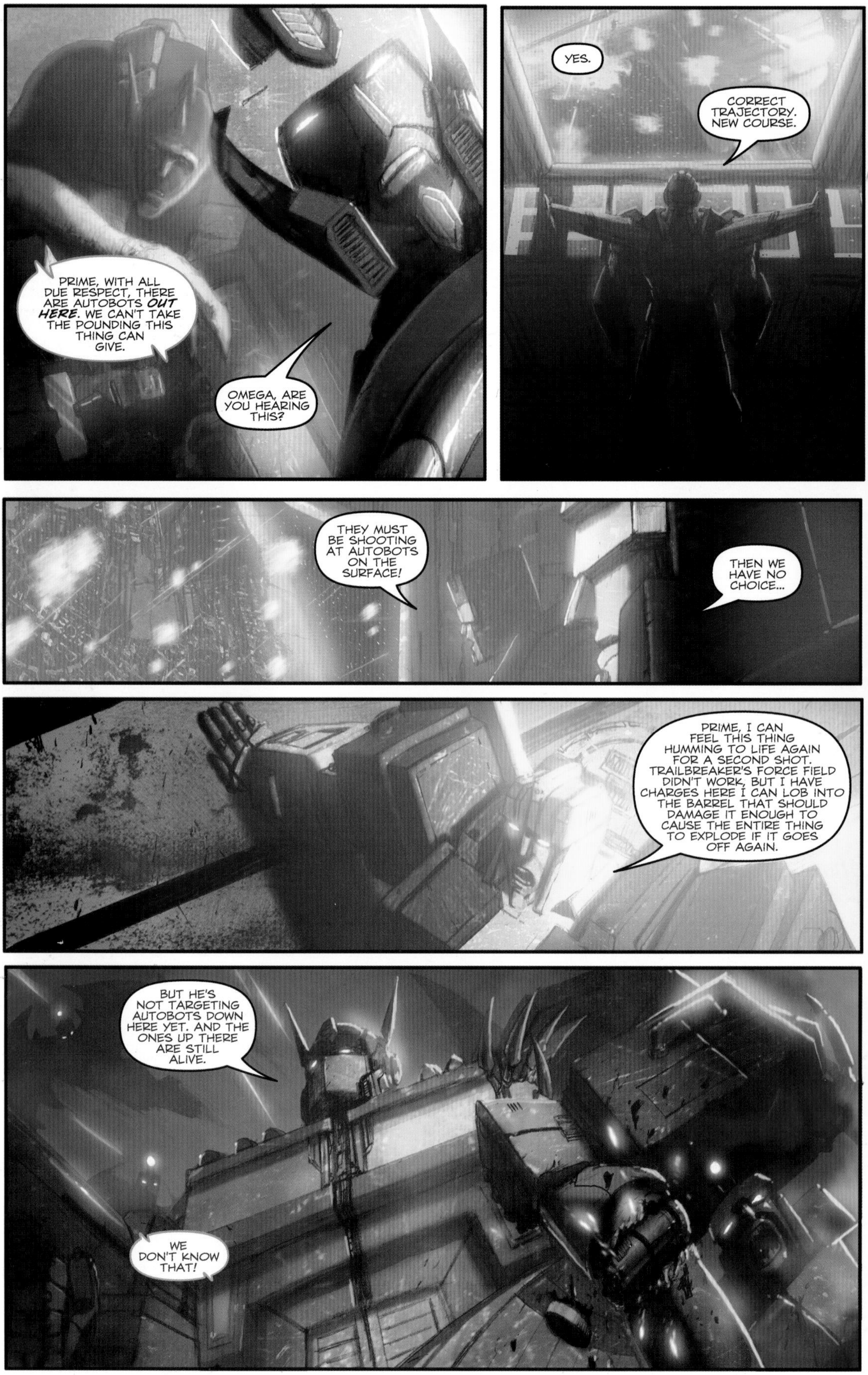
PRIME, WITH ALL DUE RESPECT, THERE ARE AUTOBOTS **OUT HERE**. WE CAN'T TAKE THE POUNDING THIS THING CAN GIVE.
OMEGA, ARE YOU HEARING THIS?
YES.
CORRECT TRAJECTORY. NEW COURSE.
THEY MUST BE SHOOTING AT AUTOBOTS ON THE SURFACE!
THEN WE HAVE NO CHOICE...
PRIME, I CAN FEEL THIS THING HUMMING TO LIFE AGAIN FOR A SECOND SHOT. TRAILBREAKER'S FORCE FIELD DIDN'T WORK, BUT I HAVE CHARGES HERE I CAN LOB INTO THE BARREL THAT SHOULD DAMAGE IT ENOUGH TO CAUSE THE ENTIRE THING TO EXPLODE IF IT GOES OFF AGAIN.
BUT HE'S NOT TARGETING AUTOBOTS DOWN HERE YET. AND THE ONES UP THERE ARE STILL ALIVE.
WE DON'T KNOW THAT!

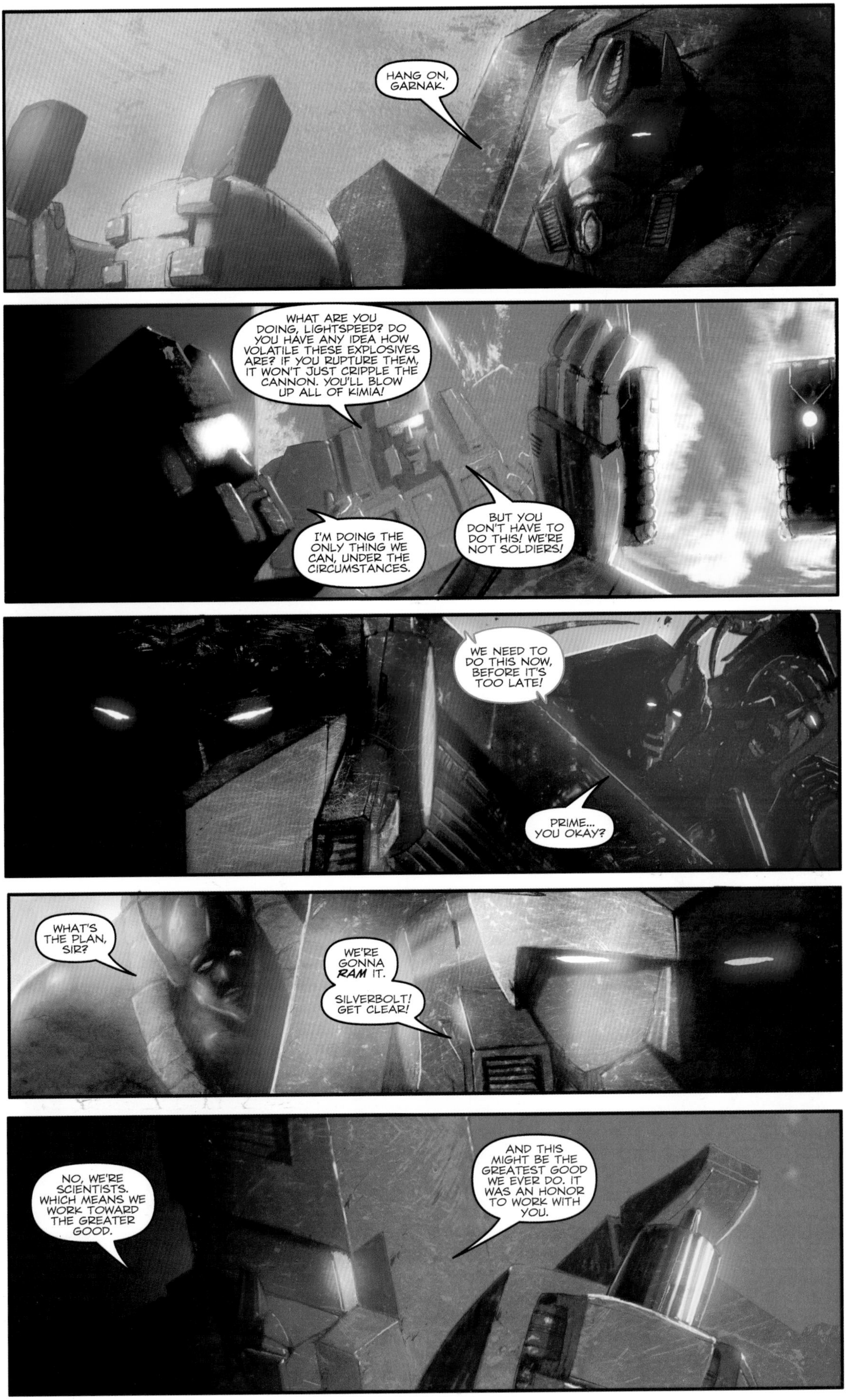

HANG ON, GARNAK.
WHAT ARE YOU DOING, LIGHTSPEED? DO YOU HAVE ANY IDEA HOW VOLATILE THESE EXPLOSIVES ARE? IF YOU RUPTURE THEM, IT WON'T JUST CRIPPLE THE CANNON. YOU'LL BLOW UP ALL OF KIMIA!
I'M DOING THE ONLY THING WE CAN, UNDER THE CIRCUMSTANCES.
BUT YOU DON'T HAVE TO DO THIS! WE'RE NOT SOLDIERS!
WE NEED TO DO THIS NOW, BEFORE IT'S TOO LATE!
PRIME... YOU OKAY?
WHAT'S THE PLAN, SIR?
WE'RE GONNA *RAM* IT.
SILVERBOLT! GET CLEAR!
NO, WE'RE SCIENTISTS. WHICH MEANS WE WORK TOWARD THE GREATER GOOD.
AND THIS MIGHT BE THE GREATEST GOOD WE EVER DO. IT WAS AN HONOR TO WORK WITH YOU.

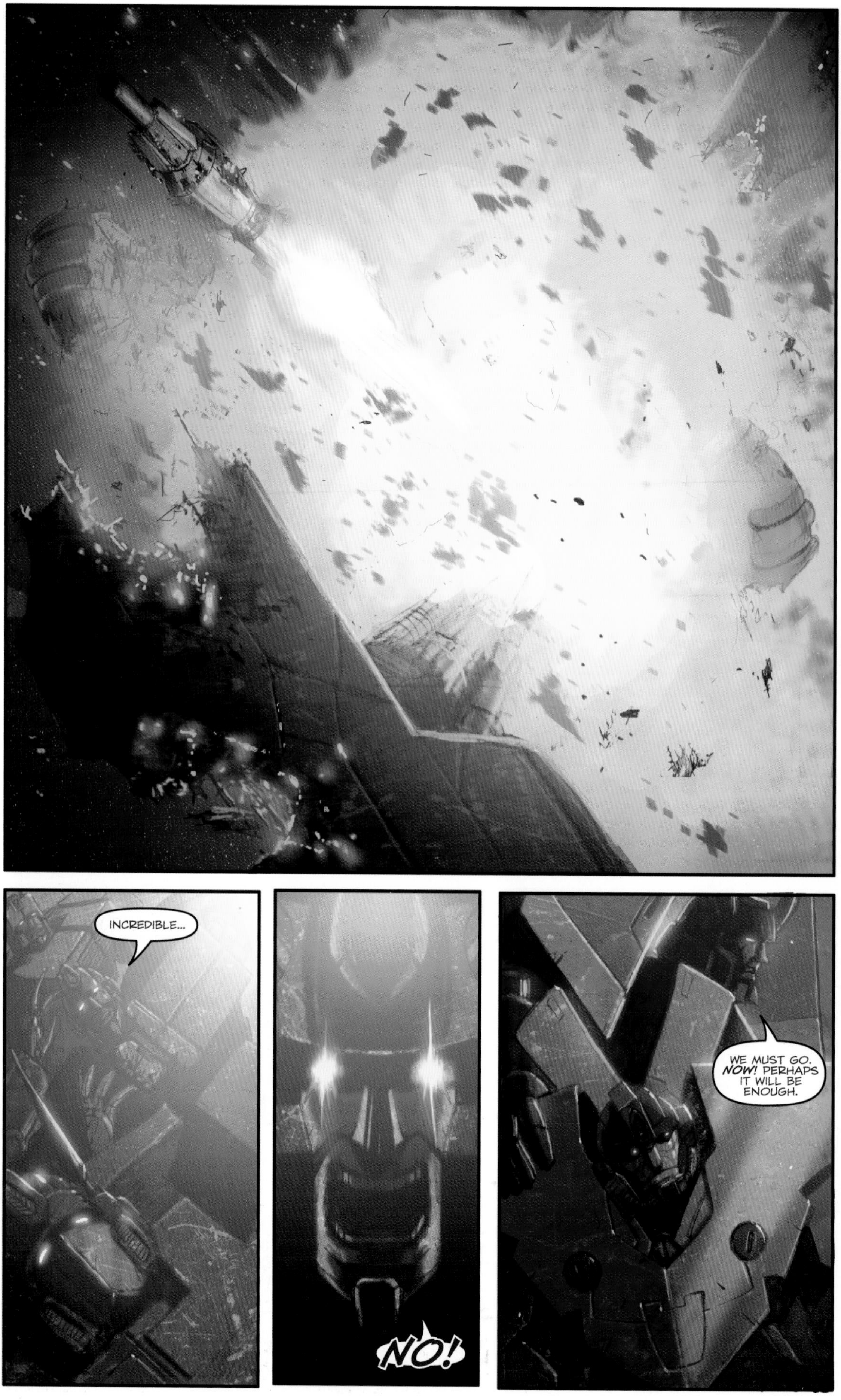
INCREDIBLE...
NO!
WE MUST GO. NOW! PERHAPS IT WILL BE ENOUGH.

PRIME!

SUNSTREAKER! I NEED A LANDING AREA! I WAS JUST TRYING TO RAM IT, HOPING I COULD KNOCK IT OFF COURSE.

BUT IT MUST HAVE EXPLODED FROM THE INSIDE, SOMEHOW. NOW OMEGA IS DAMAGED AND WE'RE COMING IN HOT FOR REPAIR. WE CAN'T STAY IN ORBIT LIKE THIS.

I'M SENDING YOU CO-ORDINATES NOW.

TRAILBREAKER'S IN BAD SHAPE. HE GOT HIT WITH A FEEDBACK WAVE WHEN KIMIA WENT OFF. GARNAK IS TAKING CARE OF HIM, BUT WE'LL NEED RATCHET.

WHERE'S PRIME?

I'M NOT SURE. HE AND IRONHIDE JUST WENT TOOLING OFF TOGETHER. I THINK THEY'RE HEADING FOR THE BLAST CRATER.

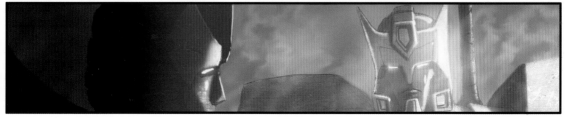

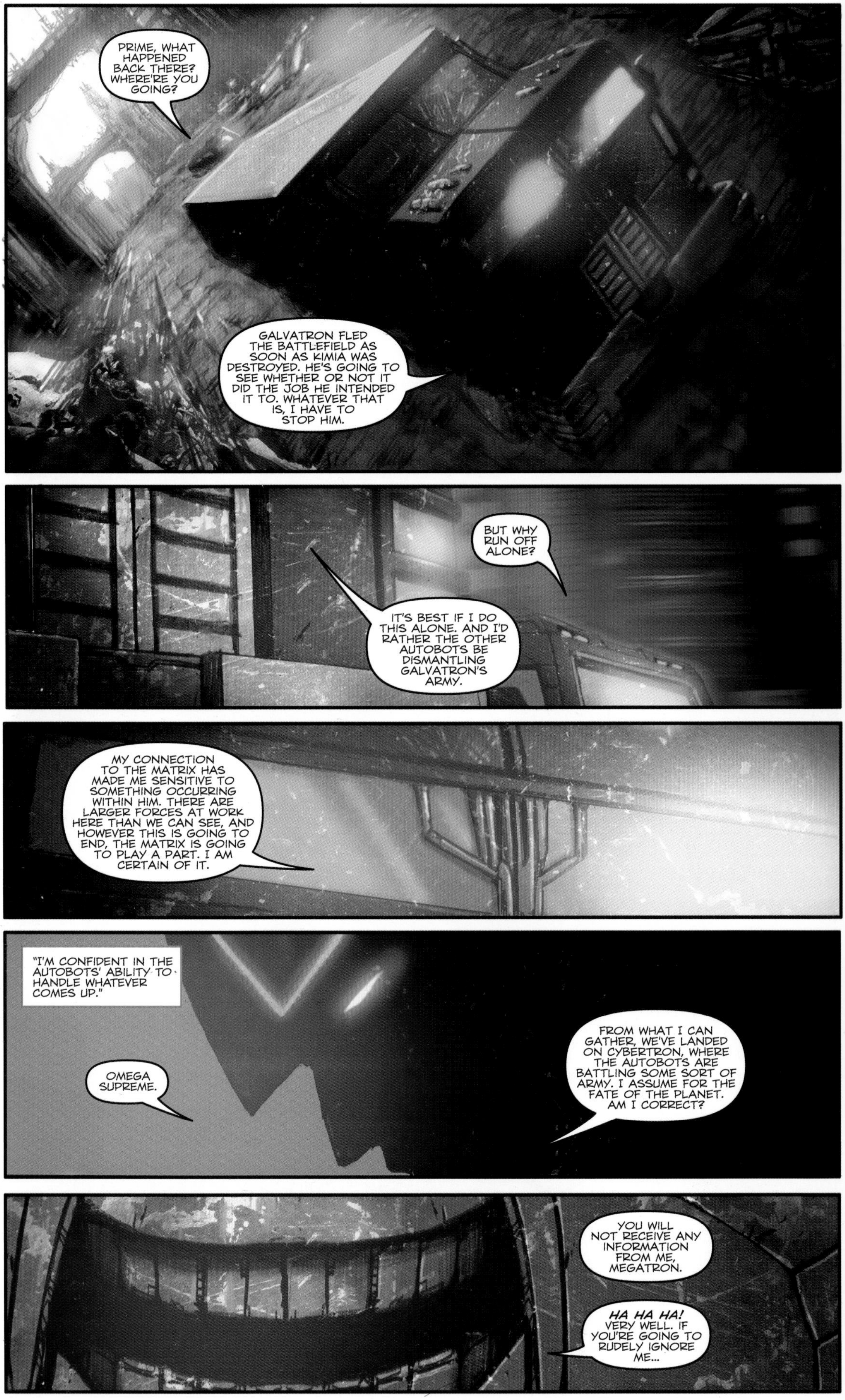
PRIME, WHAT HAPPENED BACK THERE? WHERE'RE YOU GOING?
GALVATRON FLED THE BATTLEFIELD AS SOON AS KIMIA WAS DESTROYED. HE'S GOING TO SEE WHETHER OR NOT IT DID THE JOB HE INTENDED IT TO. WHATEVER THAT IS, I HAVE TO STOP HIM.
BUT WHY RUN OFF ALONE?
IT'S BEST IF I DO THIS ALONE. AND I'D RATHER THE OTHER AUTOBOTS BE DISMANTLING GALVATRON'S ARMY.
MY CONNECTION TO THE MATRIX HAS MADE ME SENSITIVE TO SOMETHING OCCURRING WITHIN HIM. THERE ARE LARGER FORCES AT WORK HERE THAN WE CAN SEE, AND HOWEVER THIS IS GOING TO END, THE MATRIX IS GOING TO PLAY A PART. I AM CERTAIN OF IT.
"I'M CONFIDENT IN THE AUTOBOTS' ABILITY TO HANDLE WHATEVER COMES UP."
OMEGA SUPREME.
FROM WHAT I CAN GATHER, WE'VE LANDED ON CYBERTRON, WHERE THE AUTOBOTS ARE BATTLING SOME SORT OF ARMY. I ASSUME FOR THE FATE OF THE PLANET. AM I CORRECT?
YOU WILL NOT RECEIVE ANY INFORMATION FROM ME, MEGATRON.
HA HA HA! VERY WELL. IF YOU'RE GOING TO RUDELY IGNORE ME...

...I'LL JUST BE LEAVING.

HOPE YER COMFORTABLE, MR. TRAILBREAKER, SIR. DON'T RIGHTLY KNOW IF YER CAN HEAR ME, BUT MR. RODIMUS AND MR. DRIFT WENT OFF ON A CHASE SO IT'S JUST ME AND MR. SUNSTREAKER HERE FOR A TIME.

WHICH IS NICE, INNIT?

GARNAK. QUIET.

I'M SORRY, SIR. RUNNIN' ME MOUTH AGAIN AS ALWAYS.

NO, I THINK I HEAR SOMETHING.

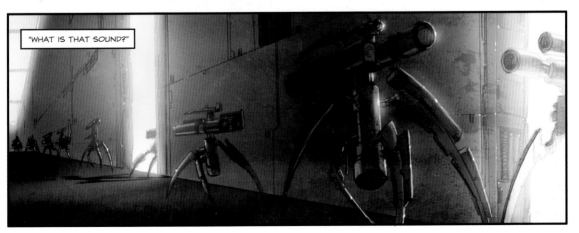

"WHAT IS THAT SOUND?"

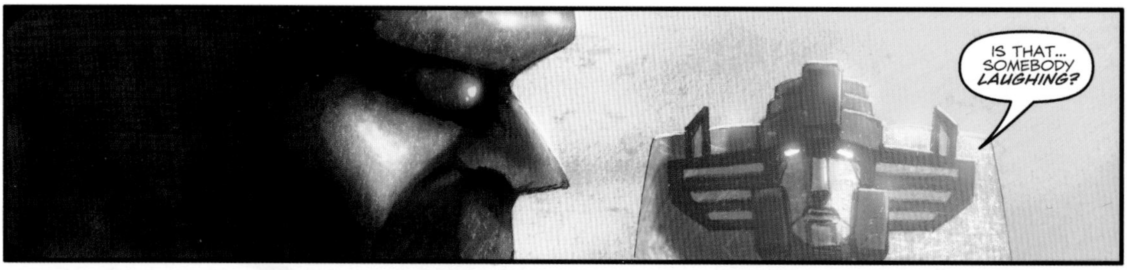
IS THAT... SOMEBODY *LAUGHING?*

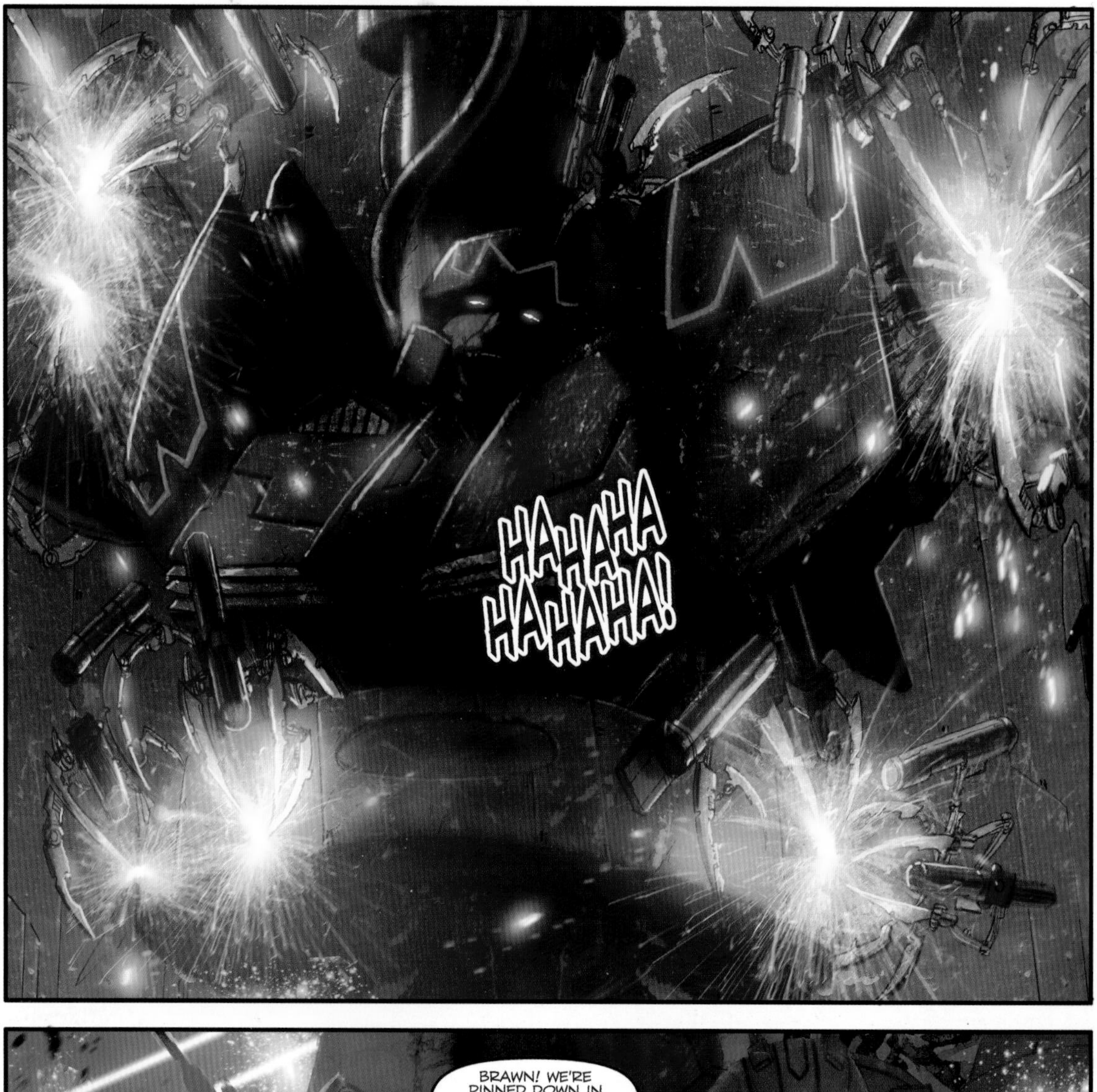
HAHAHA HAHAHA!

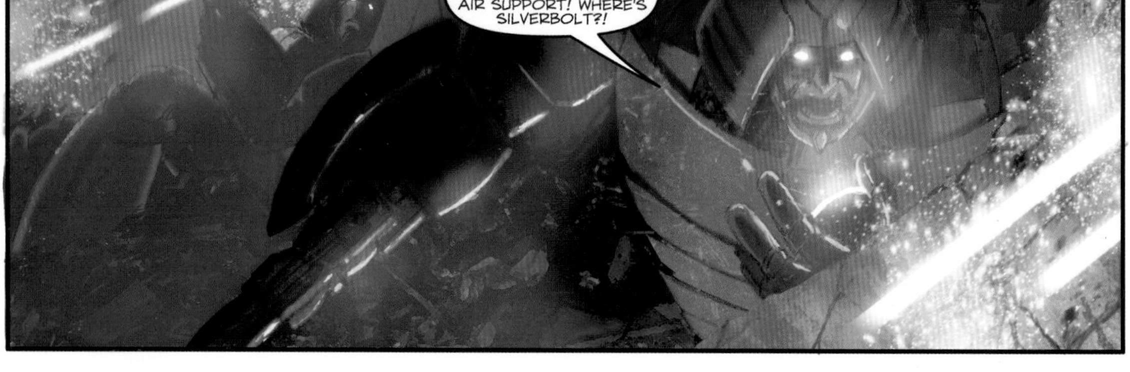
BRAWN! WE'RE PINNED DOWN IN SECTOR A55F. WE NEED AIR SUPPORT! WHERE'S SILVERBOLT?!

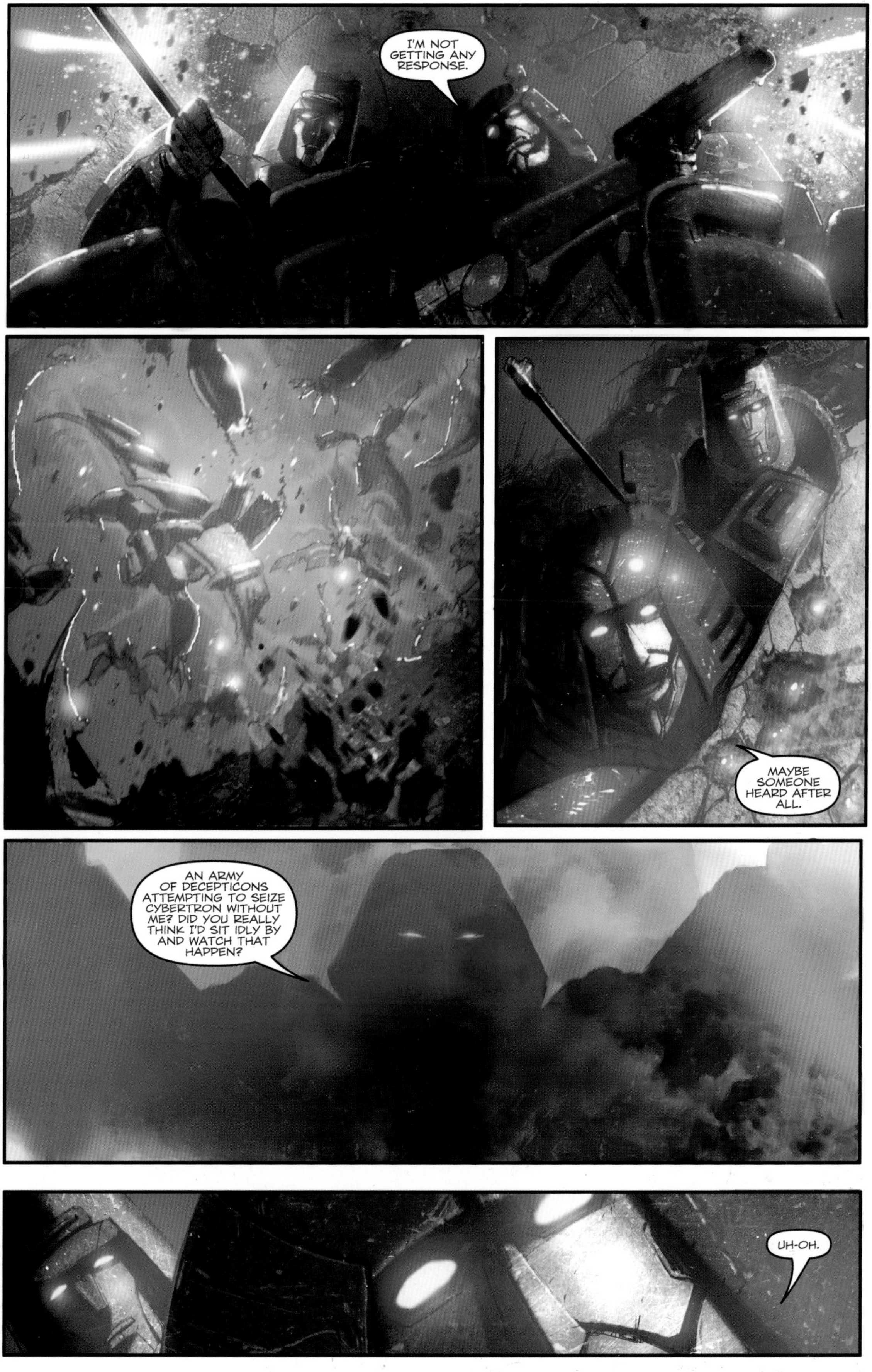
I'M NOT GETTING ANY RESPONSE.
MAYBE SOMEONE HEARD AFTER ALL.
AN ARMY OF DECEPTICONS ATTEMPTING TO SEIZE CYBERTRON WITHOUT ME? DID YOU REALLY THINK I'D SIT IDLY BY AND WATCH THAT HAPPEN?
UH-OH.

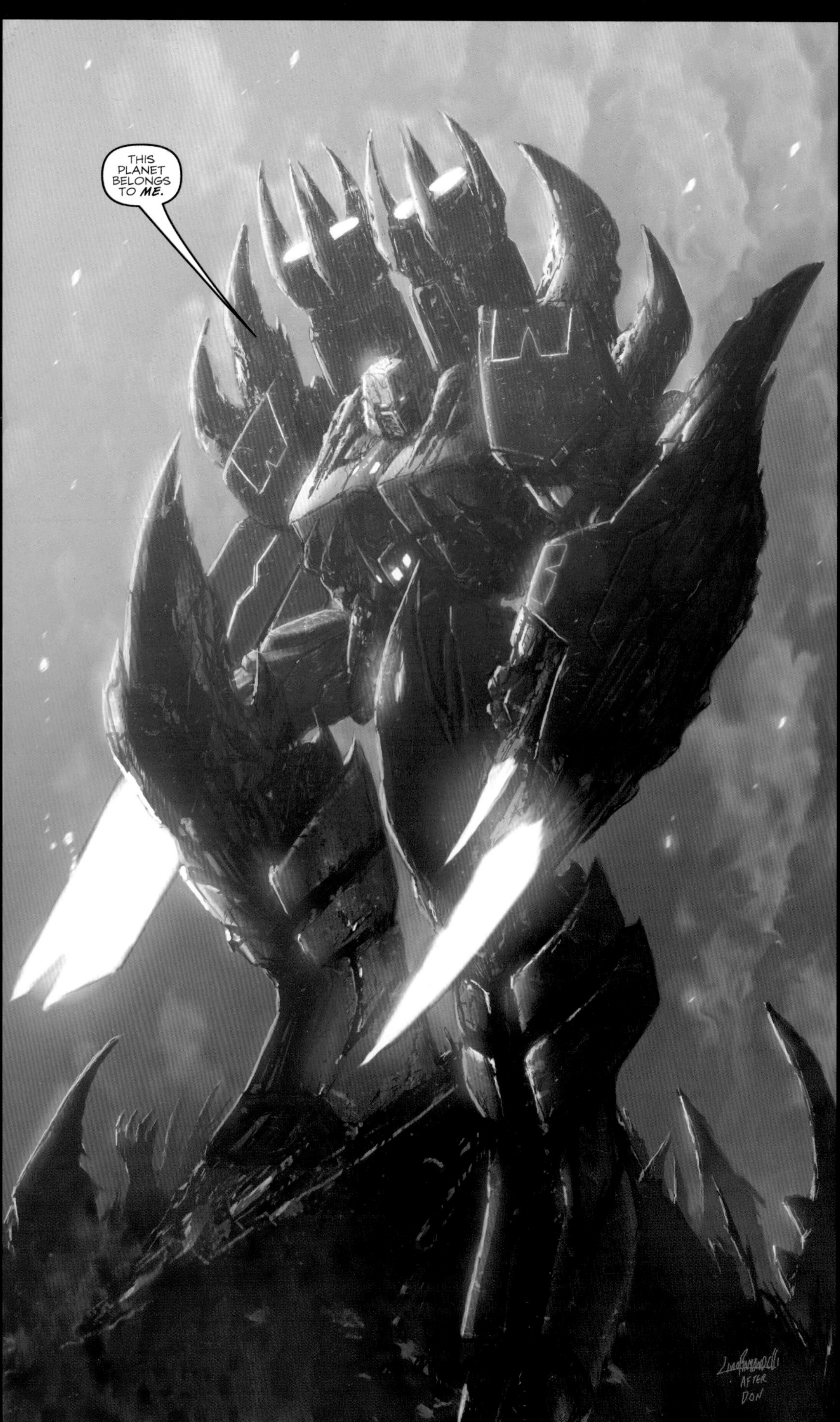
THIS PLANET BELONGS TO *ME*.
AFTER DON

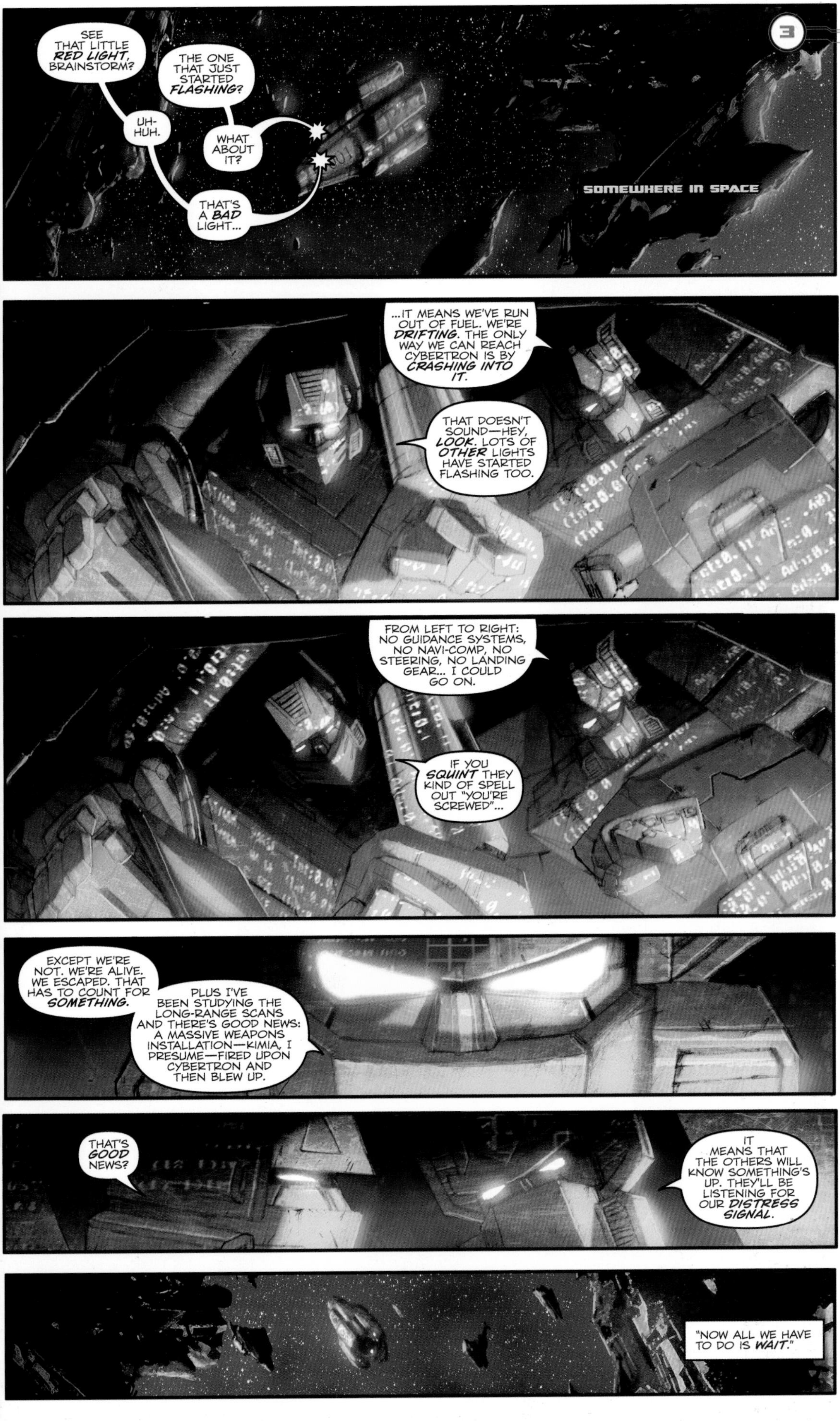
3
SEE THAT LITTLE RED LIGHT, BRAINSTORM?
UH-HUH.
THE ONE THAT JUST STARTED FLASHING?
WHAT ABOUT IT?
THAT'S A BAD LIGHT...
SOMEWHERE IN SPACE
...IT MEANS WE'VE RUN OUT OF FUEL. WE'RE DRIFTING. THE ONLY WAY WE CAN REACH CYBERTRON IS BY CRASHING INTO IT.
THAT DOESN'T SOUND—HEY, LOOK. LOTS OF OTHER LIGHTS HAVE STARTED FLASHING TOO.
FROM LEFT TO RIGHT: NO GUIDANCE SYSTEMS, NO NAVI-COMP, NO STEERING, NO LANDING GEAR... I COULD GO ON.
IF YOU SQUINT THEY KIND OF SPELL OUT "YOU'RE SCREWED"...
EXCEPT WE'RE NOT. WE'RE ALIVE. WE ESCAPED. THAT HAS TO COUNT FOR SOMETHING.
PLUS I'VE BEEN STUDYING THE LONG-RANGE SCANS AND THERE'S GOOD NEWS: A MASSIVE WEAPONS INSTALLATION—KIMIA, I PRESUME—FIRED UPON CYBERTRON AND THEN BLEW UP.
THAT'S GOOD NEWS?
IT MEANS THAT THE OTHERS WILL KNOW SOMETHING'S UP. THEY'LL BE LISTENING FOR OUR DISTRESS SIGNAL.
"NOW ALL WE HAVE TO DO IS WAIT."

CHROMEDOME, WHY ARE ESCAPE PODS ALWAYS SO SMALL? SHOULDN'T THEY BE BIG ENOUGH TO ACCOMMODATE EVERYONE WHO MIGHT, Y'KNOW, NEED TO ESCAPE? OTHERWISE IT'S A BIT, WELL, PESSIMISTIC.

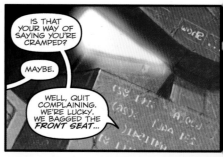

IS THAT YOUR WAY OF SAYING YOU'RE CRAMPED?

MAYBE.

WELL, QUIT COMPLAINING. WE'RE LUCKY. WE BAGGED THE *FRONT SEAT*...

"...HOW DO YOU THINK THE GUYS IN THE *BACK* FEEL?

"I'VE SEEN MORE ROOM INSIDE A—HOLD IT! *INCOMING MESSAGE!* I'M SWITCHING TO *VISUAL*."

NEED HELP, K1? I'M GOING TO DOCK WITH YOU.

OH HELL. IT'S *ARCEE*. WE'RE BEING RESCUED BY A PSYCHOPATH IN *PINK ARMOR*.

BEGGARS CAN'T BE CHOOSERS.

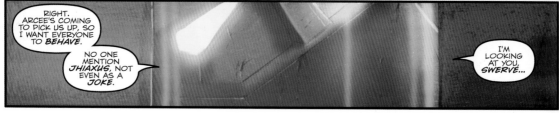

RIGHT. ARCEE'S COMING TO PICK US UP, SO I WANT EVERYONE TO *BEHAVE*.

NO ONE MENTION *JHIAXUS*, NOT EVEN AS A *JOKE*.

I'M LOOKING AT YOU, *SWERVE*...

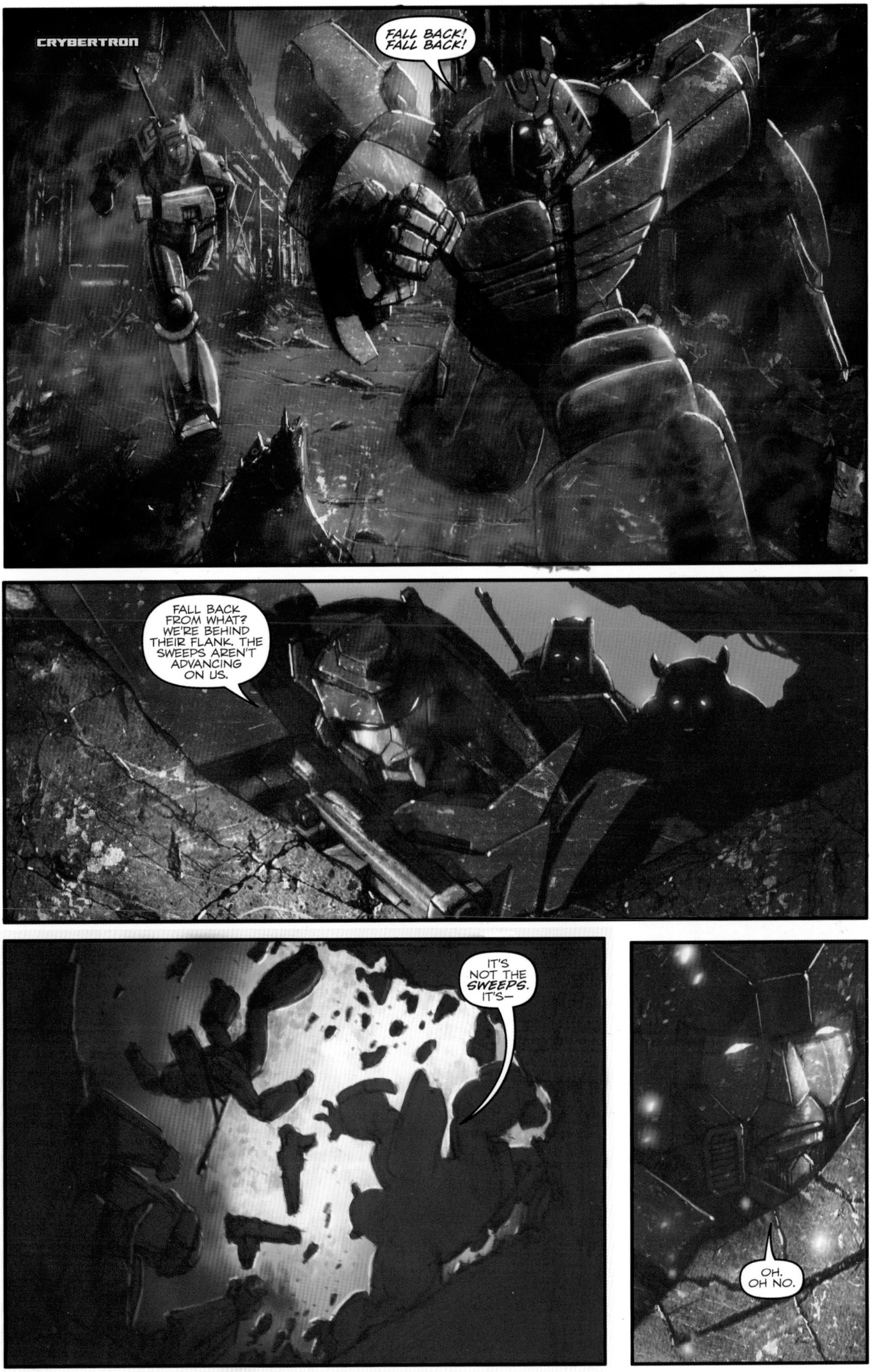
CRYBERTRON
FALL BACK! FALL BACK!
FALL BACK FROM WHAT? WE'RE BEHIND THEIR FLANK. THE SWEEPS AREN'T ADVANCING ON US.
IT'S NOT THE ***SWEEPS***. IT'S—
OH. OH NO.

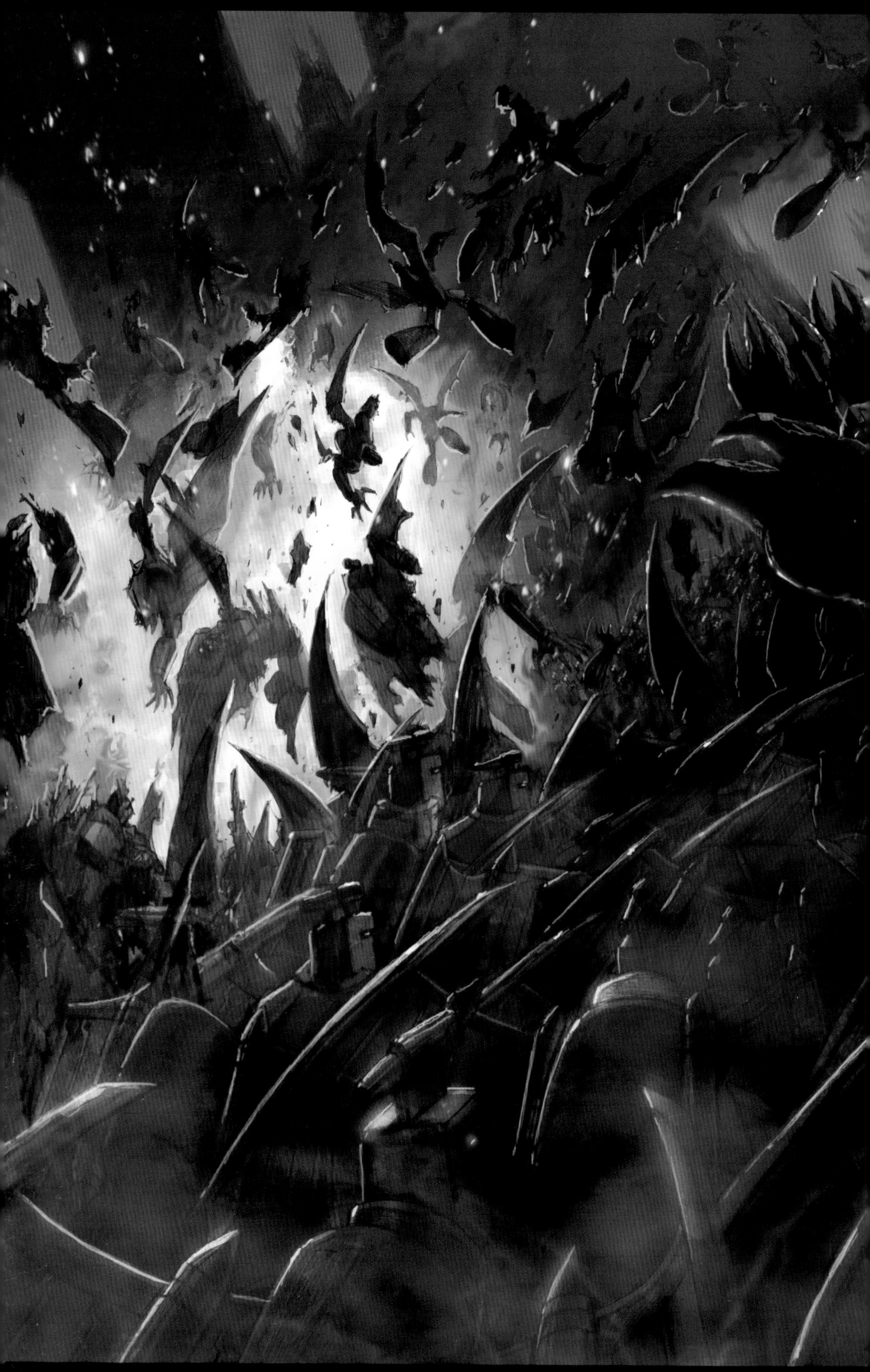

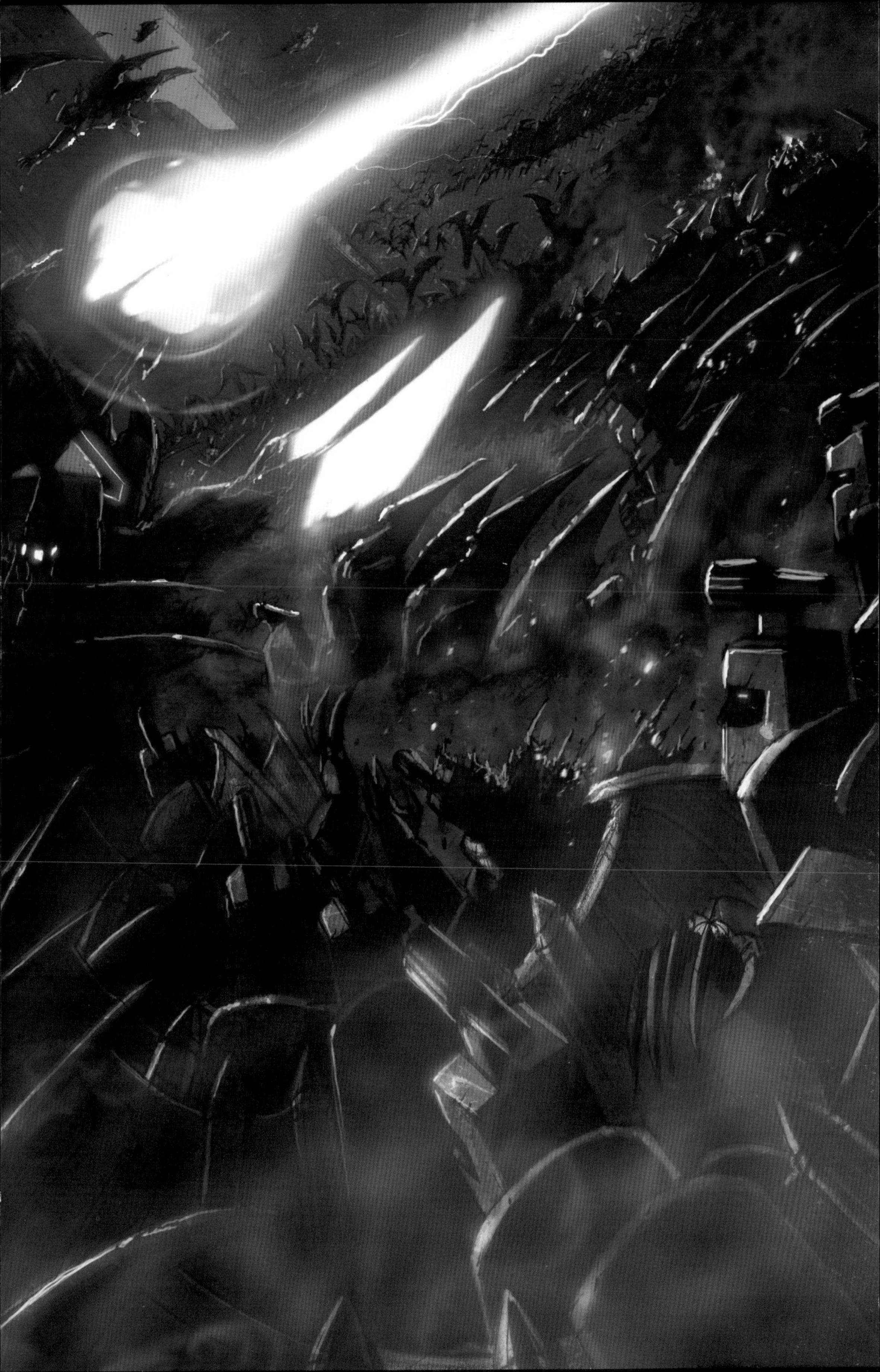

MEGATRON'S ESCAPED!

IN HINDSIGHT... WE PROBABLY SHOULD HAVE EXPECTED THAT.

A PRISONER NO LONGER MEGATRON IS STRONGER!

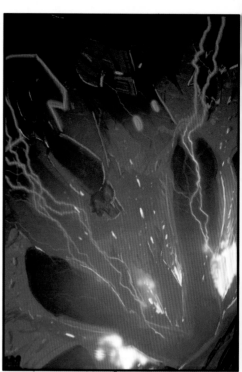

RIGHT NOW, THIS IS ACTUALLY WORKING TO OUR ADVANTAGE. HE'S OCCUPIED WITH THE SWEEPS, WHICH WERE EVENTUALLY GOING TO OVERWHELM US. IF HE'S GOING TO TAKE THEM ALL OUT, HE'S DOING US A FAVOR.

AFTER DOING THAT, EVEN *HE* HAS TO BE TIRED. THEN WE MARSHAL THE FORCES AND—

GAAH! WHAT—?

RRRRG... WHERE DID...?

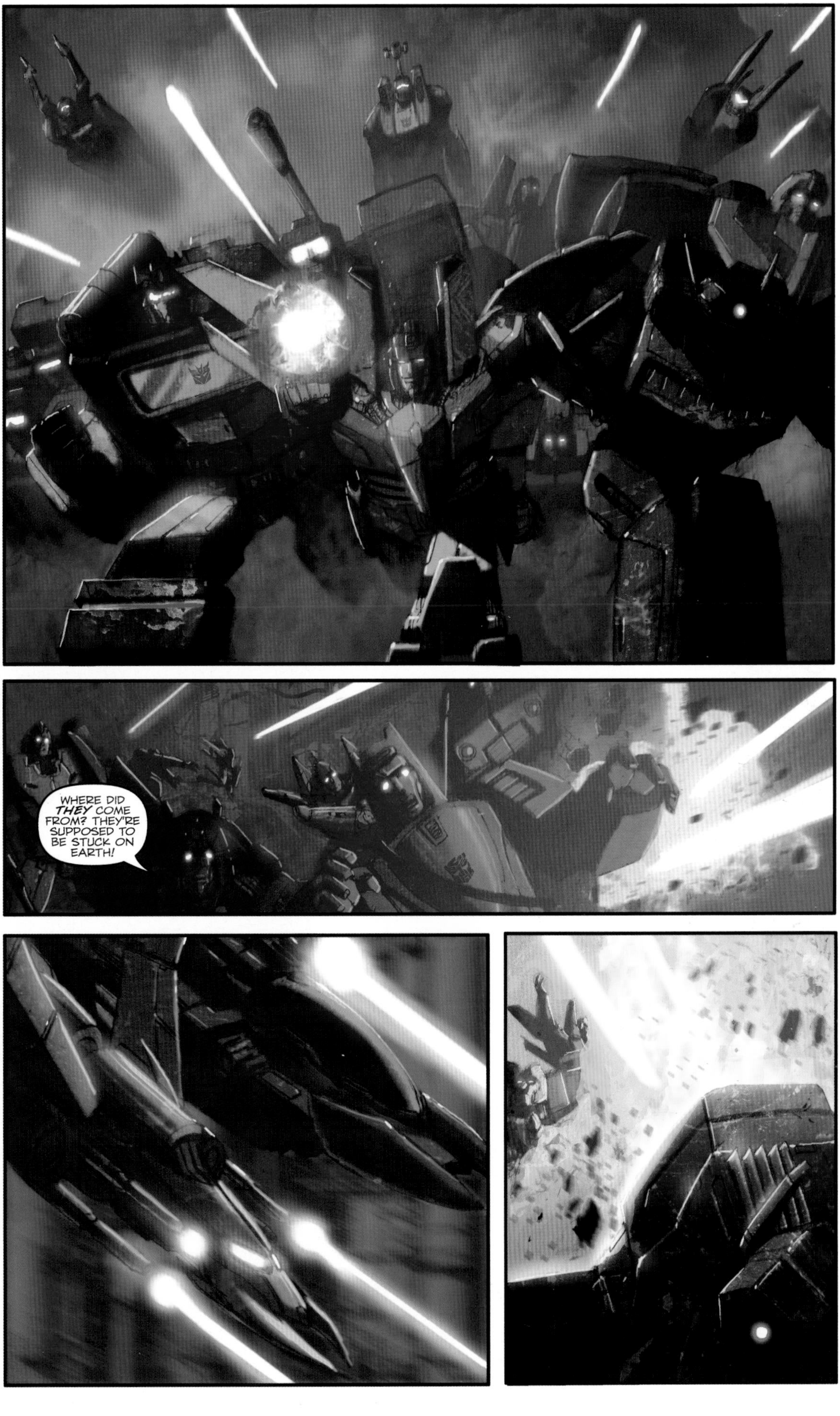
WHERE DID THEY COME FROM? THEY'RE SUPPOSED TO BE STUCK ON EARTH!

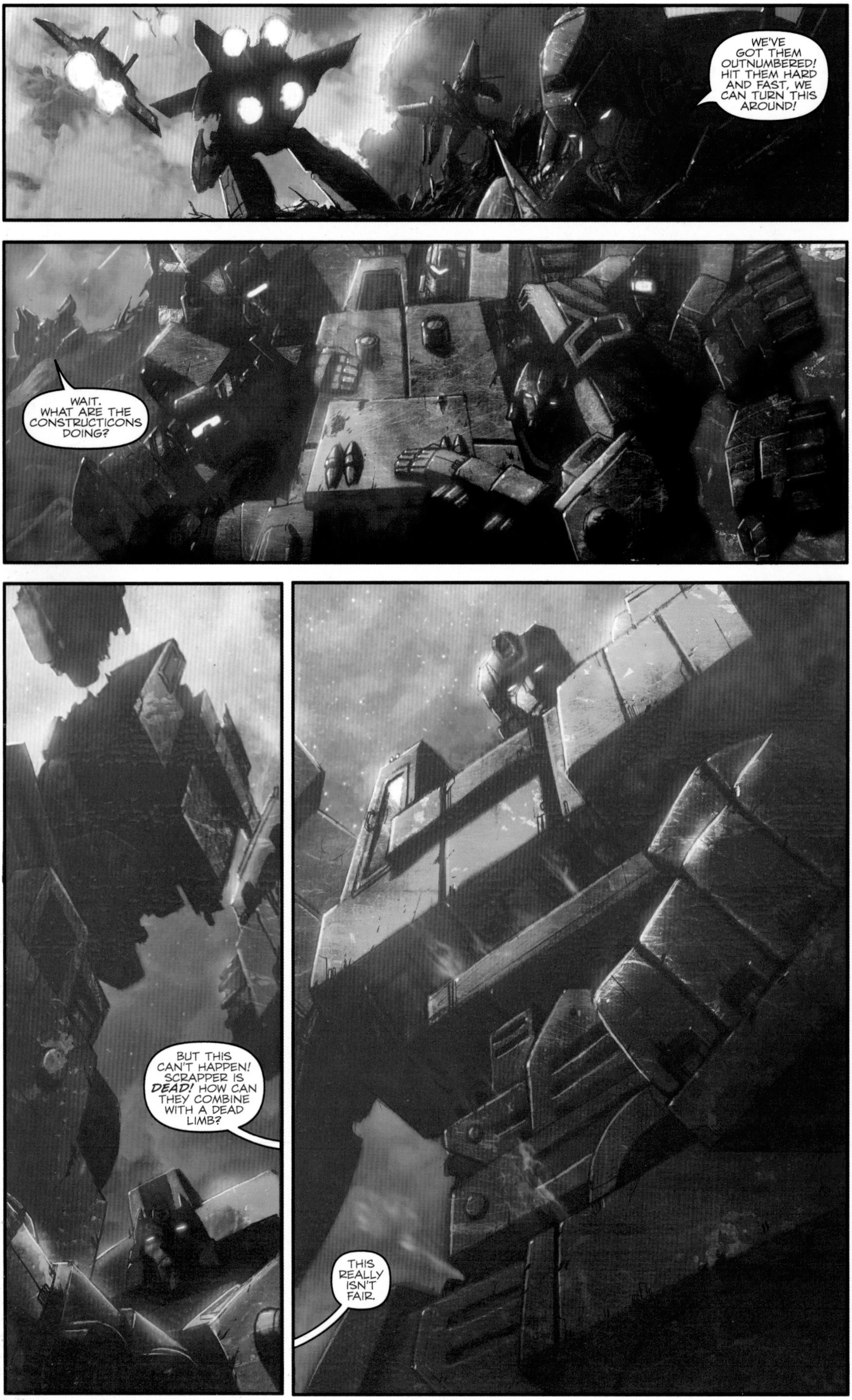
WE'VE GOT THEM OUTNUMBERED! HIT THEM HARD AND FAST, WE CAN TURN THIS AROUND!
WAIT. WHAT ARE THE CONSTRUCTICONS DOING?
BUT THIS CAN'T HAPPEN! SCRAPPER IS DEAD! HOW CAN THEY COMBINE WITH A DEAD LIMB?
THIS REALLY ISN'T FAIR.

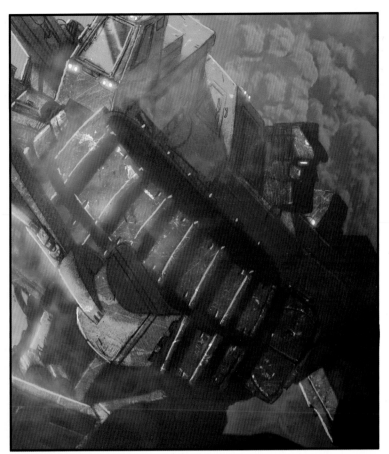

SCRAAAAAAAAAPE

HE'S *SLOW!* CAN'T USE HIS LEG! FALL BACK TO OMEGA SUPREME!

SUNSTREAKER! WE'RE RETREATING TO YOUR POSITION. *DEVASTATOR* IS HERE!

WHAT?! HOW IS THAT EVEN POSSIBLE?

JETFIRE THINKS THAT THEY MIGHT HAVE SOMEHOW BUILT A SPACE-BRIDGE BEACON INTO MEGATRON'S ACTUAL BODY, SO THEY COULD REINFORCE HIM WHEREVER HE WAS IN THE GALAXY.

GREAT. AS IF HE NEEDED REINFORCEMENT.

THEY'RE ALL OVER US AND WE NEED TO REGROUP.

WELL, DON'T BRING THEM *HERE!* OMEGA'S IN NO SHAPE TO SHELTER ANYONE. THE ONLY REASON WE SURVIVED MEGATRON'S ESCAPE IS BECAUSE WE STAYED OUT OF HIS WAY.

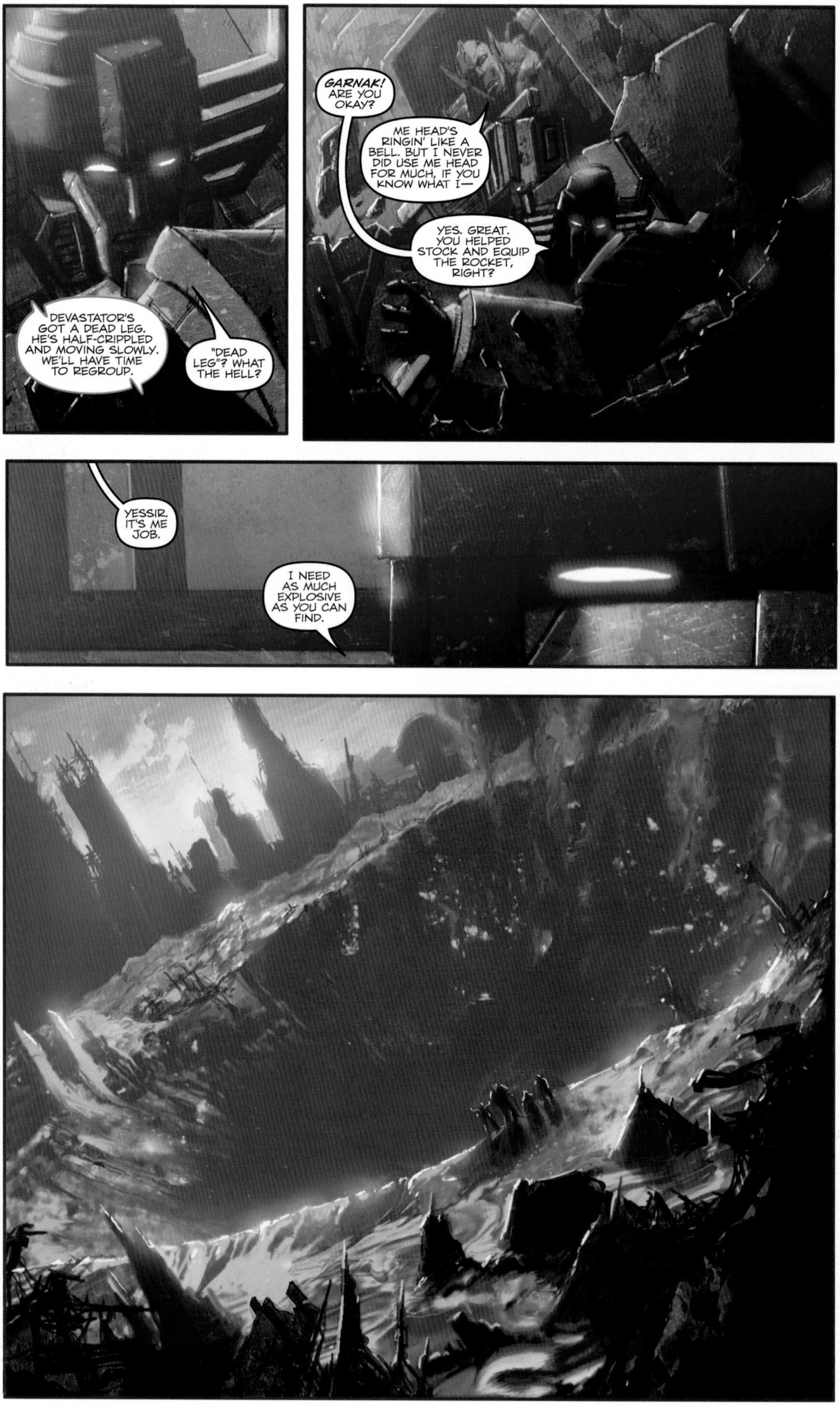

DEVASTATOR'S GOT A DEAD LEG. HE'S HALF-CRIPPLED AND MOVING SLOWLY. WE'LL HAVE TIME TO REGROUP.
"DEAD LEG"? WHAT THE HELL?
GARNAK! ARE YOU OKAY?
ME HEAD'S RINGIN' LIKE A BELL. BUT I NEVER DID USE ME HEAD FOR MUCH, IF YOU KNOW WHAT I—
YES. GREAT. YOU HELPED STOCK AND EQUIP THE ROCKET, RIGHT?
YESSIR. IT'S ME JOB.
I NEED AS MUCH EXPLOSIVE AS YOU CAN FIND.

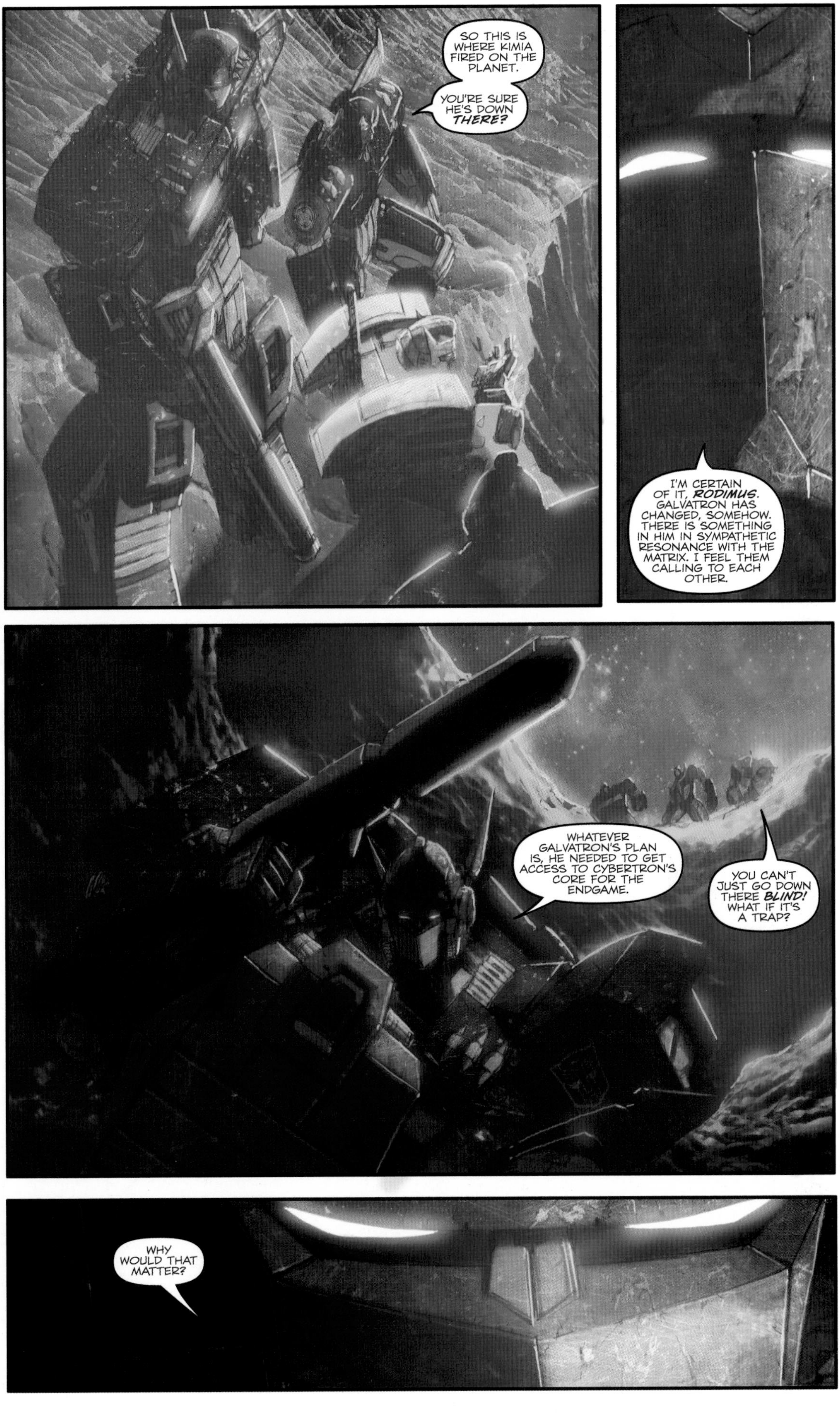
SO THIS IS WHERE KIMIA FIRED ON THE PLANET.
YOU'RE SURE HE'S DOWN *THERE?*
I'M CERTAIN OF IT, *RODIMUS*. GALVATRON HAS CHANGED, SOMEHOW. THERE IS SOMETHING IN HIM IN SYMPATHETIC RESONANCE WITH THE MATRIX. I FEEL THEM CALLING TO EACH OTHER.
WHATEVER GALVATRON'S PLAN IS, HE NEEDED TO GET ACCESS TO CYBERTRON'S CORE FOR THE ENDGAME.
YOU CAN'T JUST GO DOWN THERE *BLIND!* WHAT IF IT'S A TRAP?
WHY WOULD THAT MATTER?

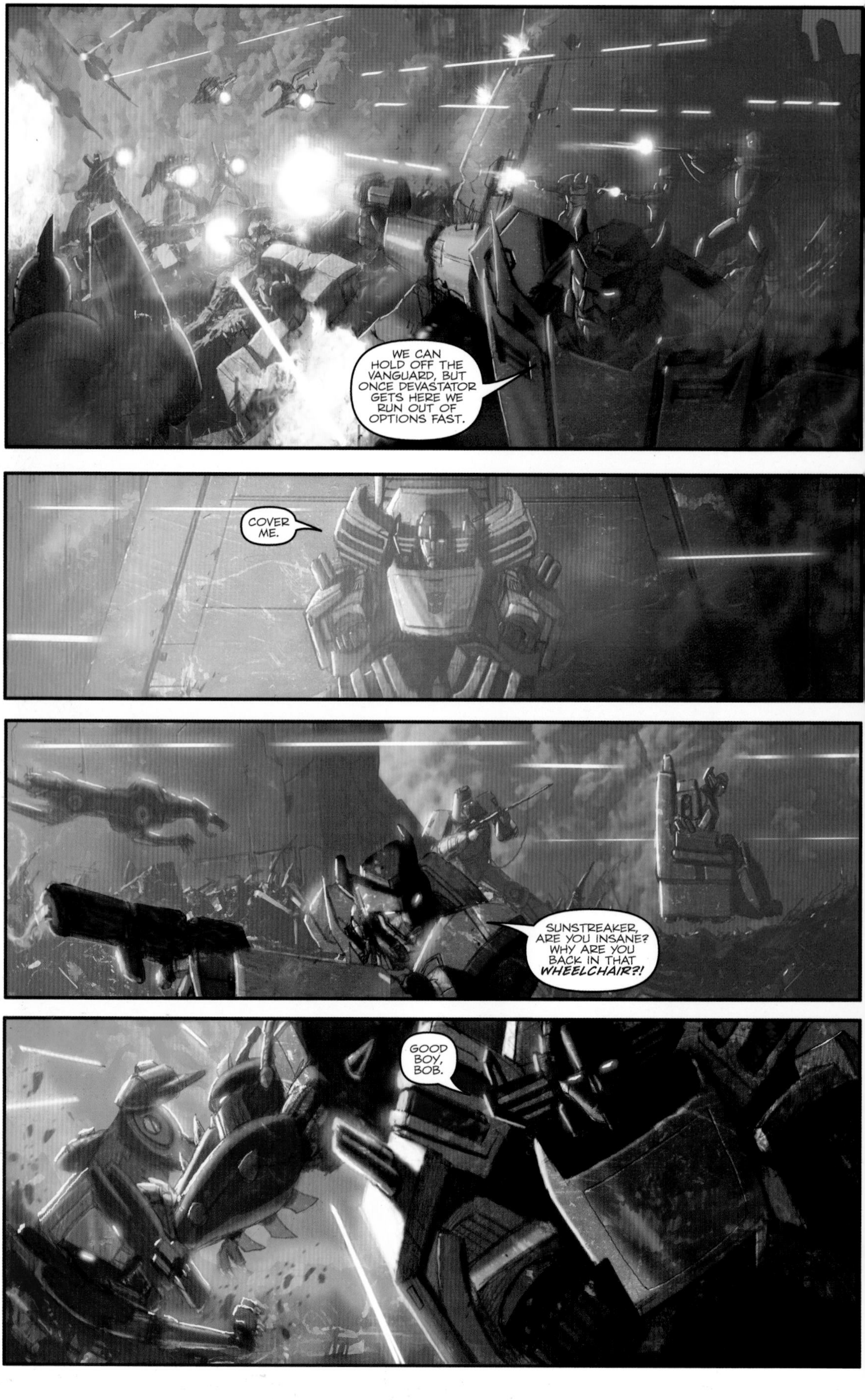

WE CAN HOLD OFF THE VANGUARD, BUT ONCE DEVASTATOR GETS HERE WE RUN OUT OF OPTIONS FAST.
COVER ME.
SUNSTREAKER, ARE YOU INSANE? WHY ARE YOU BACK IN THAT *WHEELCHAIR?!*
GOOD BOY, BOB.

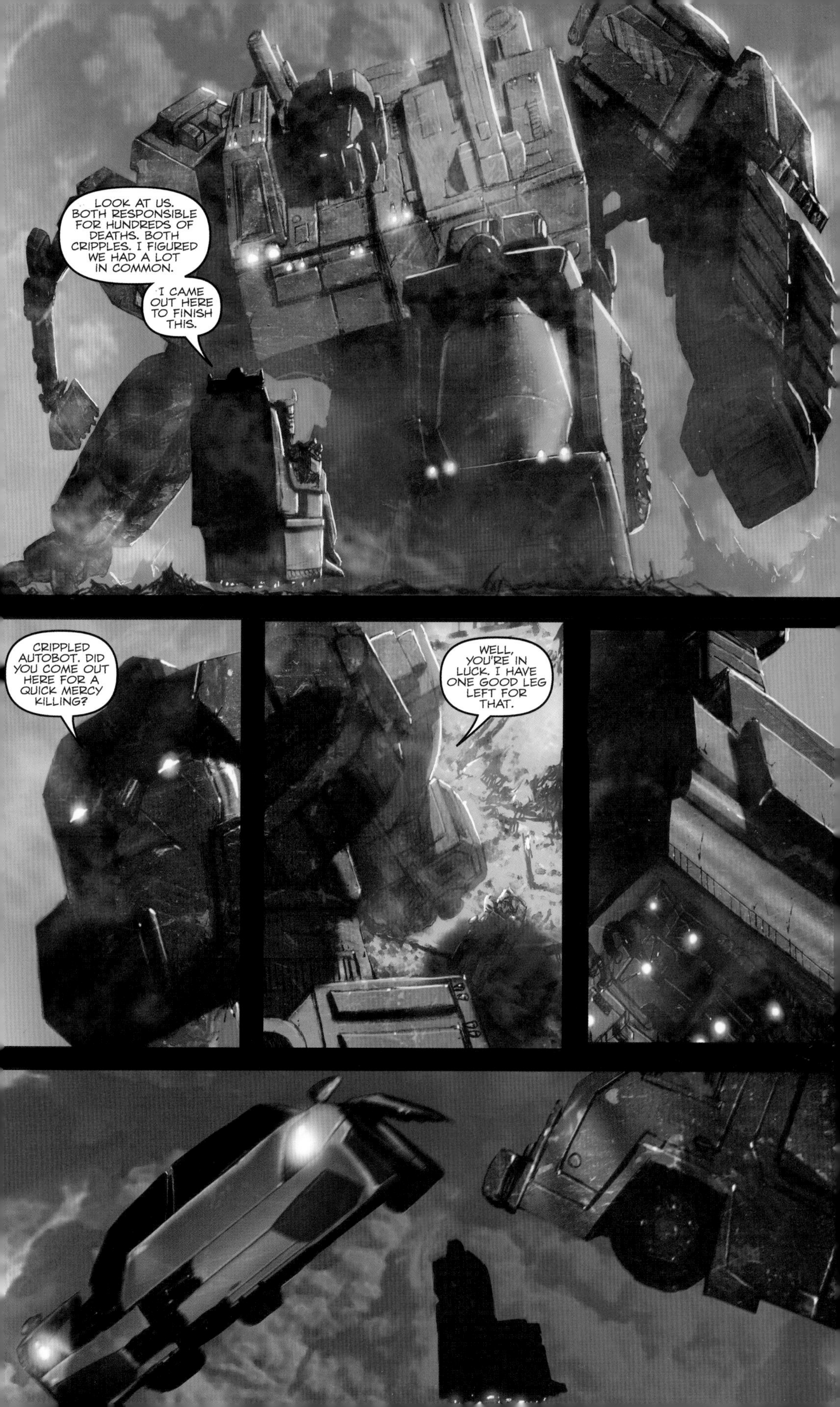
LOOK AT US. BOTH RESPONSIBLE FOR HUNDREDS OF DEATHS. BOTH CRIPPLES. I FIGURED WE HAD A LOT IN COMMON.
I CAME OUT HERE TO FINISH THIS.
CRIPPLED AUTOBOT. DID YOU COME OUT HERE FOR A QUICK MERCY KILLING?
WELL, YOU'RE IN LUCK. I HAVE ONE GOOD LEG LEFT FOR THAT.

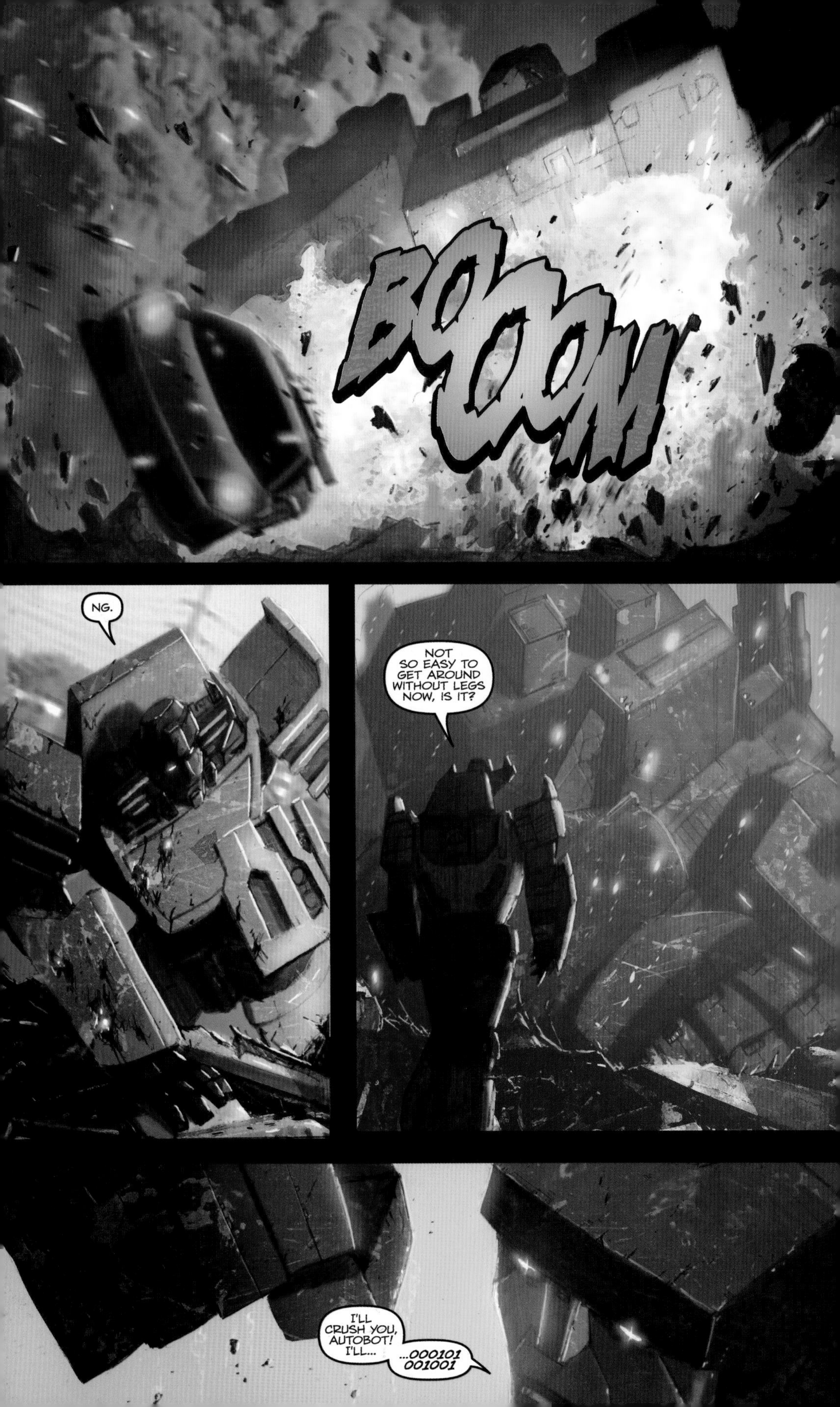
BOOOM
NG.
NOT SO EASY TO GET AROUND WITHOUT LEGS NOW, IS IT?
I'LL CRUSH YOU, AUTOBOT! I'LL...
...000101 001001

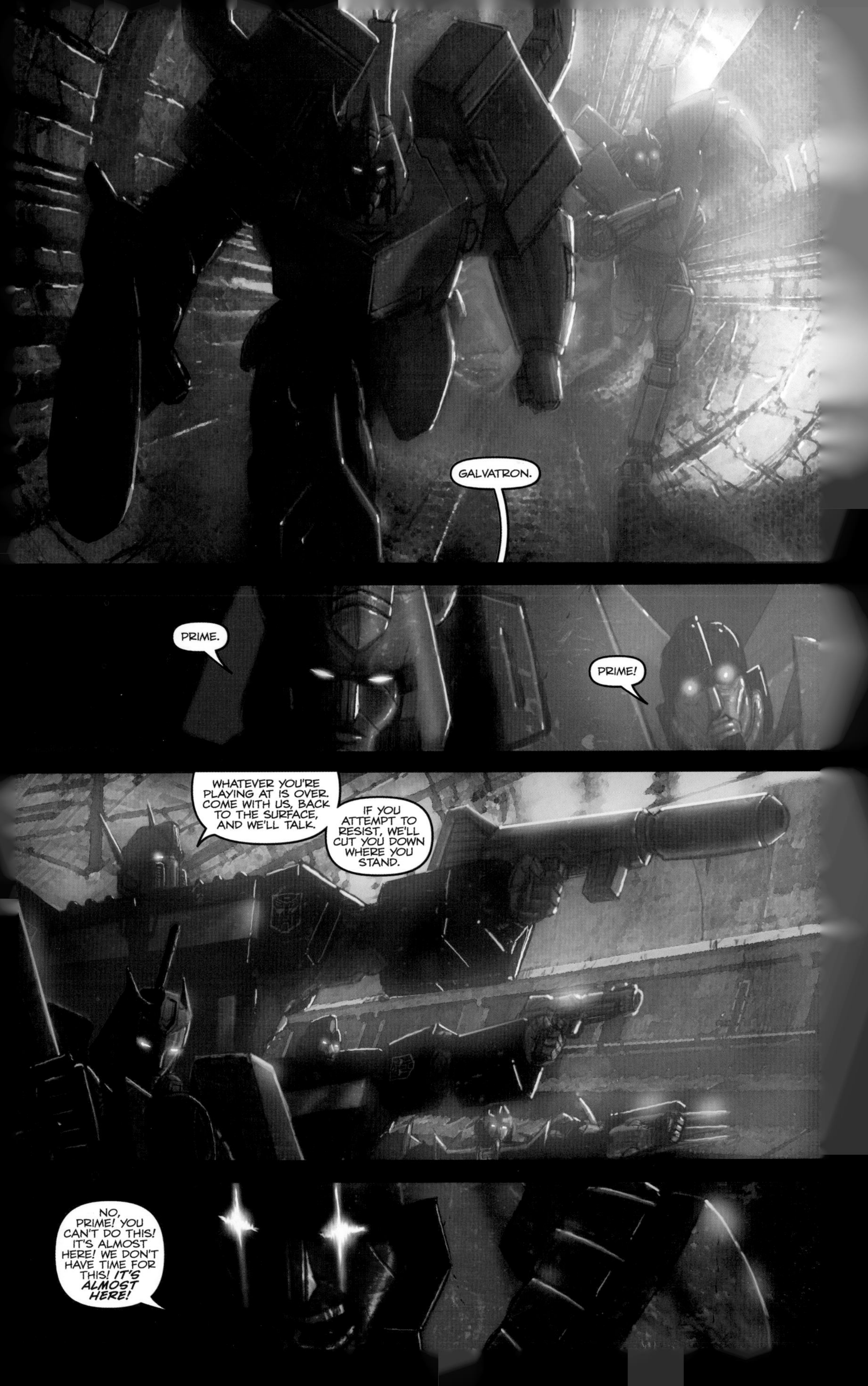
GALVATRON.
PRIME.
PRIME!
WHATEVER YOU'RE PLAYING AT IS OVER. COME WITH US, BACK TO THE SURFACE, AND WE'LL TALK.
IF YOU ATTEMPT TO RESIST, WE'LL CUT YOU DOWN WHERE YOU STAND.
NO, PRIME! YOU CAN'T DO THIS! IT'S ALMOST HERE! WE DON'T HAVE TIME FOR THIS! *IT'S ALMOST HERE!*

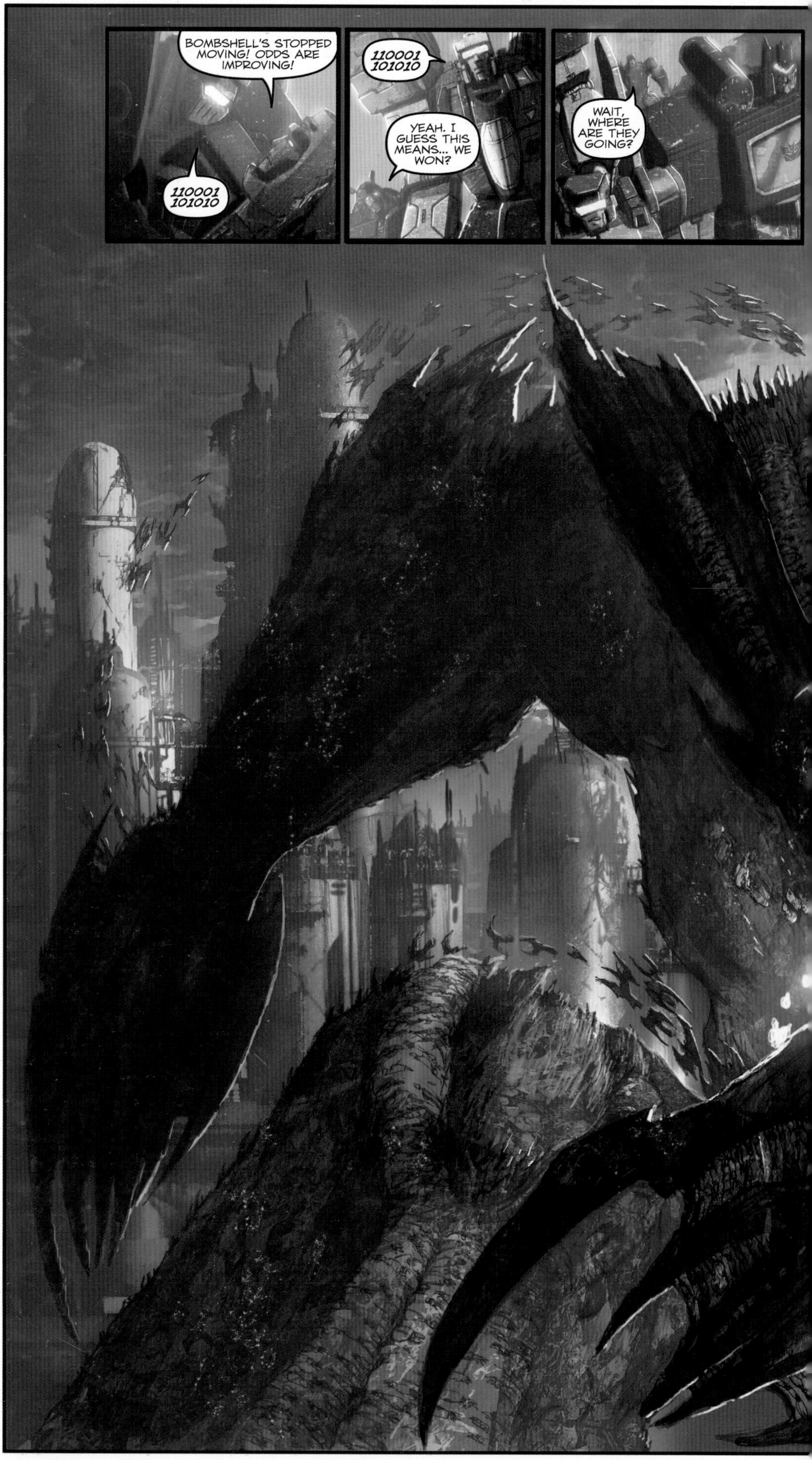
BOMBSHELL'S STOPPED MOVING! ODDS ARE IMPROVING!
110001 101010
110001 101010
YEAH. I GUESS THIS MEANS... WE WON?
WAIT, WHERE ARE THEY GOING?

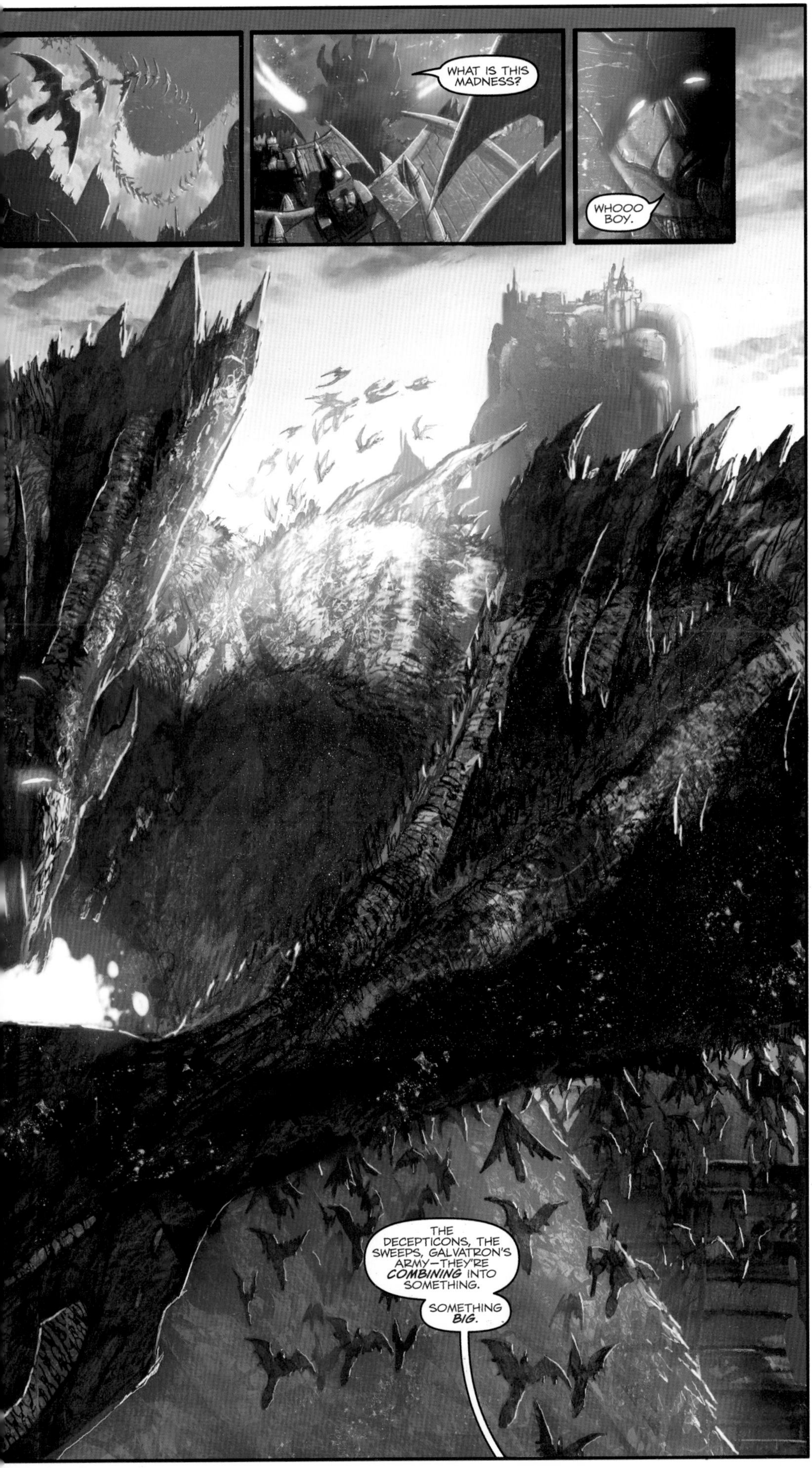
WHAT IS THIS MADNESS?
WHOOO BOY.
THE DECEPTICONS, THE SWEEPS, GALVATRON'S ARMY—THEY'RE *COMBINING* INTO SOMETHING.
SOMETHING *BIG*.

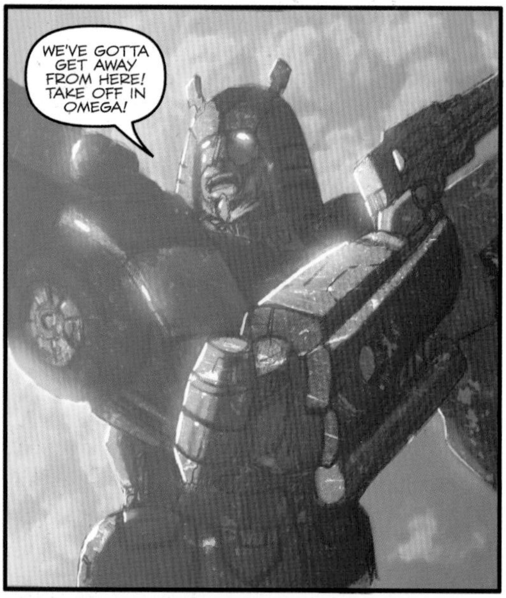
WE'VE GOTTA GET AWAY FROM HERE! TAKE OFF IN OMEGA!

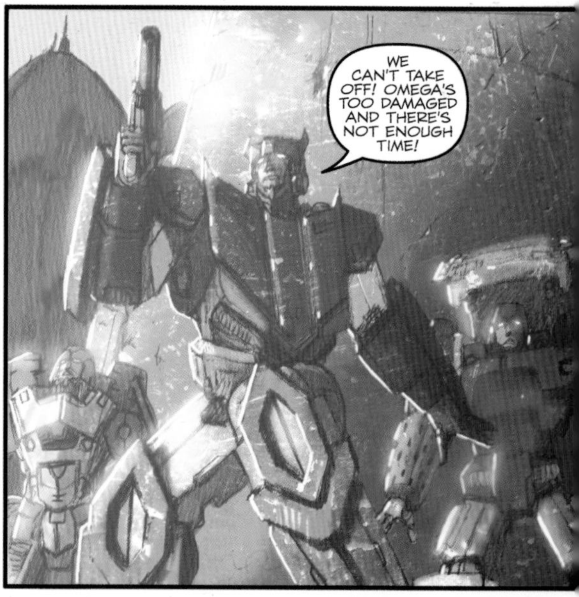
WE CAN'T TAKE OFF! OMEGA'S TOO DAMAGED AND THERE'S NOT ENOUGH TIME!

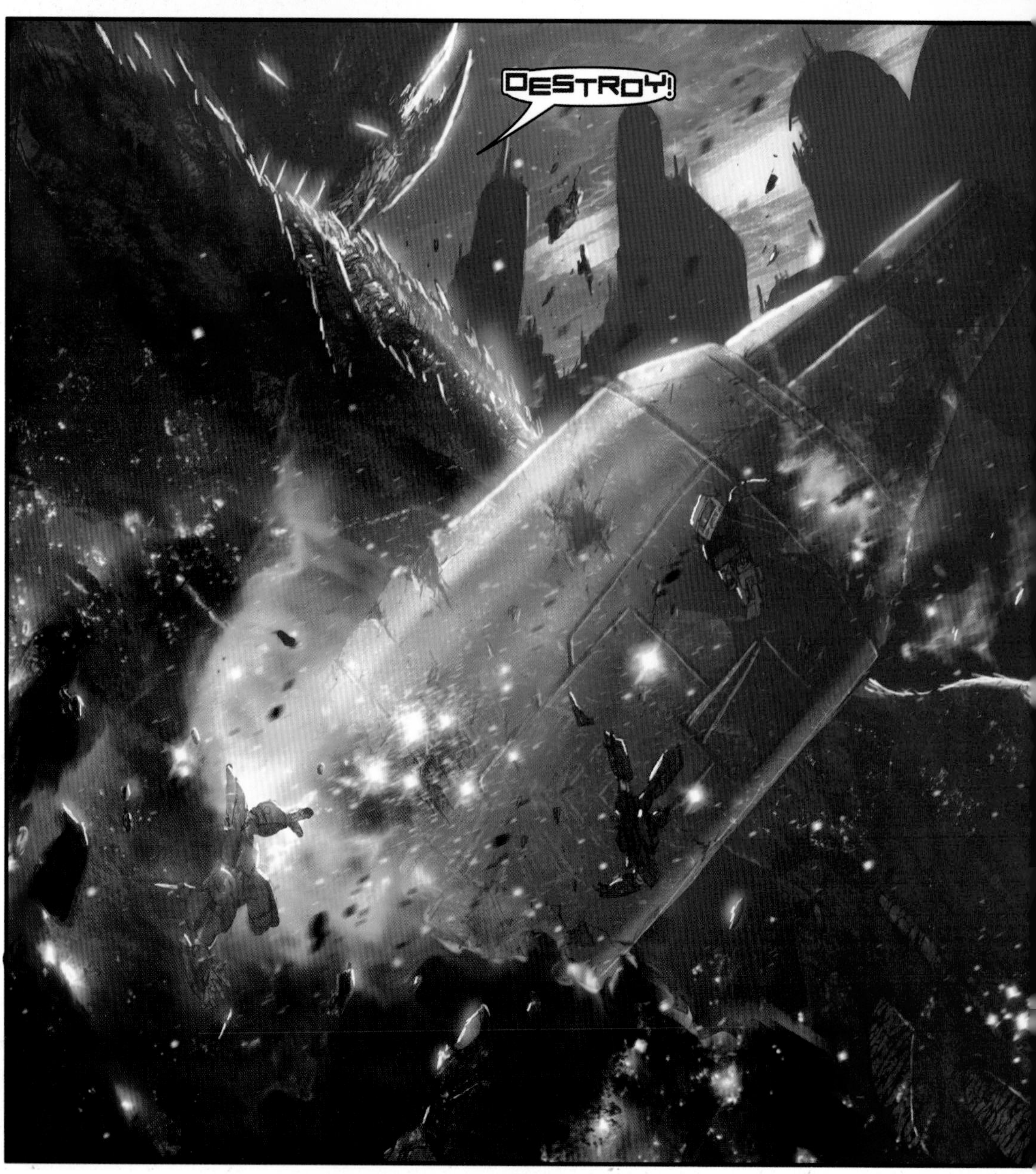
DESTROY!

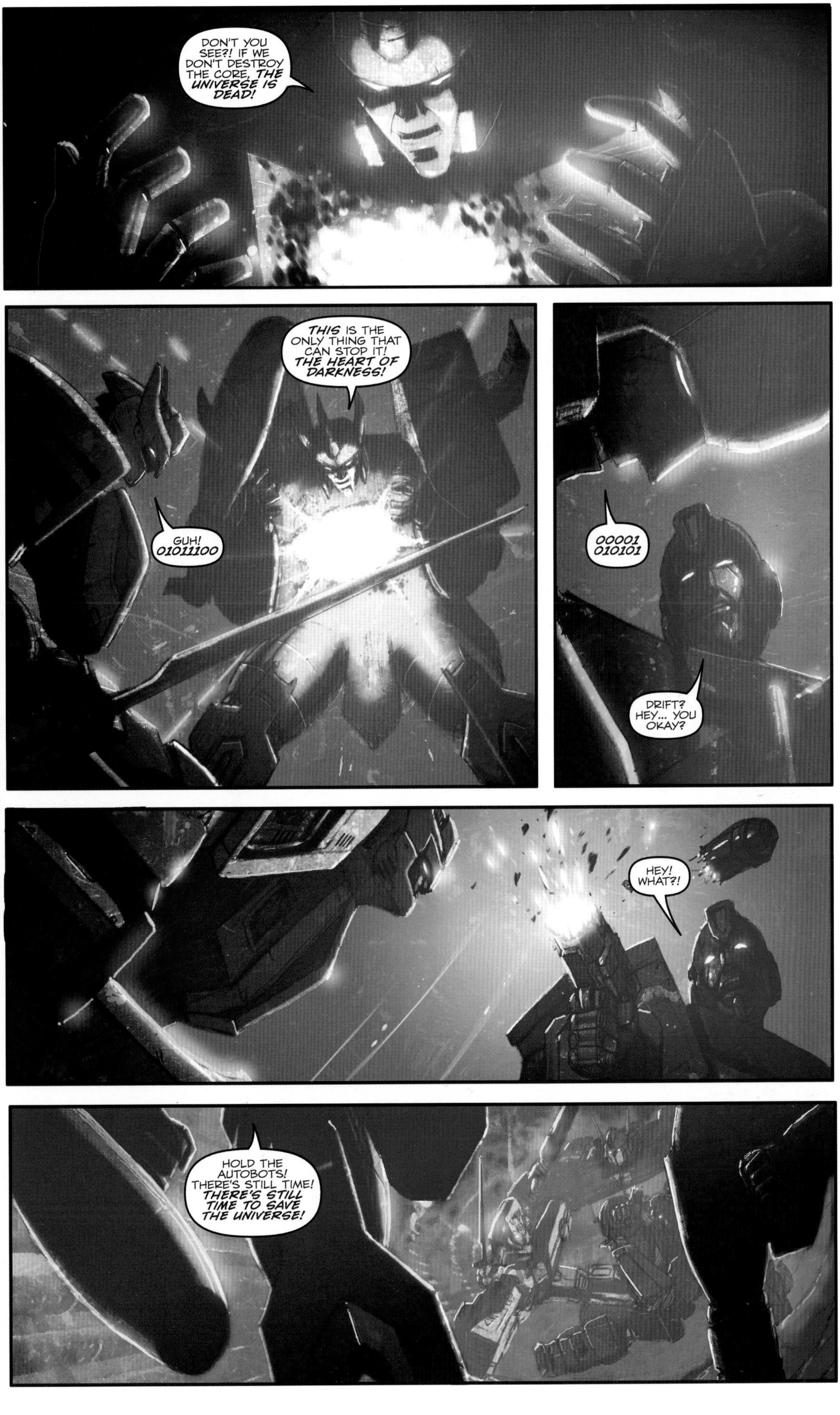
DON'T YOU SEE?! IF WE DON'T DESTROY THE CORE, THE UNIVERSE IS DEAD!
THIS IS THE ONLY THING THAT CAN STOP IT! THE HEART OF DARKNESS!
GUH! 01011100
00001 010101
DRIFT? HEY... YOU OKAY?
HEY! WHAT?!
HOLD THE AUTOBOTS! THERE'S STILL TIME! THERE'S STILL TIME TO SAVE THE UNIVERSE!

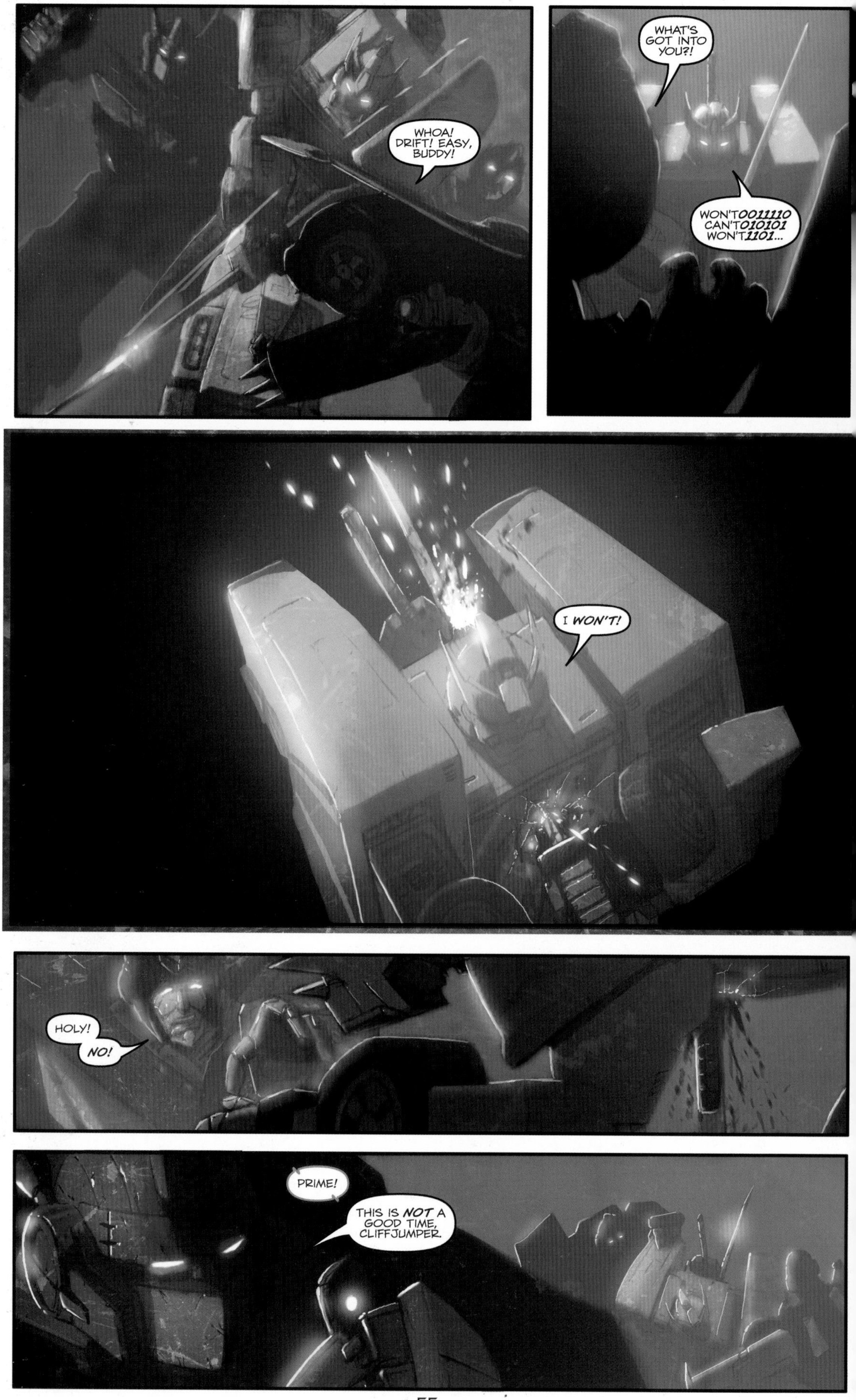
WHOA! DRIFT! EASY, BUDDY!
WHAT'S GOT INTO YOU?!
WON'T0011110 CAN'T010101 WON'T1101...
I WON'T!
HOLY!
NO!
PRIME!
THIS IS NOT A GOOD TIME, CLIFFJUMPER.

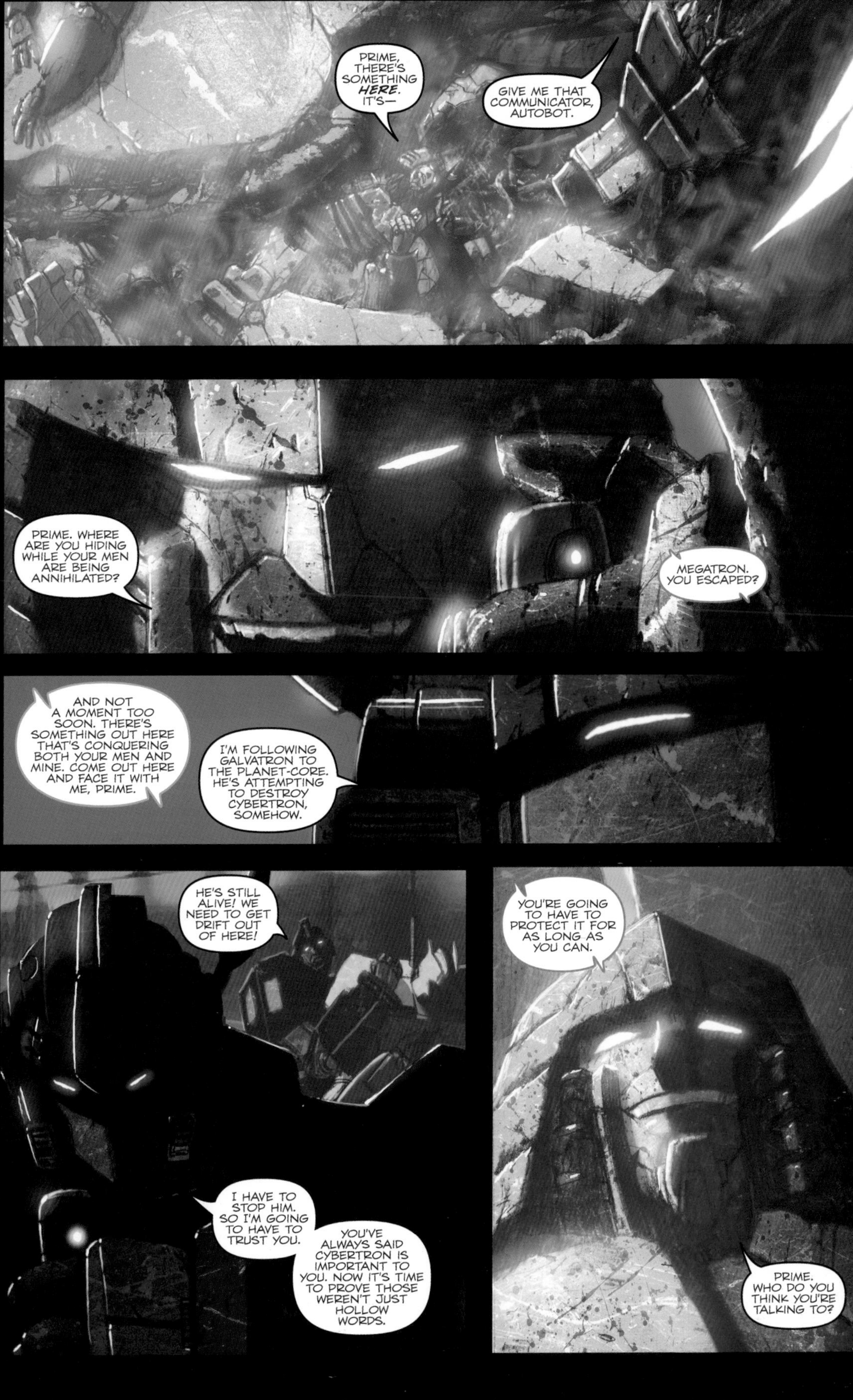
PRIME, THERE'S SOMETHING *HERE*. IT'S—
GIVE ME THAT COMMUNICATOR, AUTOBOT.
PRIME. WHERE ARE YOU HIDING WHILE YOUR MEN ARE BEING ANNIHILATED?
MEGATRON. YOU ESCAPED?
AND NOT A MOMENT TOO SOON. THERE'S SOMETHING OUT HERE THAT'S CONQUERING BOTH YOUR MEN AND MINE. COME OUT HERE AND FACE IT WITH ME, PRIME.
I'M FOLLOWING GALVATRON TO THE PLANET-CORE. HE'S ATTEMPTING TO DESTROY CYBERTRON, SOMEHOW.
HE'S STILL ALIVE! WE NEED TO GET DRIFT OUT OF HERE!
I HAVE TO STOP HIM. SO I'M GOING TO HAVE TO TRUST YOU.
YOU'VE ALWAYS SAID CYBERTRON IS IMPORTANT TO YOU. NOW IT'S TIME TO PROVE THOSE WEREN'T JUST HOLLOW WORDS.
YOU'RE GOING TO HAVE TO PROTECT IT FOR AS LONG AS YOU CAN.
PRIME. WHO DO YOU THINK YOU'RE TALKING TO?

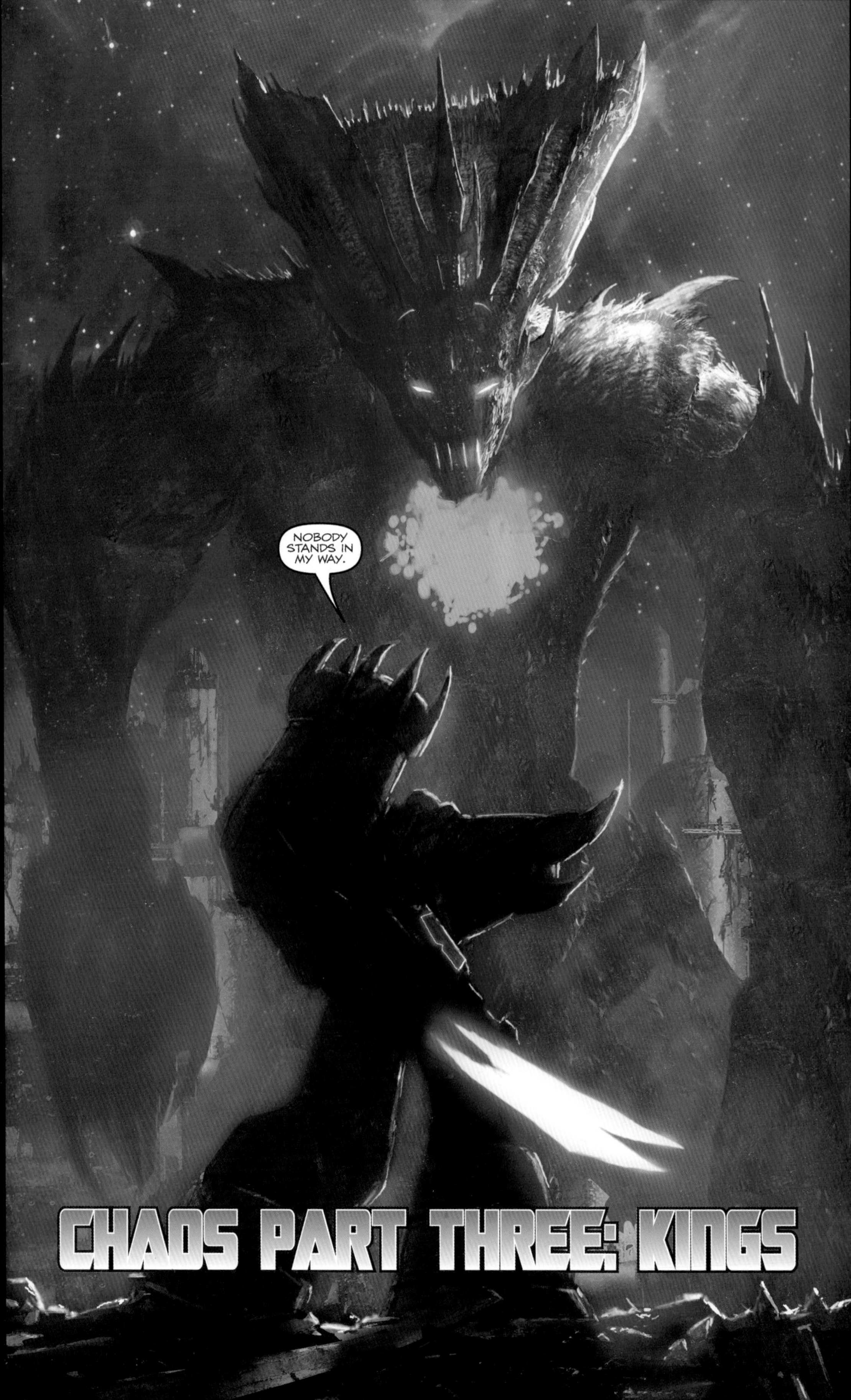
NOBODY STANDS IN MY WAY.
CHAOS PART THREE: KINGS

CAN WE JUST GO THROUGH IT *ONE MORE TIME?*

4

BY THE GREAT WELD, *BRAINSTORM!* WE'VE BEEN THROUGH IT *FIVE TIMES* ALREADY! YOU'RE SUPPOSED TO BE THE *SMART ONE!*

OH, I'M SURE IT ALL MAKES PERFECT SENSE TO *YOU, ARCEE!*

YOU AND *HARDHEAD* HAVE HAD *AGES* TO THINK ABOUT IT SINCE YOU LEFT *GORLAM PRIME.* FOR US, IT'S LIKE— IT'S LIKE A MASSIVE... WHAT DO YOU CALL IT?

INFO DUMP?

YES! EXACTLY!

LOOK, I ONLY KNOW THIS STUFF BECAUSE *GALVATRON* RUMMAGED AROUND IN MY MIND. THE CONNECTION MUST'VE WORKED BOTH WAYS, 'COS I WAS ABLE TO SEE WHAT *HE* WAS THINKING.

THAT MIND-MELD AND THE TIME I SPENT IN THE *DEAD UNIVERSE* HAVE GIVEN ME A CERTAIN *INSIGHT* INTO THE *BIGGER PICTURE.*

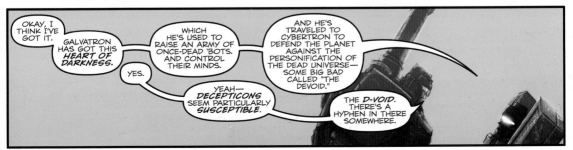

OKAY, I THINK I'VE GOT IT.

GALVATRON HAS GOT THIS *HEART OF DARKNESS.*

WHICH HE'S USED TO RAISE AN ARMY OF ONCE-DEAD 'BOTS. AND CONTROL THEIR MINDS.

AND HE'S TRAVELED TO CYBERTRON TO DEFEND THE PLANET AGAINST THE PERSONIFICATION OF THE DEAD UNIVERSE— SOME BIG BAD CALLED "THE DEVOID."

YES.

YEAH— *DECEPTICONS* SEEM PARTICULARLY *SUSCEPTIBLE.*

THE *D-VOID.* THERE'S A HYPHEN IN THERE SOMEWHERE.

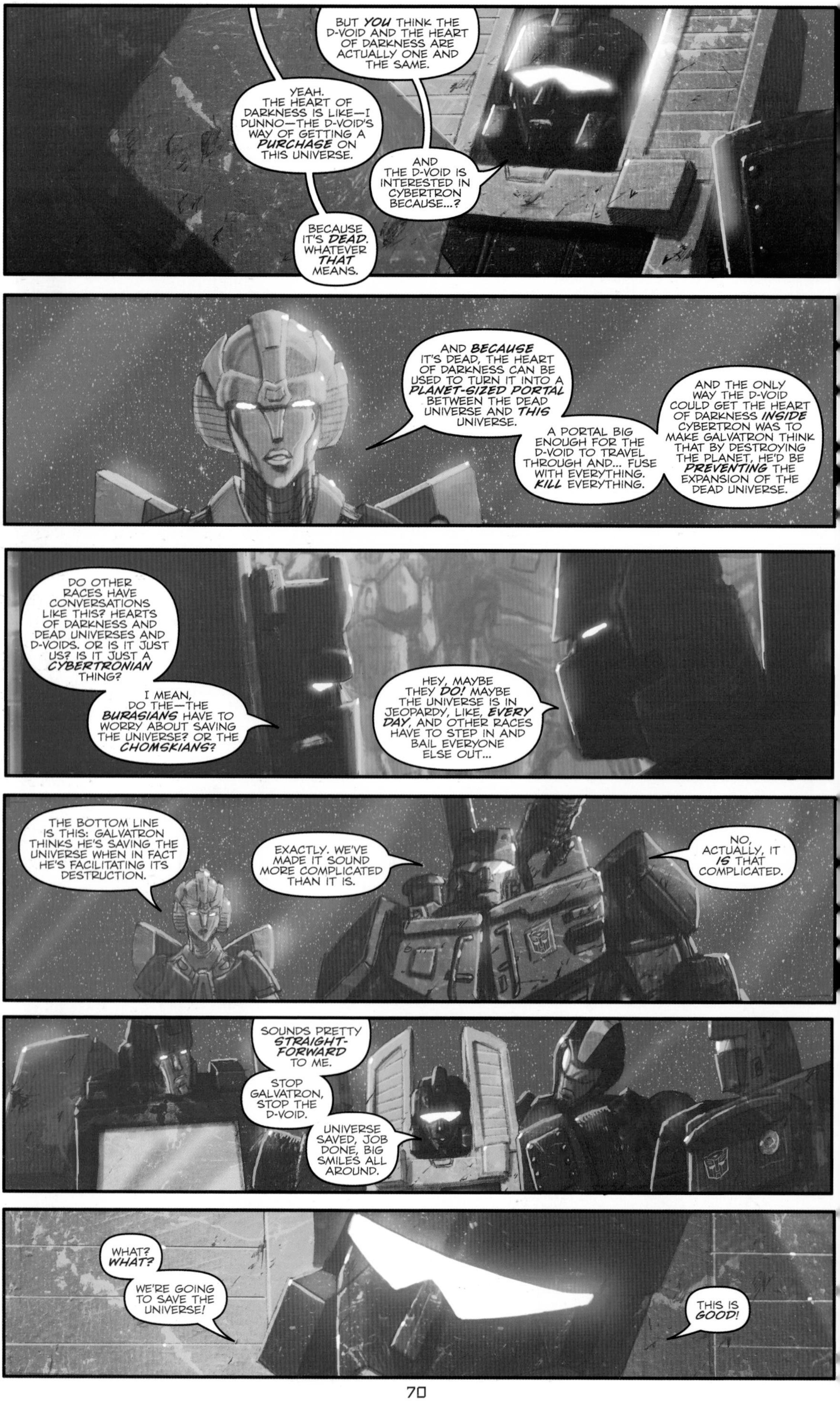
BUT YOU THINK THE D-VOID AND THE HEART OF DARKNESS ARE ACTUALLY ONE AND THE SAME.
YEAH. THE HEART OF DARKNESS IS LIKE—I DUNNO—THE D-VOID'S WAY OF GETTING A PURCHASE ON THIS UNIVERSE.
AND THE D-VOID IS INTERESTED IN CYBERTRON BECAUSE...?
BECAUSE IT'S DEAD. WHATEVER THAT MEANS.
AND BECAUSE IT'S DEAD, THE HEART OF DARKNESS CAN BE USED TO TURN IT INTO A PLANET-SIZED PORTAL BETWEEN THE DEAD UNIVERSE AND THIS UNIVERSE.
A PORTAL BIG ENOUGH FOR THE D-VOID TO TRAVEL THROUGH AND... FUSE WITH EVERYTHING. KILL EVERYTHING.
AND THE ONLY WAY THE D-VOID COULD GET THE HEART OF DARKNESS INSIDE CYBERTRON WAS TO MAKE GALVATRON THINK THAT BY DESTROYING THE PLANET, HE'D BE PREVENTING THE EXPANSION OF THE DEAD UNIVERSE.
DO OTHER RACES HAVE CONVERSATIONS LIKE THIS? HEARTS OF DARKNESS AND DEAD UNIVERSES AND D-VOIDS. OR IS IT JUST US? IS IT JUST A CYBERTRONIAN THING?
I MEAN, DO THE—THE BURASIANS HAVE TO WORRY ABOUT SAVING THE UNIVERSE? OR THE CHOMSKIANS?
HEY, MAYBE THEY DO! MAYBE THE UNIVERSE IS IN JEOPARDY, LIKE, EVERY DAY, AND OTHER RACES HAVE TO STEP IN AND BAIL EVERYONE ELSE OUT...
THE BOTTOM LINE IS THIS: GALVATRON THINKS HE'S SAVING THE UNIVERSE WHEN IN FACT HE'S FACILITATING ITS DESTRUCTION.
EXACTLY. WE'VE MADE IT SOUND MORE COMPLICATED THAN IT IS.
NO, ACTUALLY, IT IS THAT COMPLICATED.
SOUNDS PRETTY STRAIGHT-FORWARD TO ME.
STOP GALVATRON, STOP THE D-VOID.
UNIVERSE SAVED, JOB DONE, BIG SMILES ALL AROUND.
WHAT? WHAT?
WE'RE GOING TO SAVE THE UNIVERSE!
THIS IS GOOD!

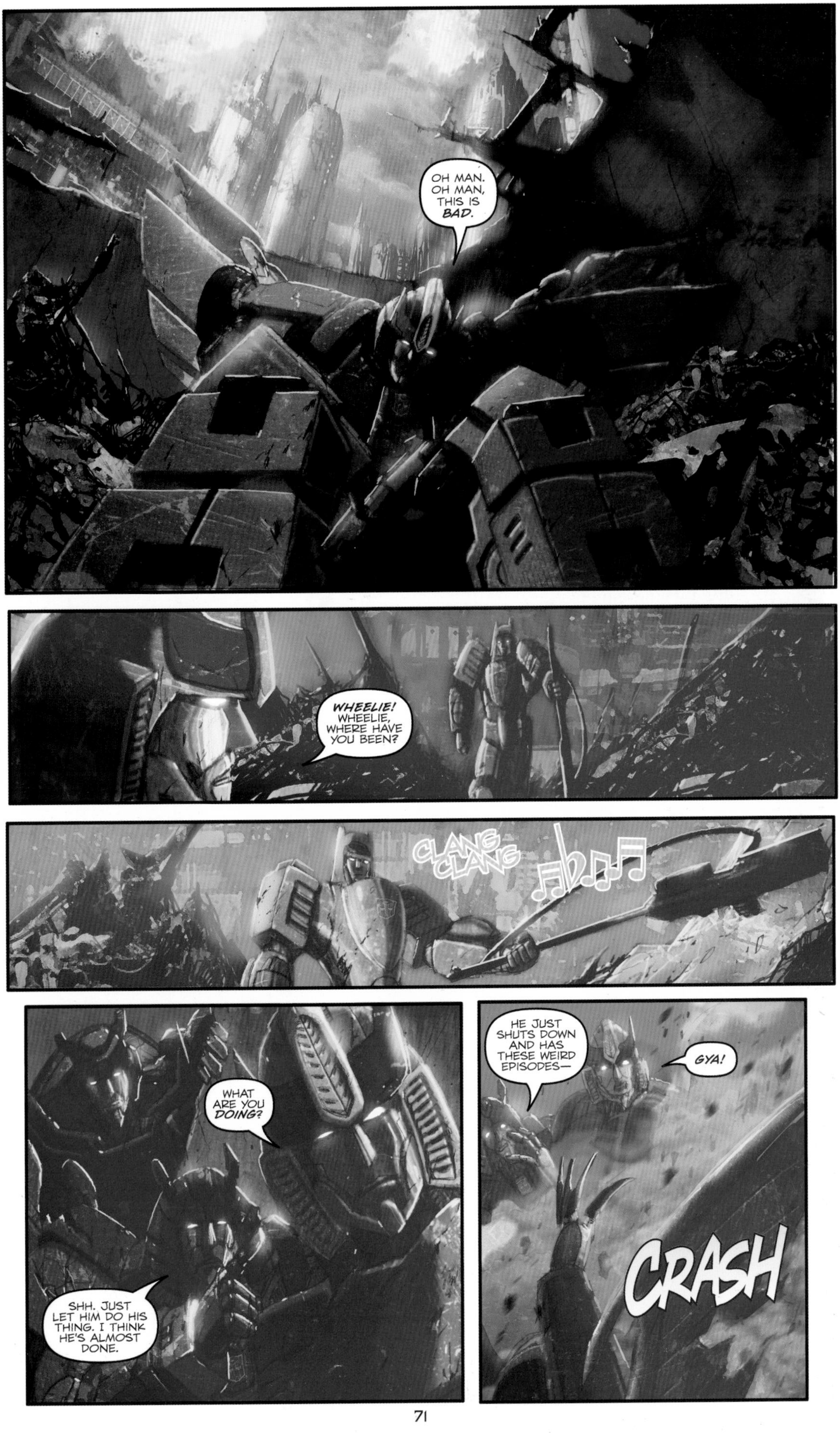

OH MAN. OH MAN, THIS IS BAD.
WHEELIE! WHEELIE, WHERE HAVE YOU BEEN?
CLANG CLANG
WHAT ARE YOU DOING?
SHH. JUST LET HIM DO HIS THING. I THINK HE'S ALMOST DONE.
HE JUST SHUTS DOWN AND HAS THESE WEIRD EPISODES—
GYA!
CRASH

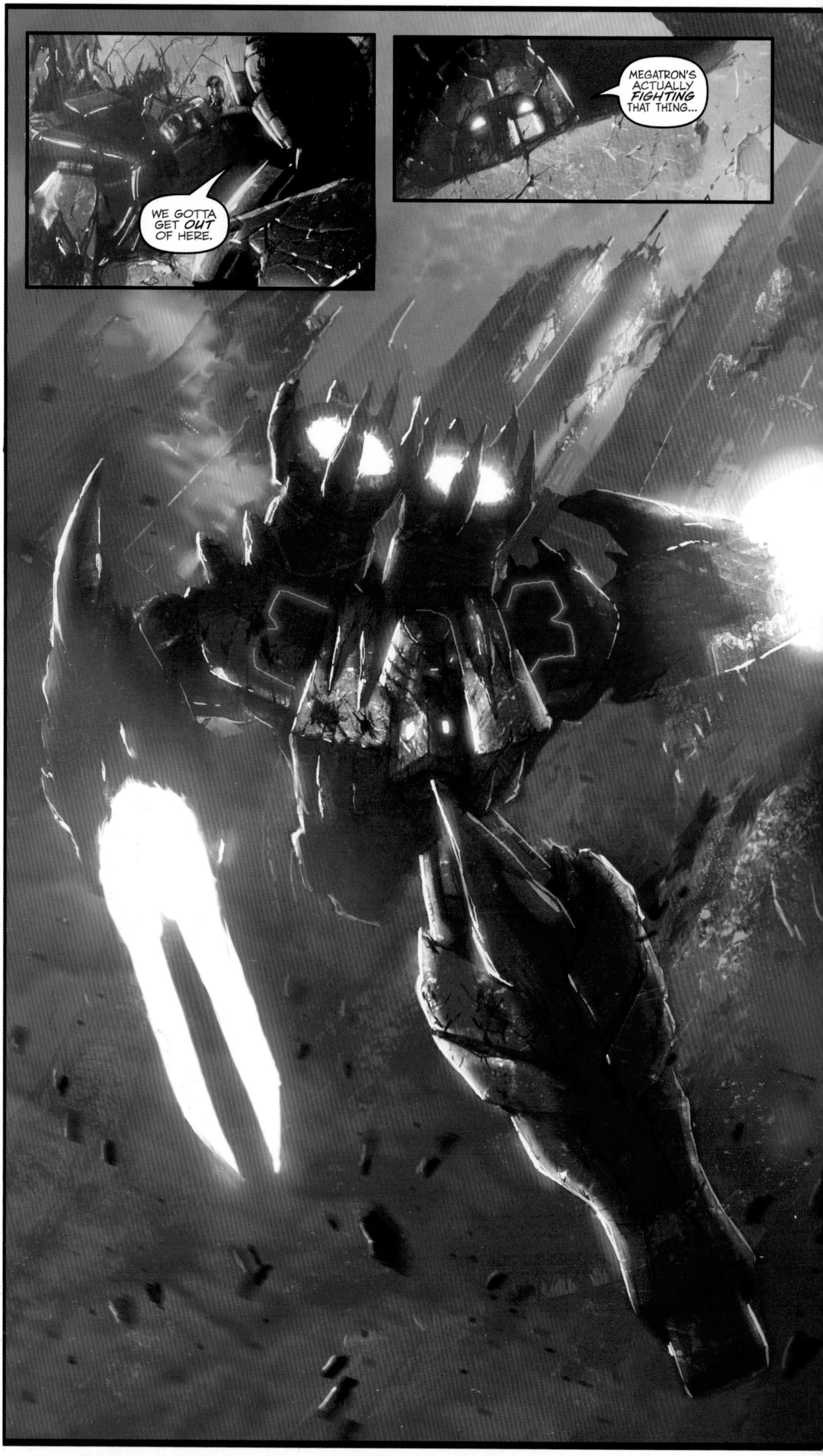
WE GOTTA GET OUT OF HERE.
MEGATRON'S ACTUALLY FIGHTING THAT THING...

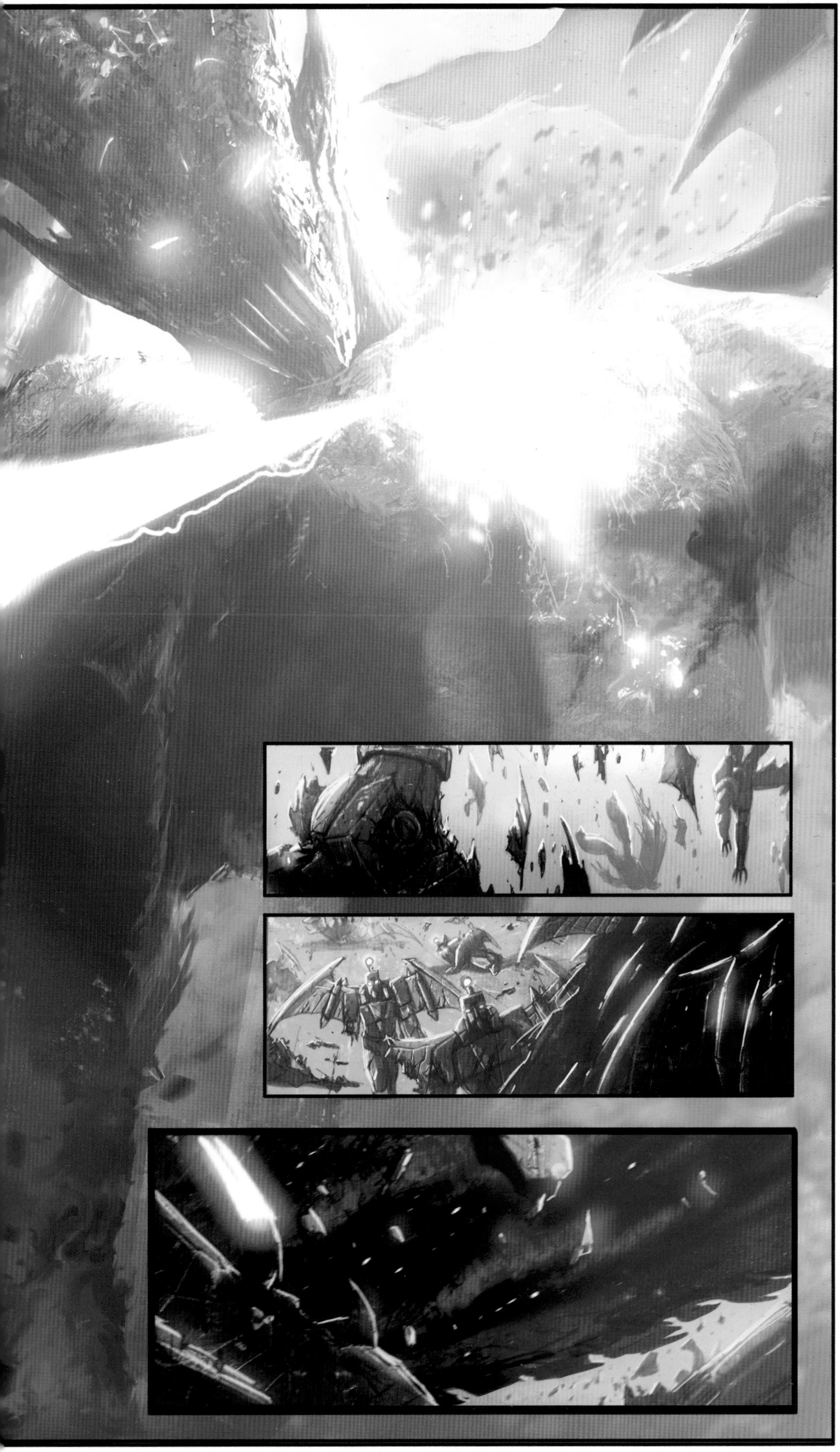

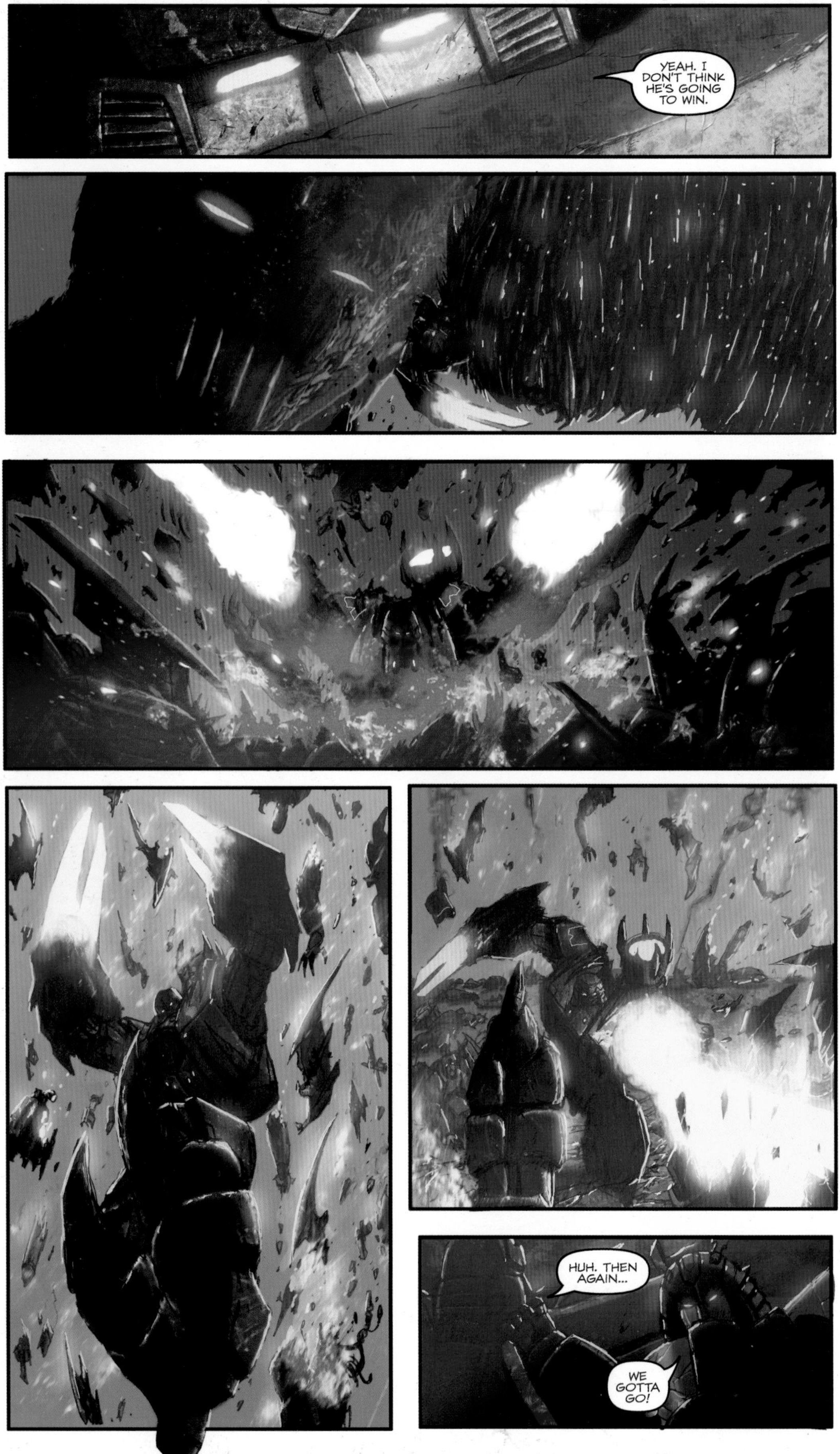
YEAH. I DON'T THINK HE'S GOING TO WIN.
HUH. THEN AGAIN...
WE GOTTA GO!

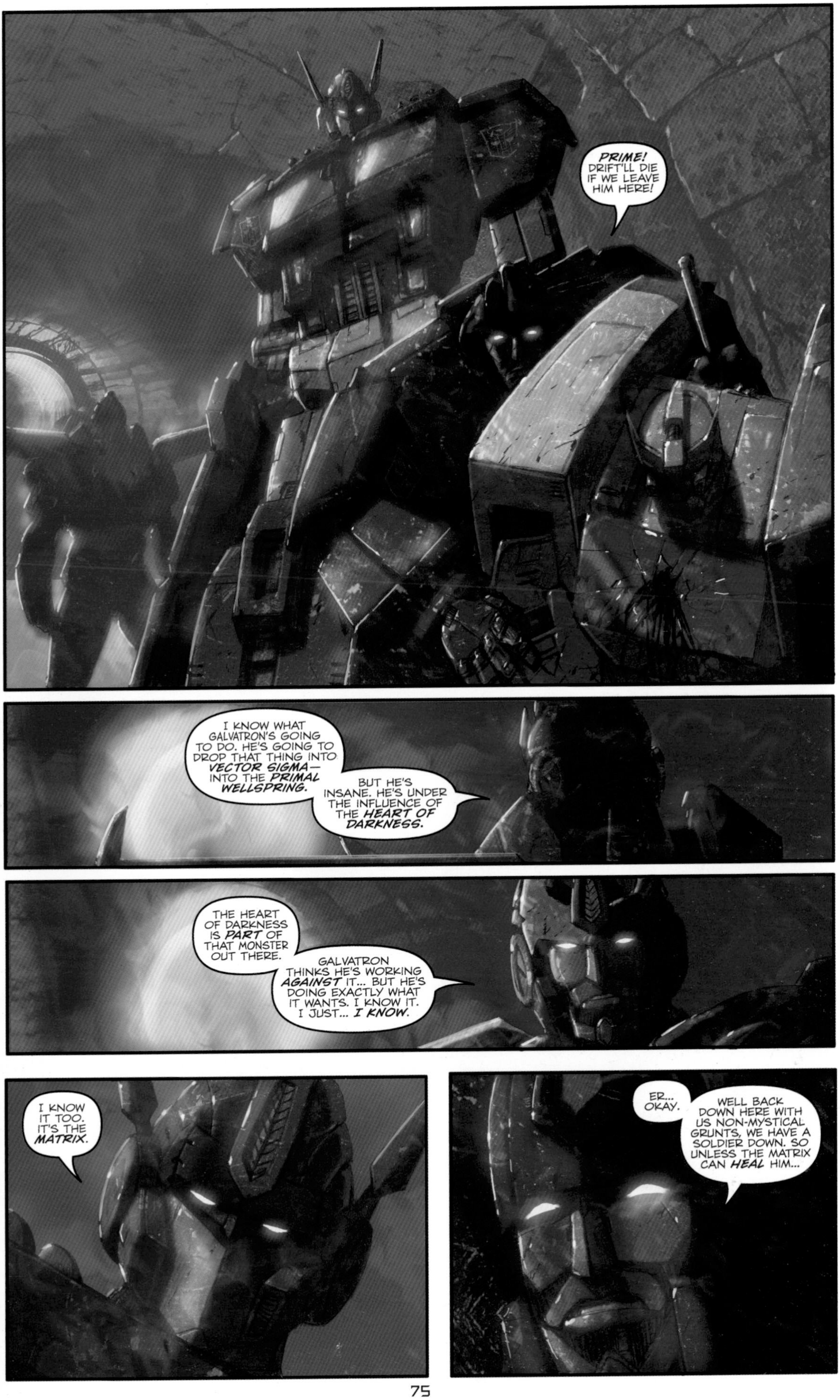
PRIME! DRIFT'LL DIE IF WE LEAVE HIM HERE!
I KNOW WHAT GALVATRON'S GOING TO DO. HE'S GOING TO DROP THAT THING INTO VECTOR SIGMA— INTO THE PRIMAL WELLSPRING.
BUT HE'S INSANE. HE'S UNDER THE INFLUENCE OF THE HEART OF DARKNESS.
THE HEART OF DARKNESS IS PART OF THAT MONSTER OUT THERE.
GALVATRON THINKS HE'S WORKING AGAINST IT... BUT HE'S DOING EXACTLY WHAT IT WANTS. I KNOW IT. I JUST... I KNOW.
I KNOW IT TOO. IT'S THE MATRIX.
ER... OKAY.
WELL BACK DOWN HERE WITH US NON-MYSTICAL GRUNTS, WE HAVE A SOLDIER DOWN. SO UNLESS THE MATRIX CAN HEAL HIM...

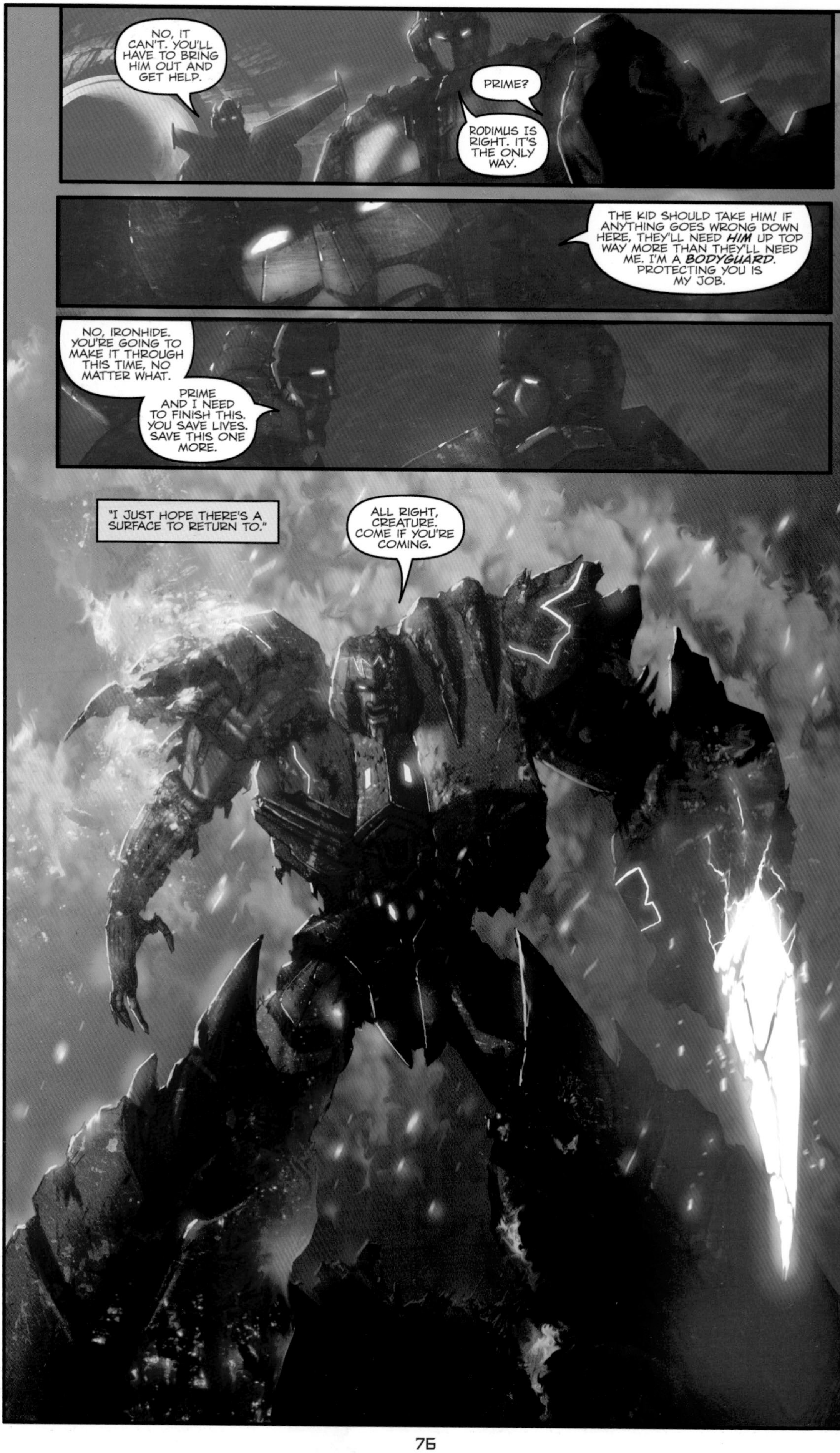
NO, IT CAN'T. YOU'LL HAVE TO BRING HIM OUT AND GET HELP.
PRIME?
RODIMUS IS RIGHT. IT'S THE ONLY WAY.
THE KID SHOULD TAKE HIM! IF ANYTHING GOES WRONG DOWN HERE, THEY'LL NEED *HIM* UP TOP WAY MORE THAN THEY'LL NEED ME. I'M A *BODYGUARD*. PROTECTING YOU IS MY JOB.
NO, IRONHIDE. YOU'RE GOING TO MAKE IT THROUGH THIS TIME, NO MATTER WHAT.
PRIME AND I NEED TO FINISH THIS. YOU SAVE LIVES. SAVE THIS ONE MORE.
"I JUST HOPE THERE'S A SURFACE TO RETURN TO."
ALL RIGHT, CREATURE. COME IF YOU'RE COMING.

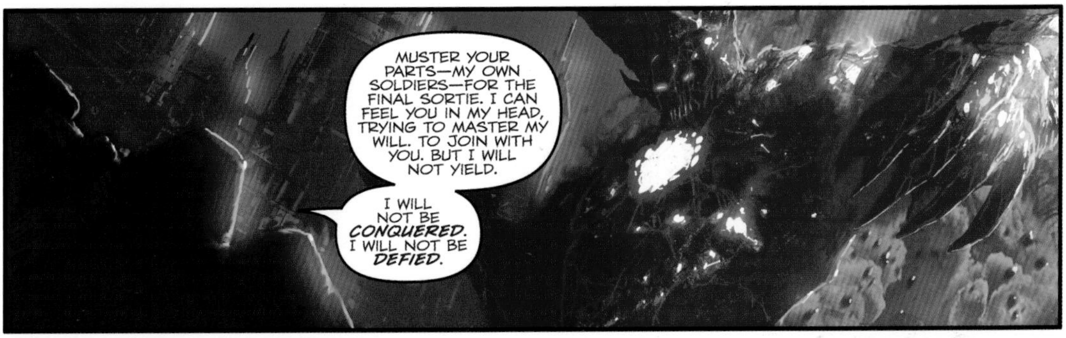
MUSTER YOUR PARTS—MY OWN SOLDIERS—FOR THE FINAL SORTIE. I CAN FEEL YOU IN MY HEAD, TRYING TO MASTER MY WILL. TO JOIN WITH YOU. BUT I WILL NOT YIELD.
I WILL NOT BE CONQUERED. I WILL NOT BE DEFIED.

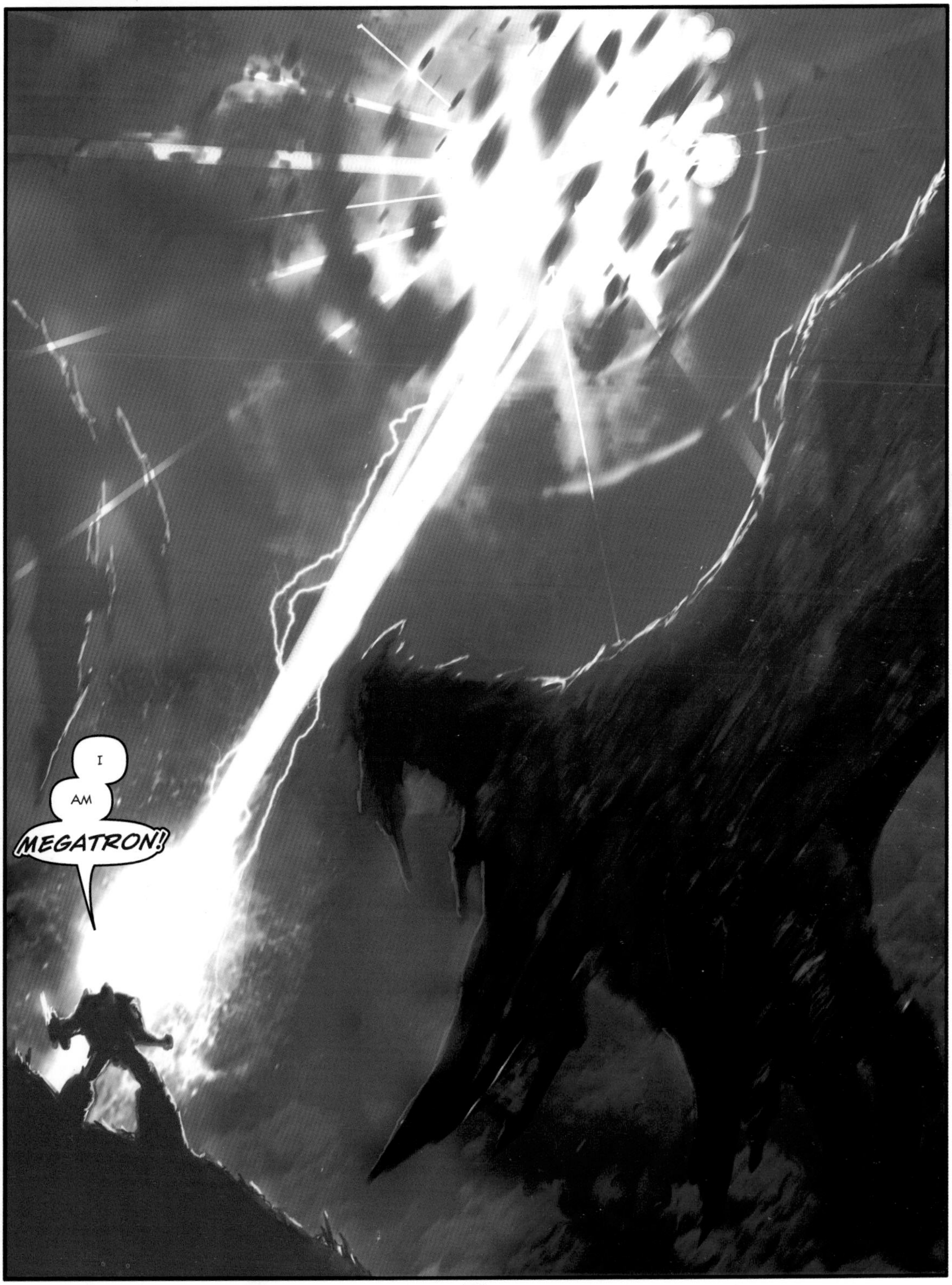
I
AM
MEGATRON!

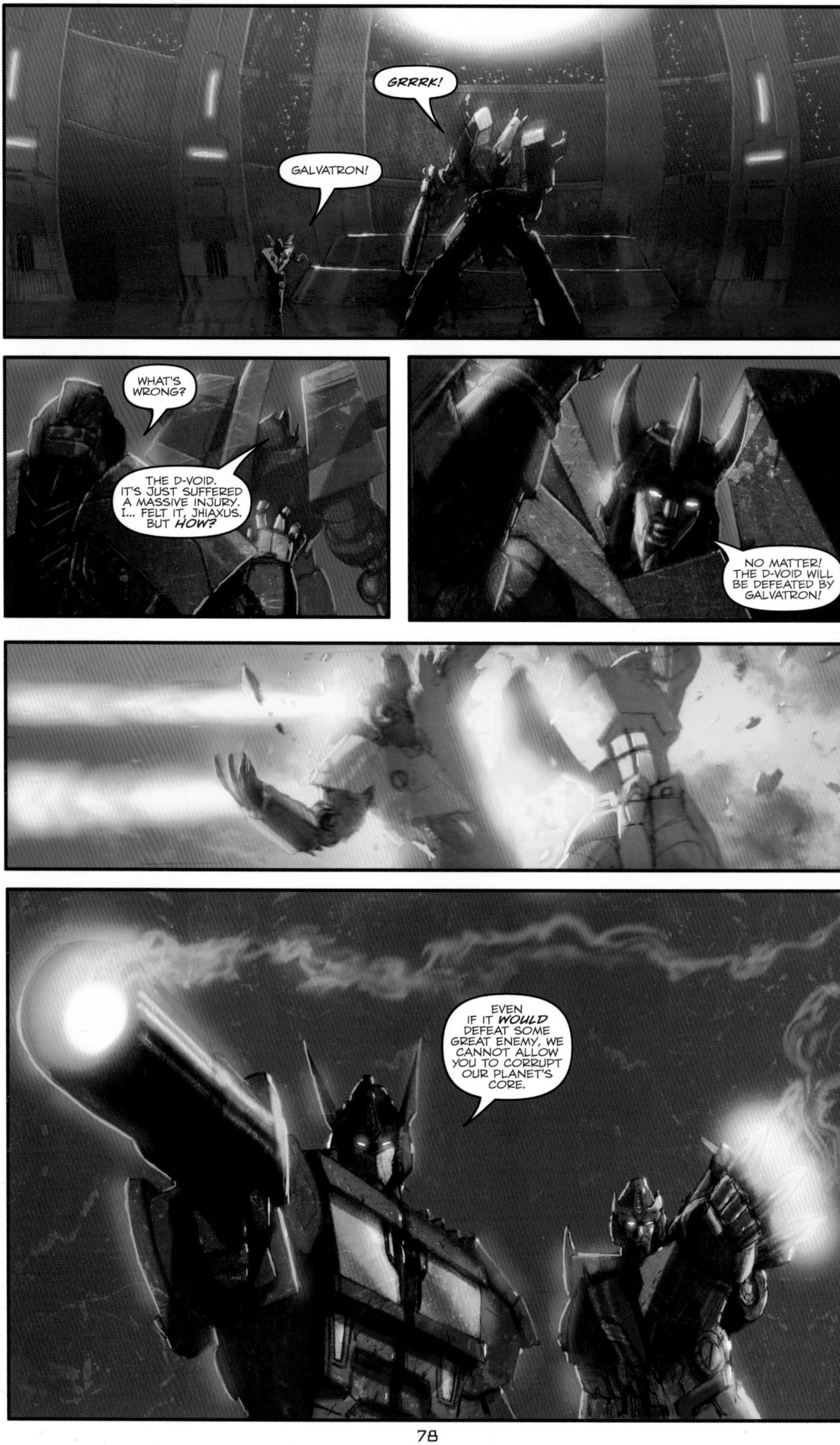
GRRRK!
GALVATRON!
WHAT'S WRONG?
THE D-VOID. IT'S JUST SUFFERED A MASSIVE INJURY. I... FELT IT, JHIAXUS. BUT HOW?
NO MATTER! THE D-VOID WILL BE DEFEATED BY GALVATRON!
EVEN IF IT WOULD DEFEAT SOME GREAT ENEMY, WE CANNOT ALLOW YOU TO CORRUPT OUR PLANET'S CORE.

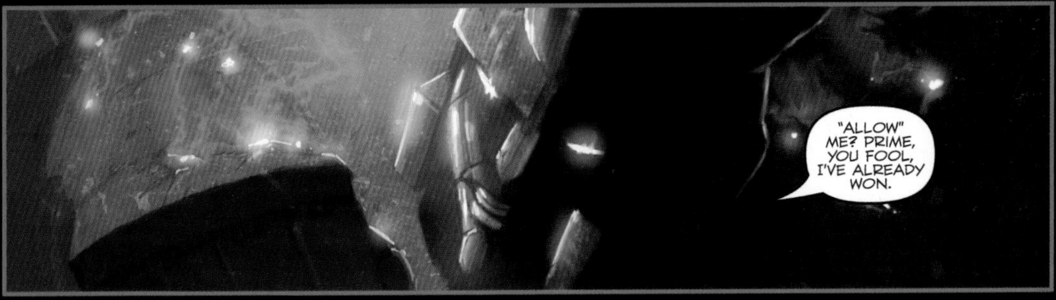
"ALLOW" ME? PRIME, YOU FOOL, I'VE ALREADY WON.

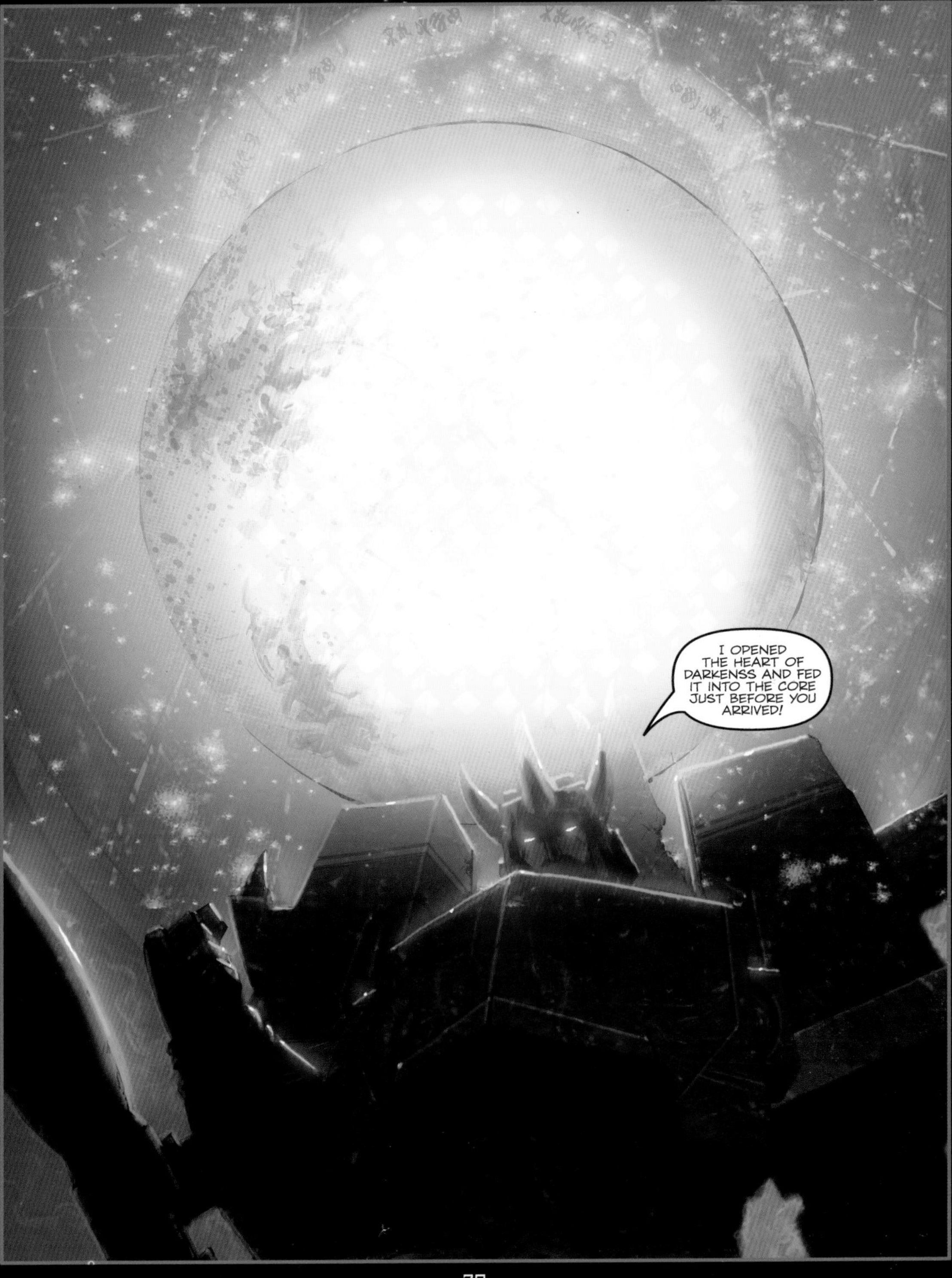
I OPENED THE HEART OF DARKENSS AND FED IT INTO THE CORE JUST BEFORE YOU ARRIVED!

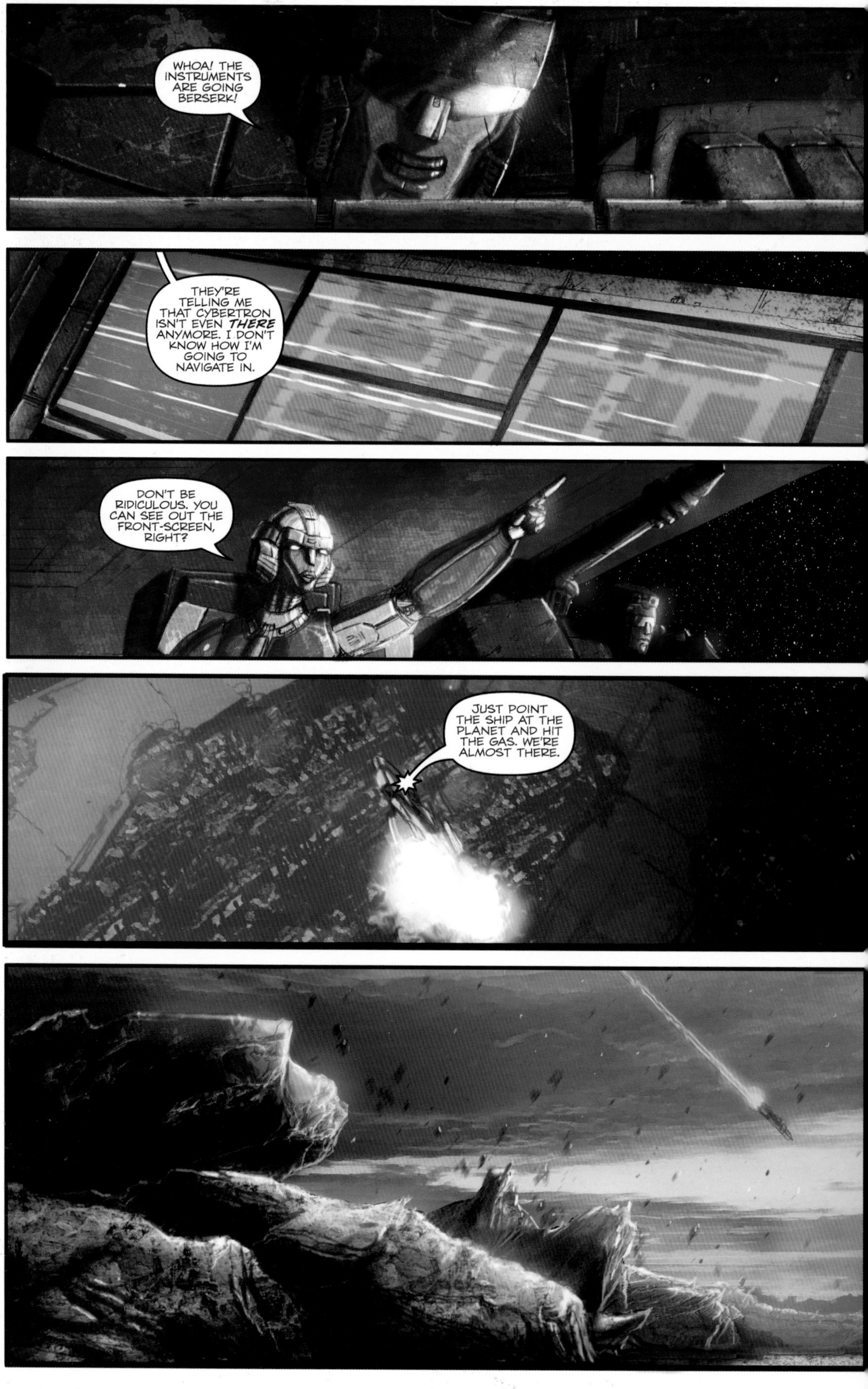
WHOA! THE INSTRUMENTS ARE GOING BERSERK!
THEY'RE TELLING ME THAT CYBERTRON ISN'T EVEN *THERE* ANYMORE. I DON'T KNOW HOW I'M GOING TO NAVIGATE IN.
DON'T BE RIDICULOUS. YOU CAN SEE OUT THE FRONT-SCREEN, RIGHT?
JUST POINT THE SHIP AT THE PLANET AND HIT THE GAS. WE'RE ALMOST THERE.

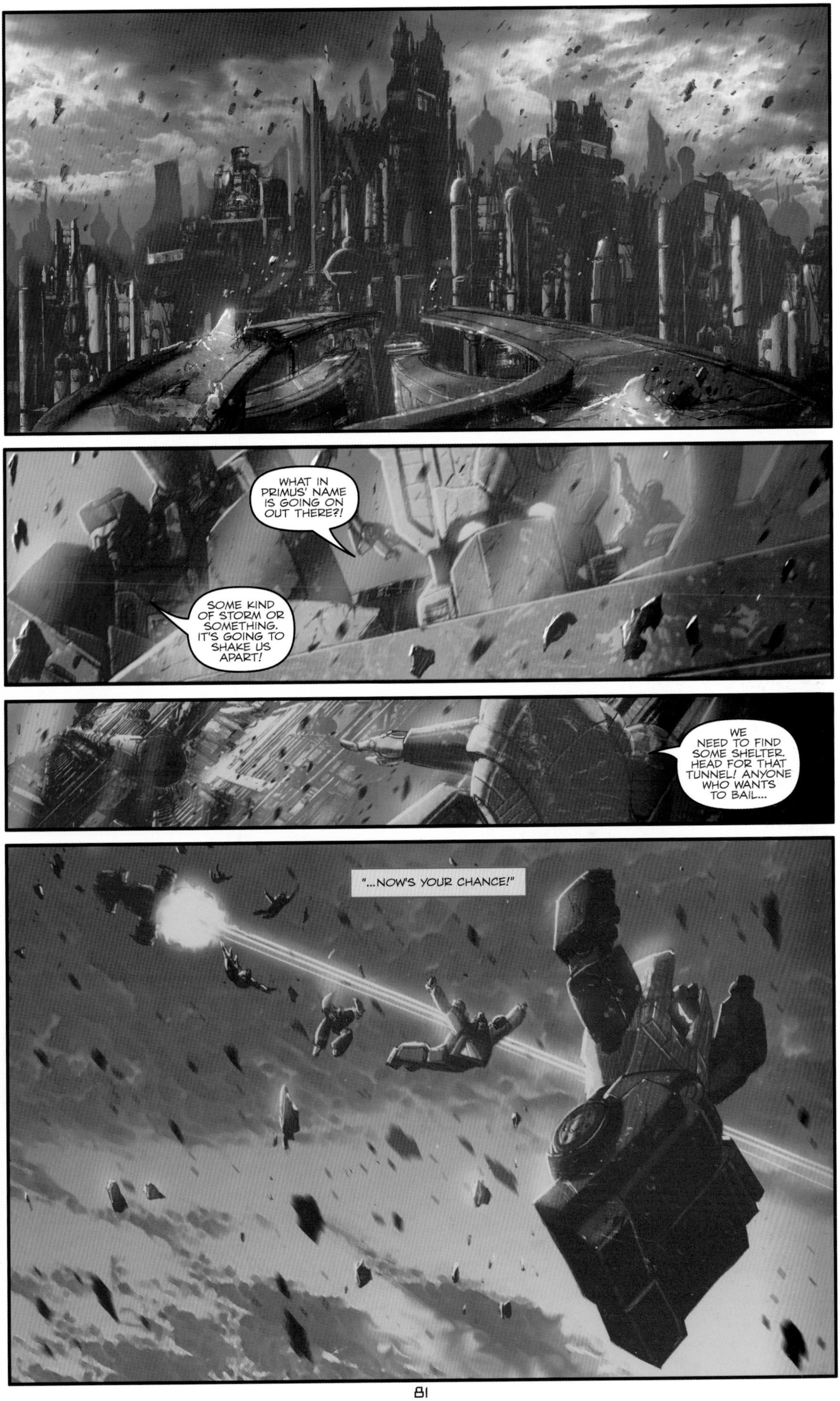
WHAT IN PRIMUS' NAME IS GOING ON OUT THERE?!
SOME KIND OF STORM OR SOMETHING. IT'S GOING TO SHAKE US APART!
WE NEED TO FIND SOME SHELTER. HEAD FOR THAT TUNNEL! ANYONE WHO WANTS TO BAIL...
"...NOW'S YOUR CHANCE!"

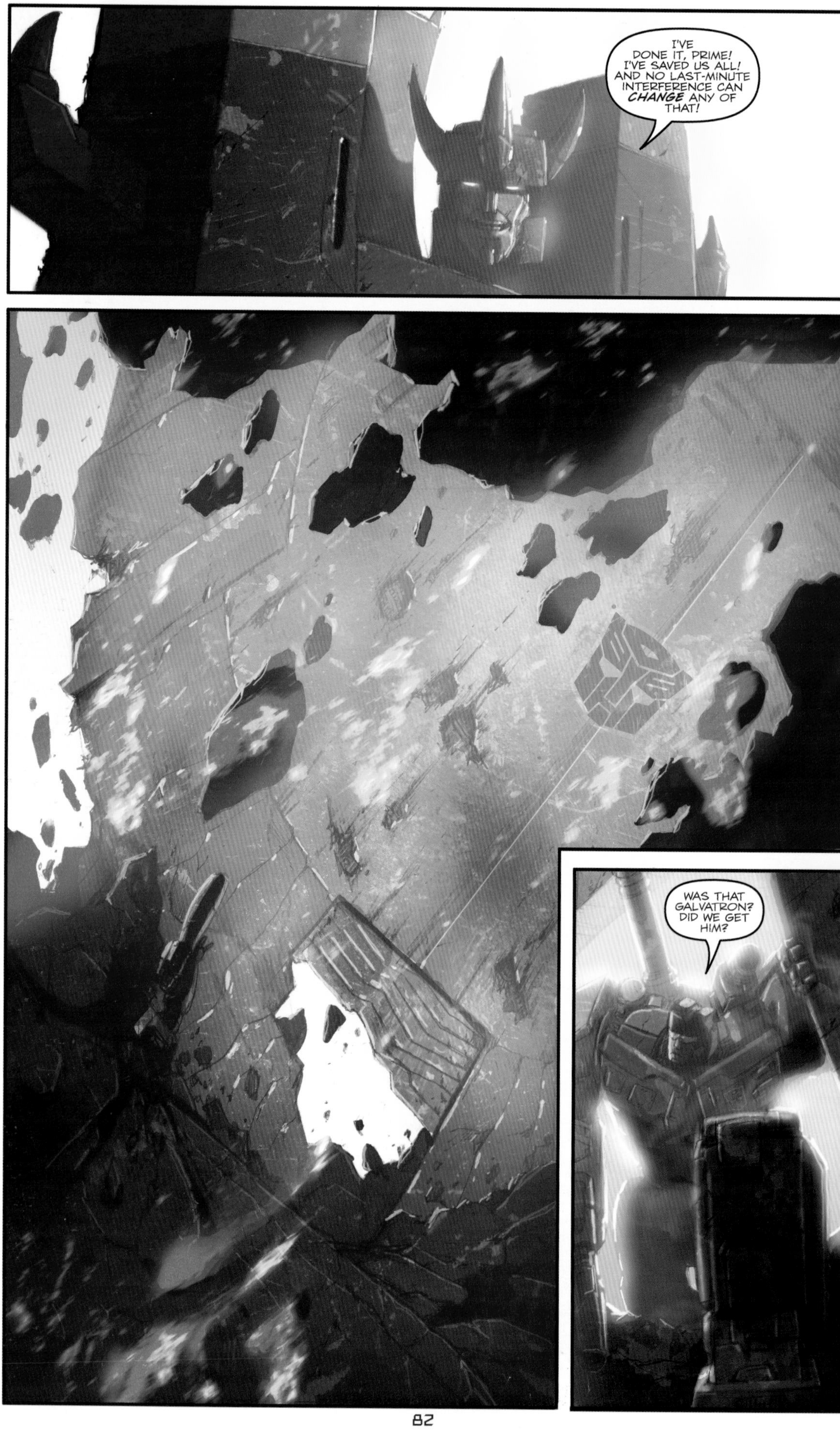
I'VE DONE IT, PRIME! I'VE SAVED US ALL! AND NO LAST-MINUTE INTERFERENCE CAN *CHANGE* ANY OF THAT!
WAS THAT GALVATRON? DID WE GET HIM?

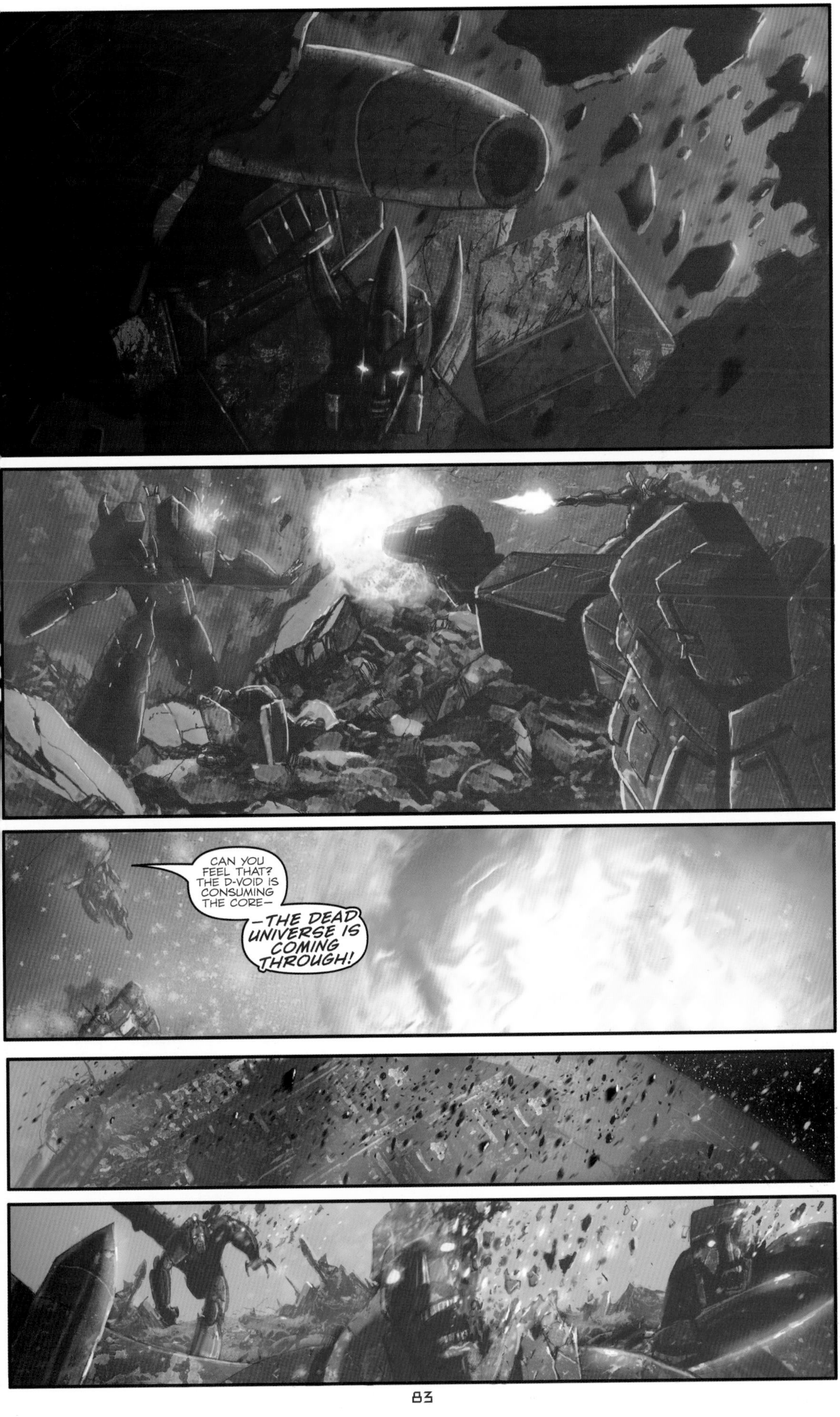
CAN YOU FEEL THAT? THE D-VOID IS CONSUMING THE CORE—
—THE DEAD UNIVERSE IS COMING THROUGH!

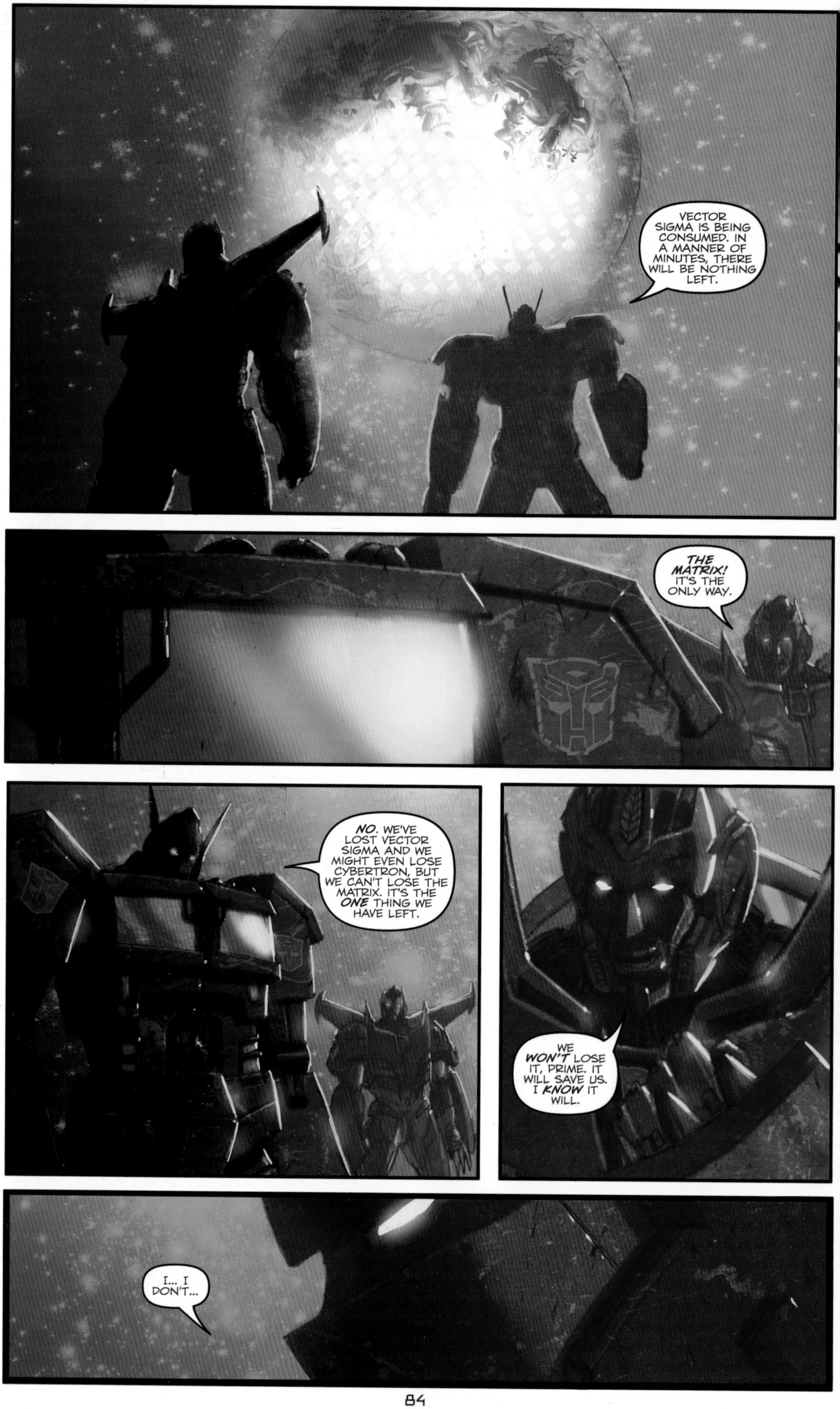
VECTOR SIGMA IS BEING CONSUMED. IN A MANNER OF MINUTES, THERE WILL BE NOTHING LEFT.
THE MATRIX! IT'S THE ONLY WAY.
NO. WE'VE LOST VECTOR SIGMA AND WE MIGHT EVEN LOSE CYBERTRON, BUT WE CAN'T LOSE THE MATRIX. IT'S THE ONE THING WE HAVE LEFT.
WE WON'T LOSE IT, PRIME. IT WILL SAVE US. I KNOW IT WILL.
I... I DON'T...

NOT LIKE YOU TO *HESITATE*, PRIME. YOU'VE CHANGED, AND NOT FOR THE BETTER.

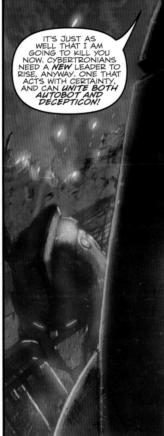

IT'S JUST AS WELL THAT I AM GOING TO KILL YOU NOW. CYBERTRONIANS NEED A *NEW* LEADER TO RISE, ANYWAY. ONE THAT ACTS WITH CERTAINTY, AND CAN *UNITE BOTH AUTOBOT AND DECEPTICON!*

NO MORE SECRET ALLIES TO AMBUSH ME NOW, PRIME.

UNKK!

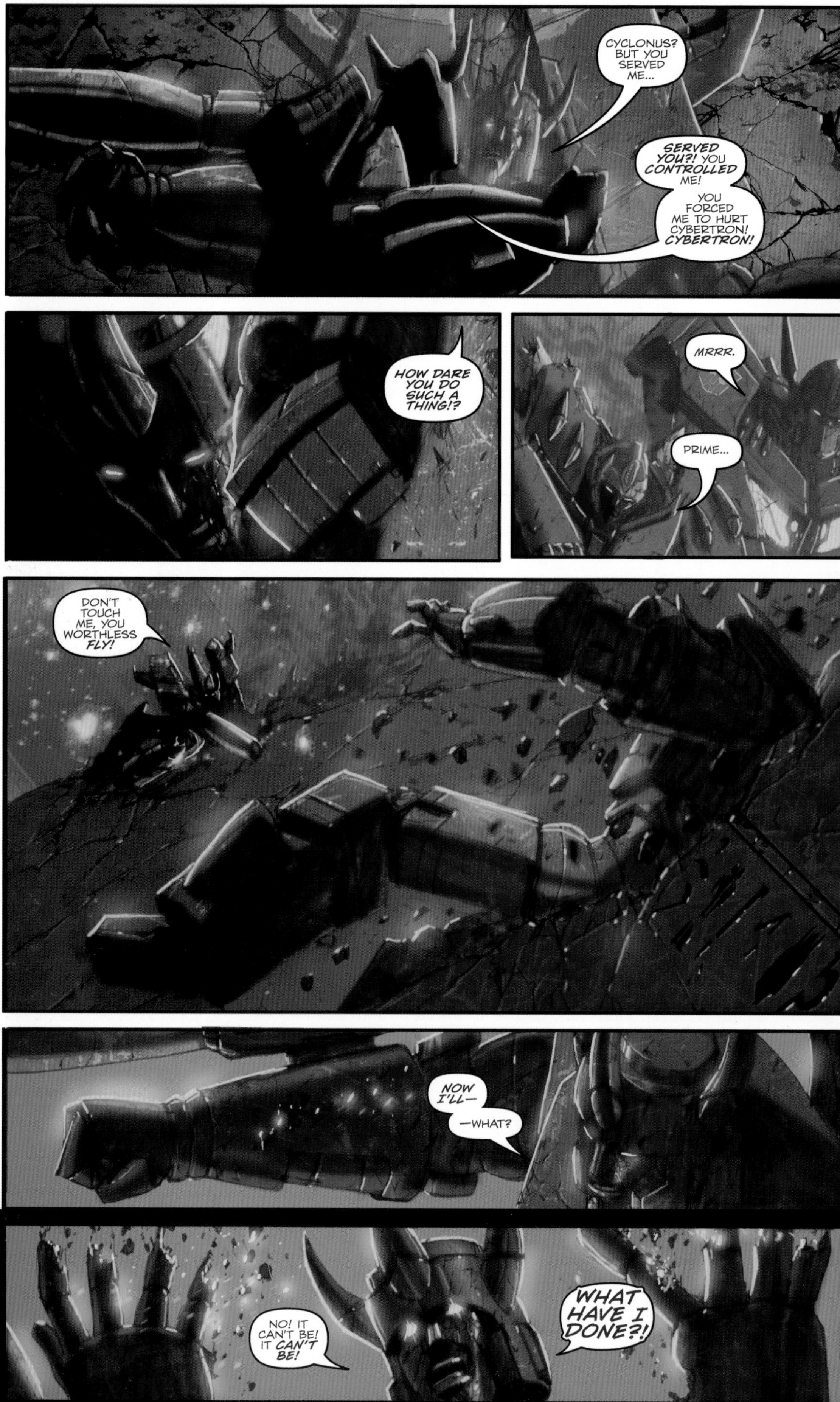
CYCLONUS? BUT YOU SERVED ME...
SERVED YOU?! YOU CONTROLLED ME!
YOU FORCED ME TO HURT CYBERTRON! CYBERTRON!
HOW DARE YOU DO SUCH A THING!?
MRRR.
PRIME...
DON'T TOUCH ME, YOU WORTHLESS FLY!
NOW I'LL—
—WHAT?
NO! IT CAN'T BE! IT CAN'T BE!
WHAT HAVE I DONE?!

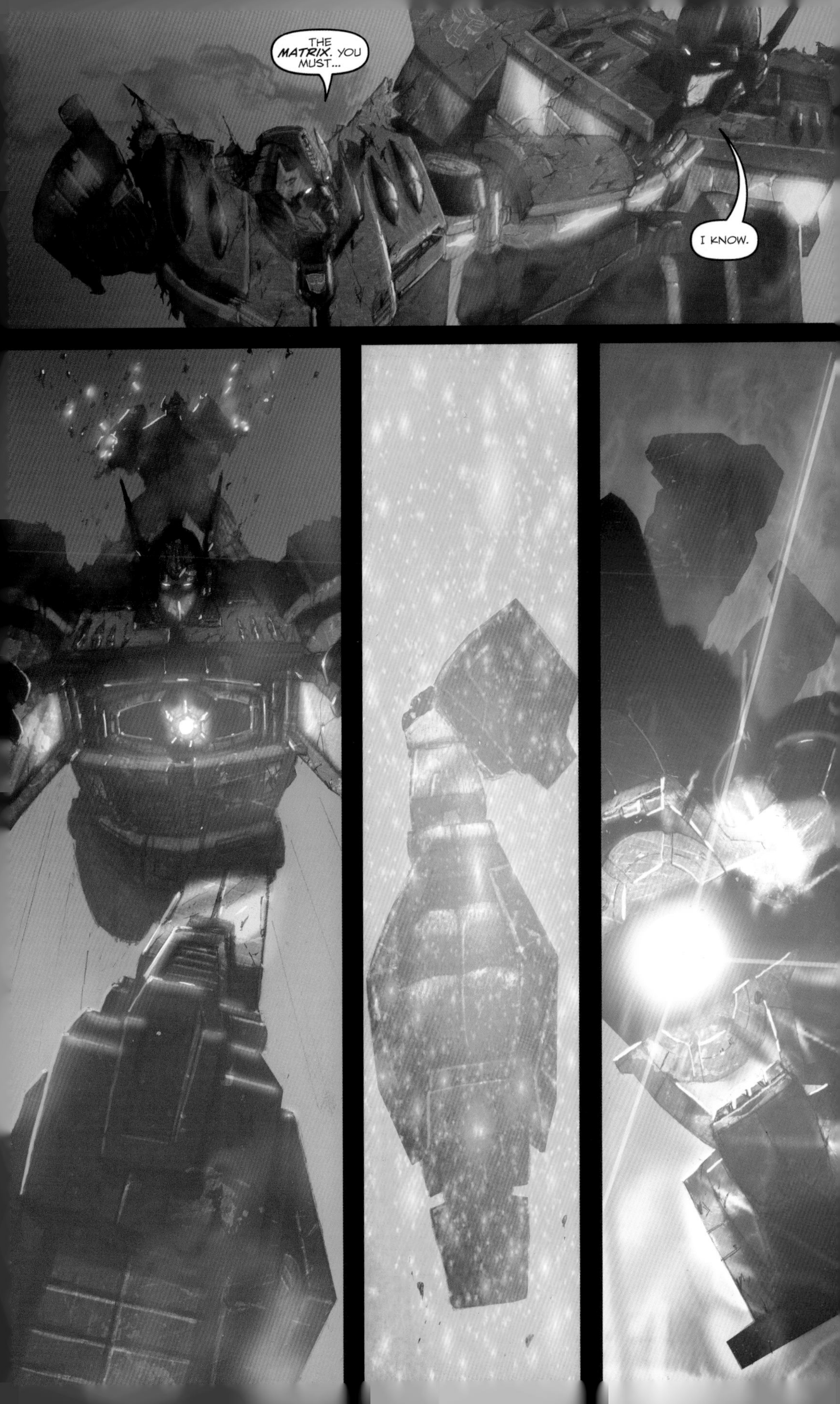
THE MATRIX. YOU MUST...
I KNOW.

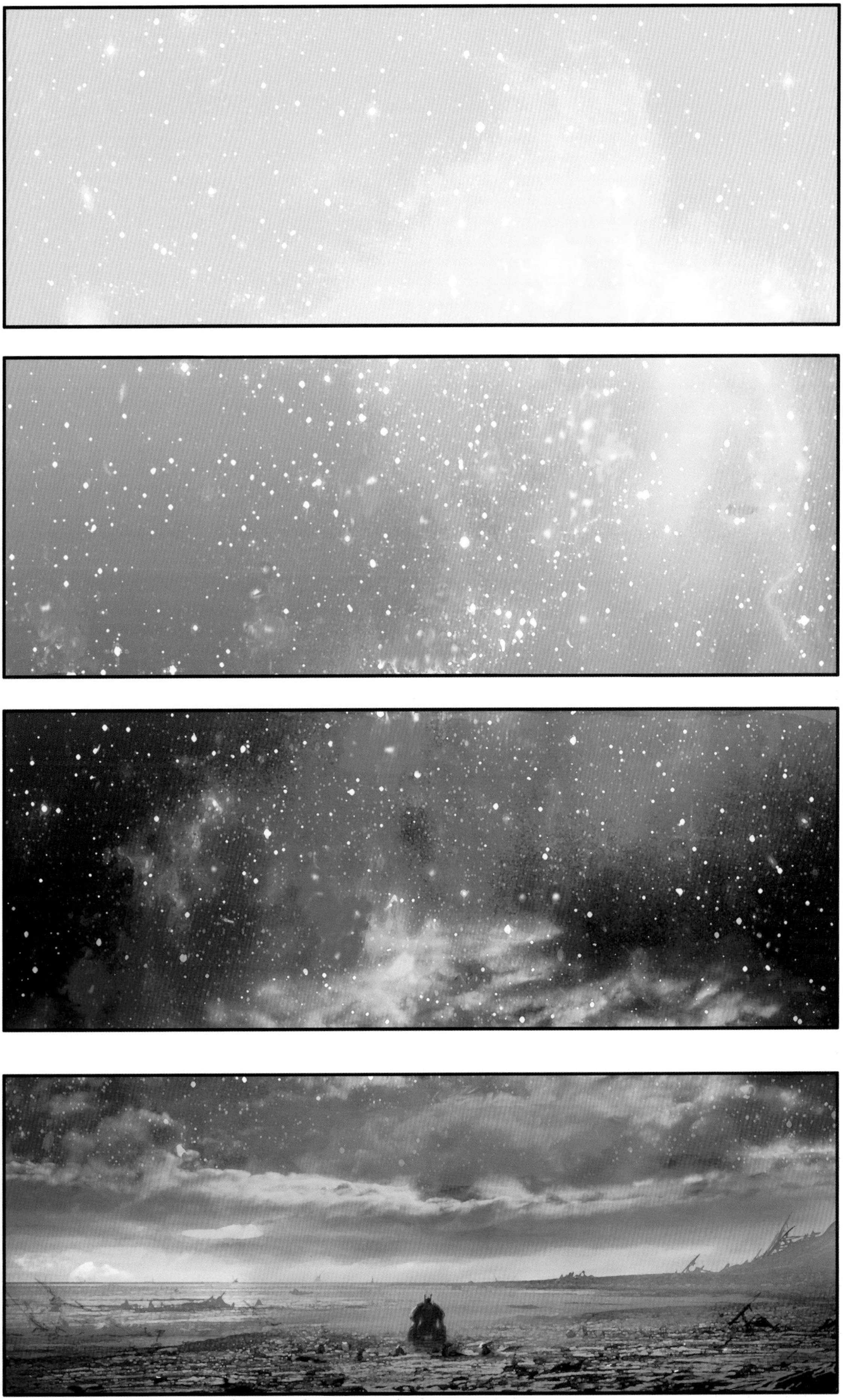

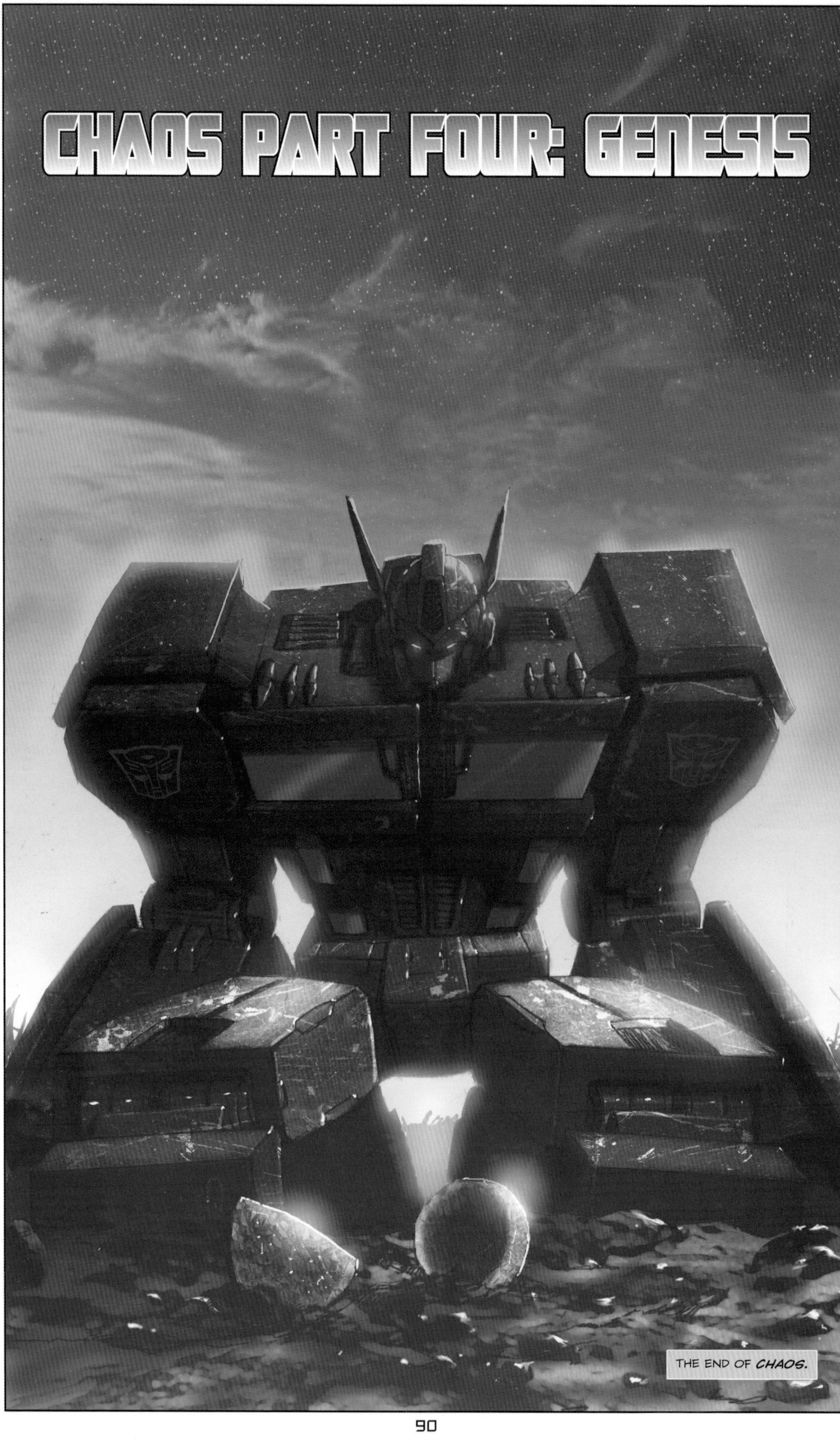
CHAOS PART FOUR: GENESIS
THE END OF CHAOS.

"TELL US A STORY."

5

"YEAH! TELL US A STORY! A *GOOD* ONE. WITH LOTS OF FIGHTING.

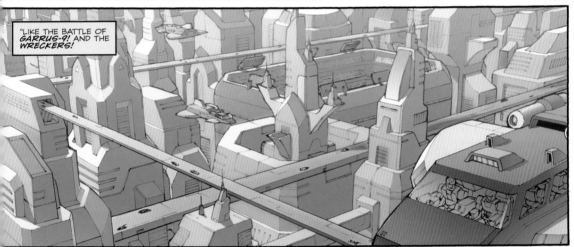

"LIKE THE BATTLE OF *GARRUS-9!* AND THE *WRECKERS!*

"TELL US ABOUT THE *MATRIX* AGAIN! WHEN IT *DIDN'T WORK* BUT THEN IT *DID.*

"IT'S *REMEMBRANCE* DAY, AND YOU KNOW MORE STORIES THAN *ANYONE.*"

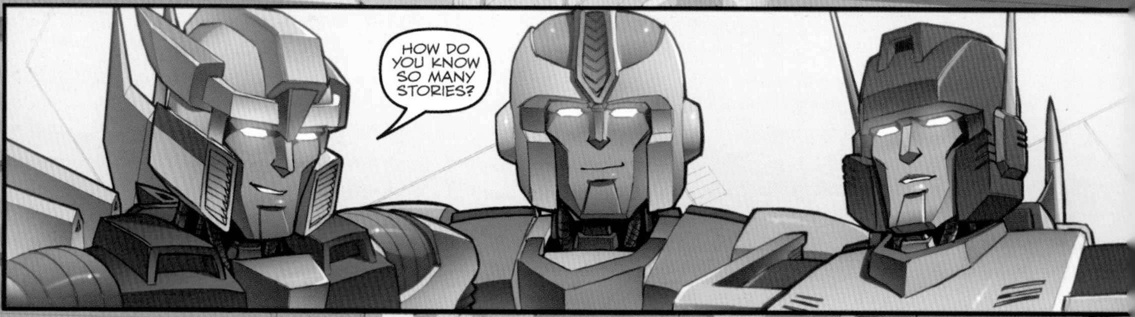
HOW DO YOU KNOW SO MANY STORIES?

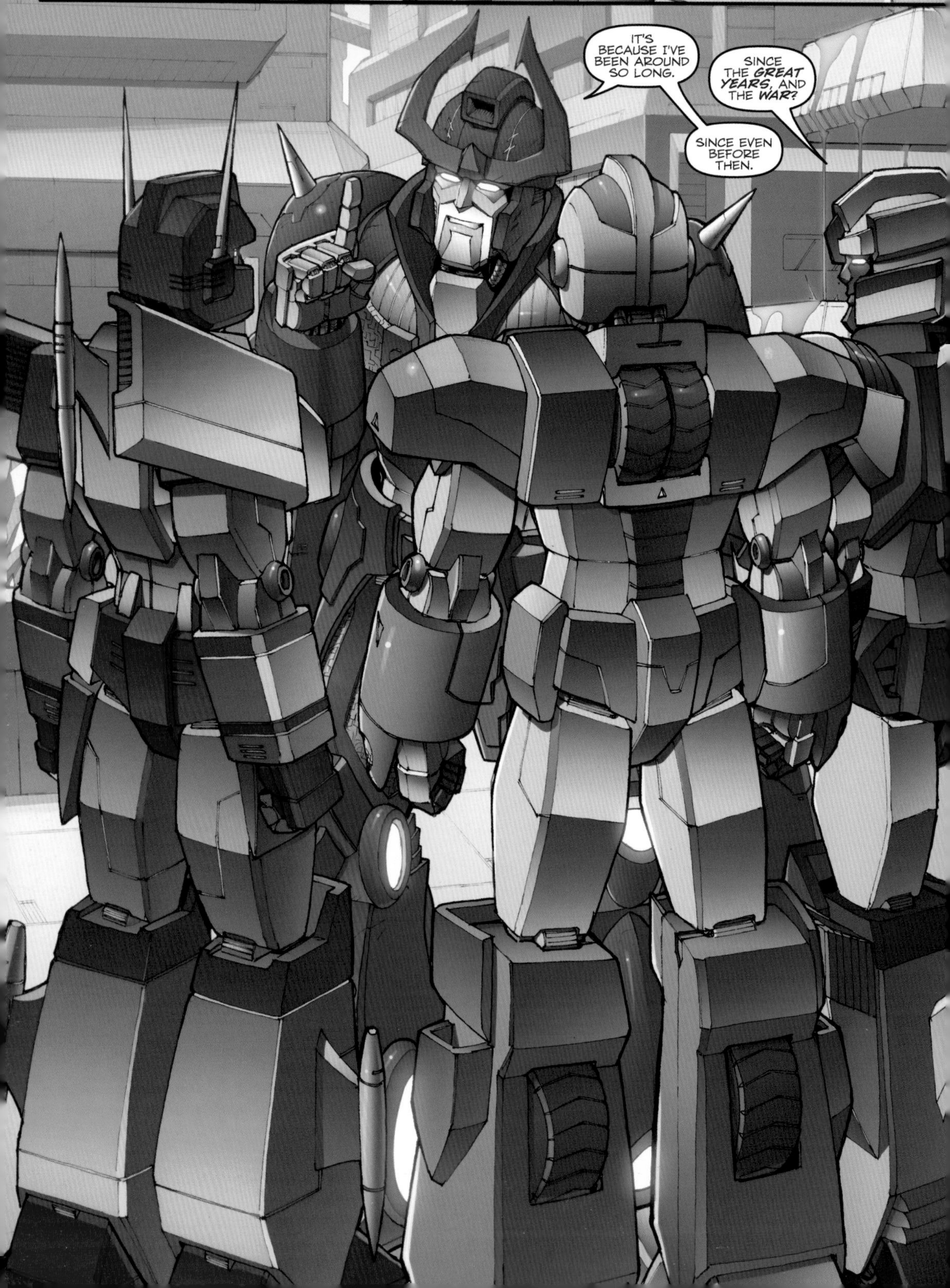
IT'S BECAUSE I'VE BEEN AROUND SO LONG.
SINCE THE ***GREAT YEARS,*** AND THE ***WAR?***
SINCE EVEN BEFORE THEN.

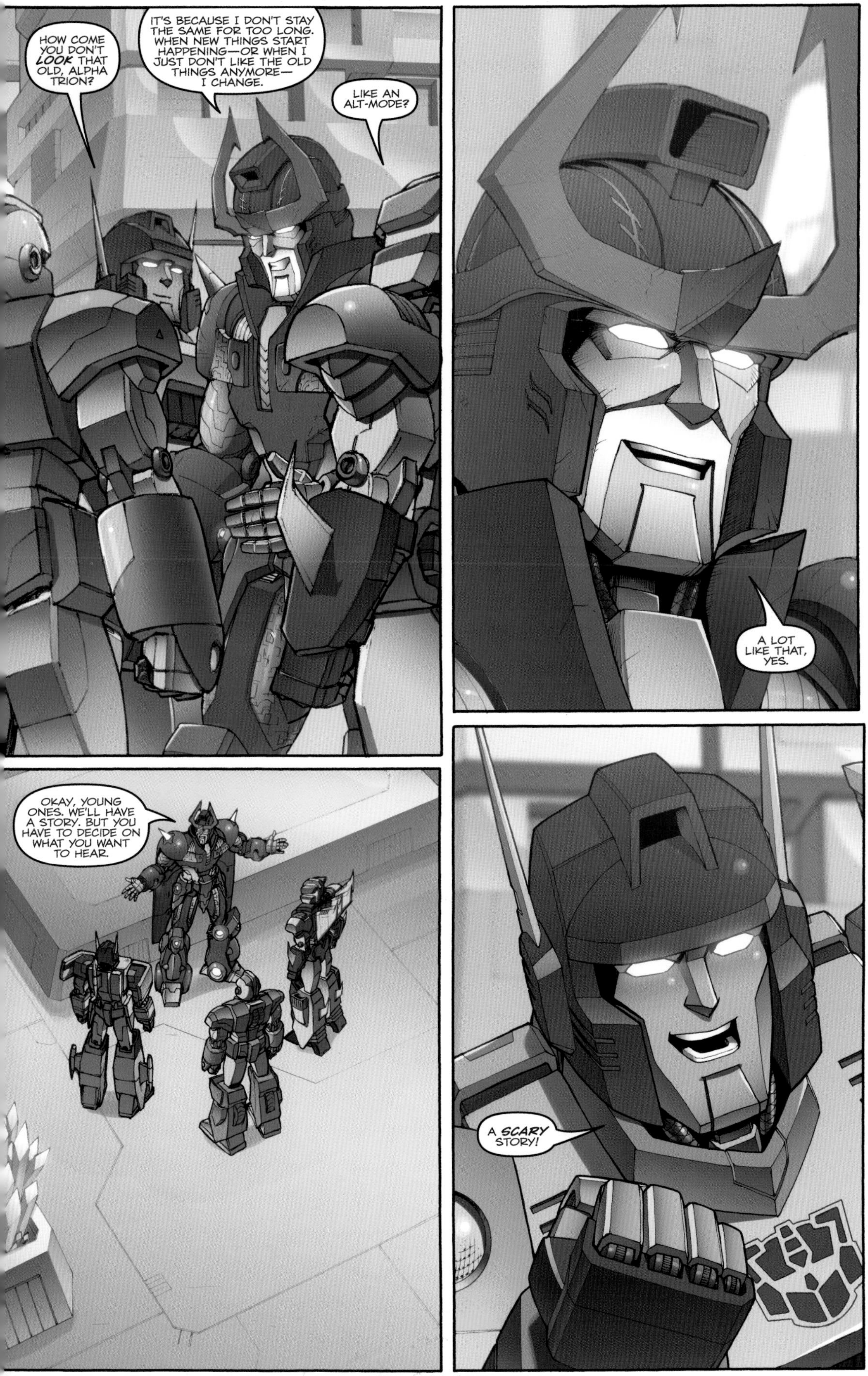
HOW COME YOU DON'T LOOK THAT OLD, ALPHA TRION?
IT'S BECAUSE I DON'T STAY THE SAME FOR TOO LONG. WHEN NEW THINGS START HAPPENING—OR WHEN I JUST DON'T LIKE THE OLD THINGS ANYMORE—I CHANGE.
LIKE AN ALT-MODE?
A LOT LIKE THAT, YES.
OKAY, YOUNG ONES. WE'LL HAVE A STORY. BUT YOU HAVE TO DECIDE ON WHAT YOU WANT TO HEAR.
A SCARY STORY!

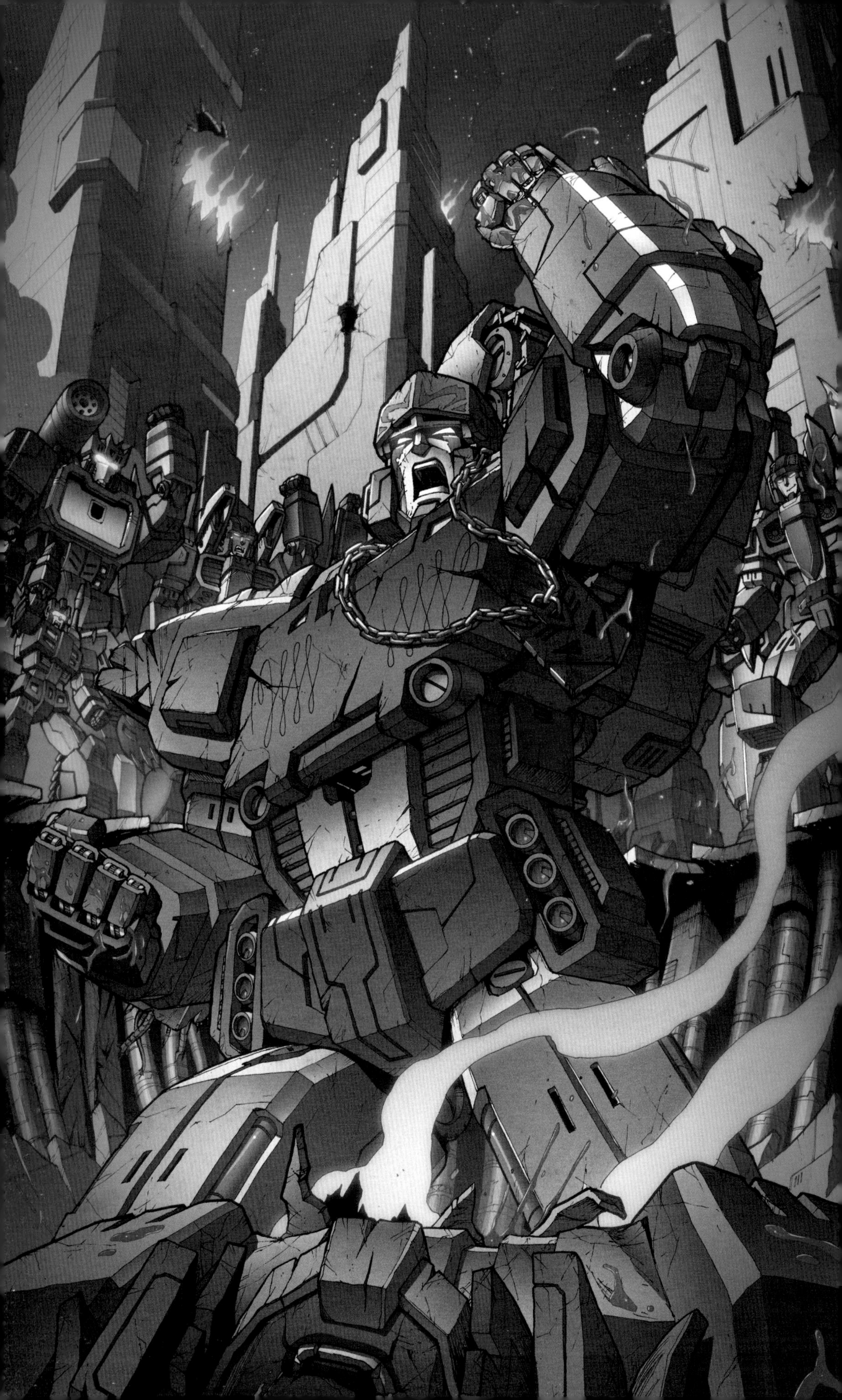

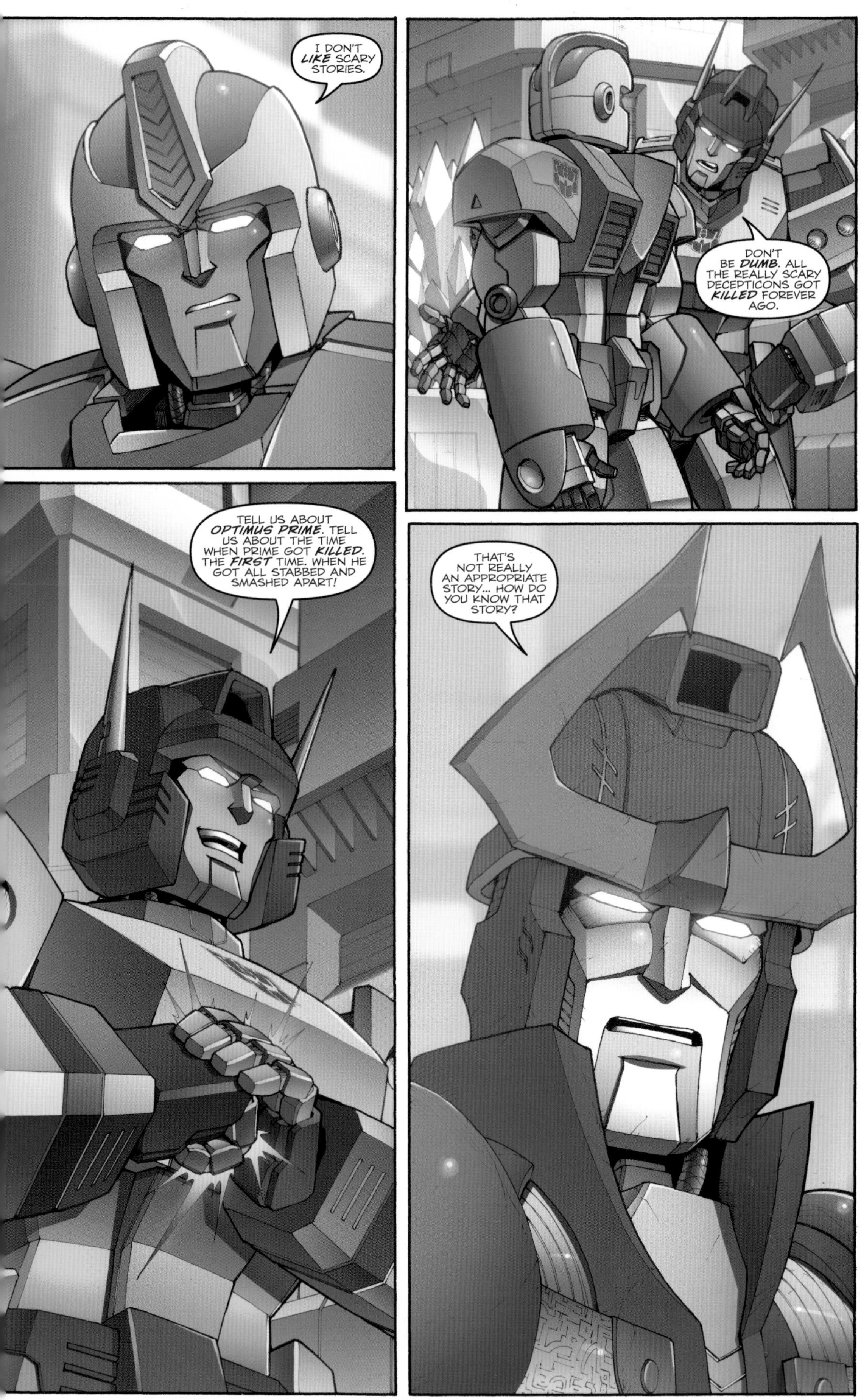
I DON'T LIKE SCARY STORIES.
DON'T BE DUMB. ALL THE REALLY SCARY DECEPTICONS GOT KILLED FOREVER AGO.
TELL US ABOUT OPTIMUS PRIME. TELL US ABOUT THE TIME WHEN PRIME GOT KILLED. THE FIRST TIME. WHEN HE GOT ALL STABBED AND SMASHED APART!
THAT'S NOT REALLY AN APPROPRIATE STORY... HOW DO YOU KNOW THAT STORY?

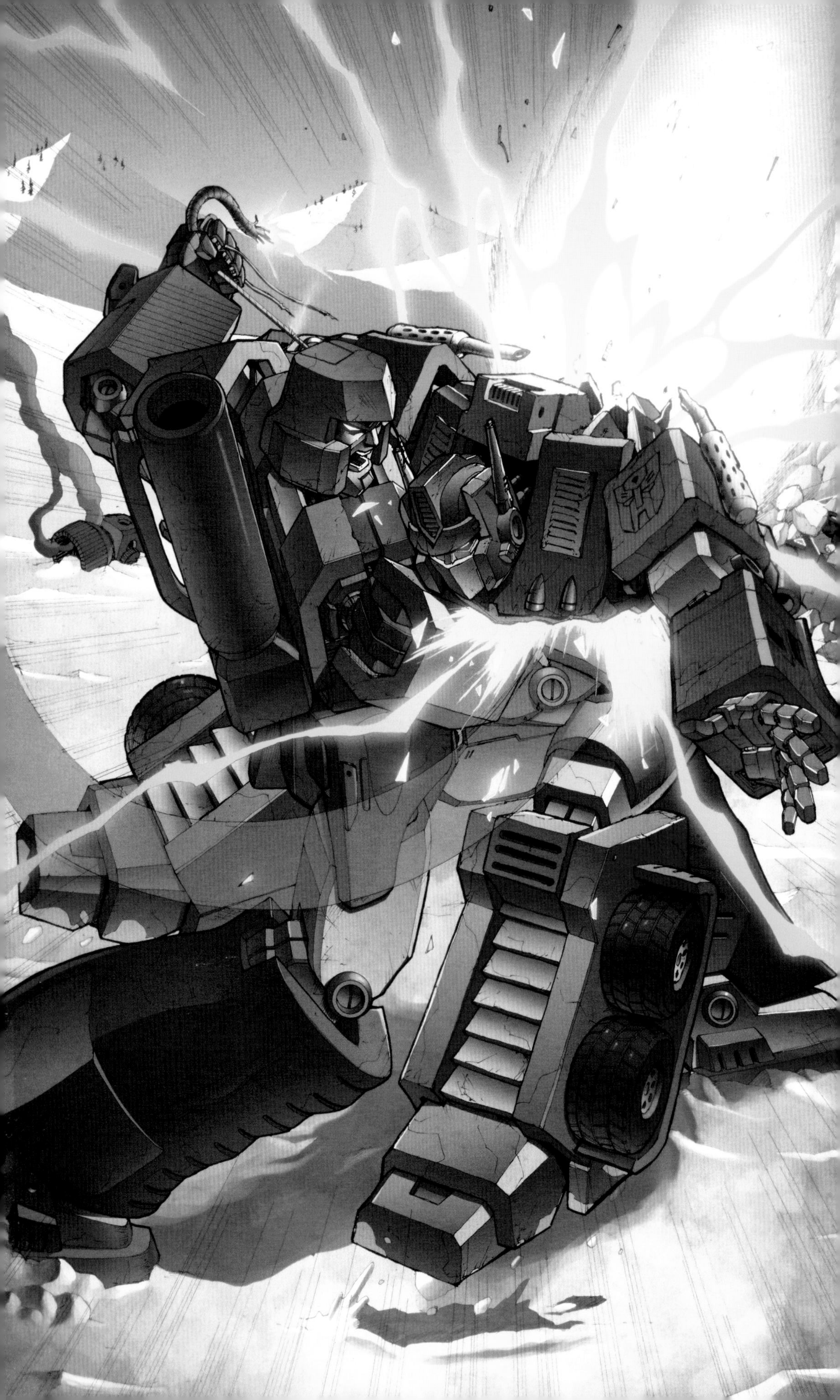

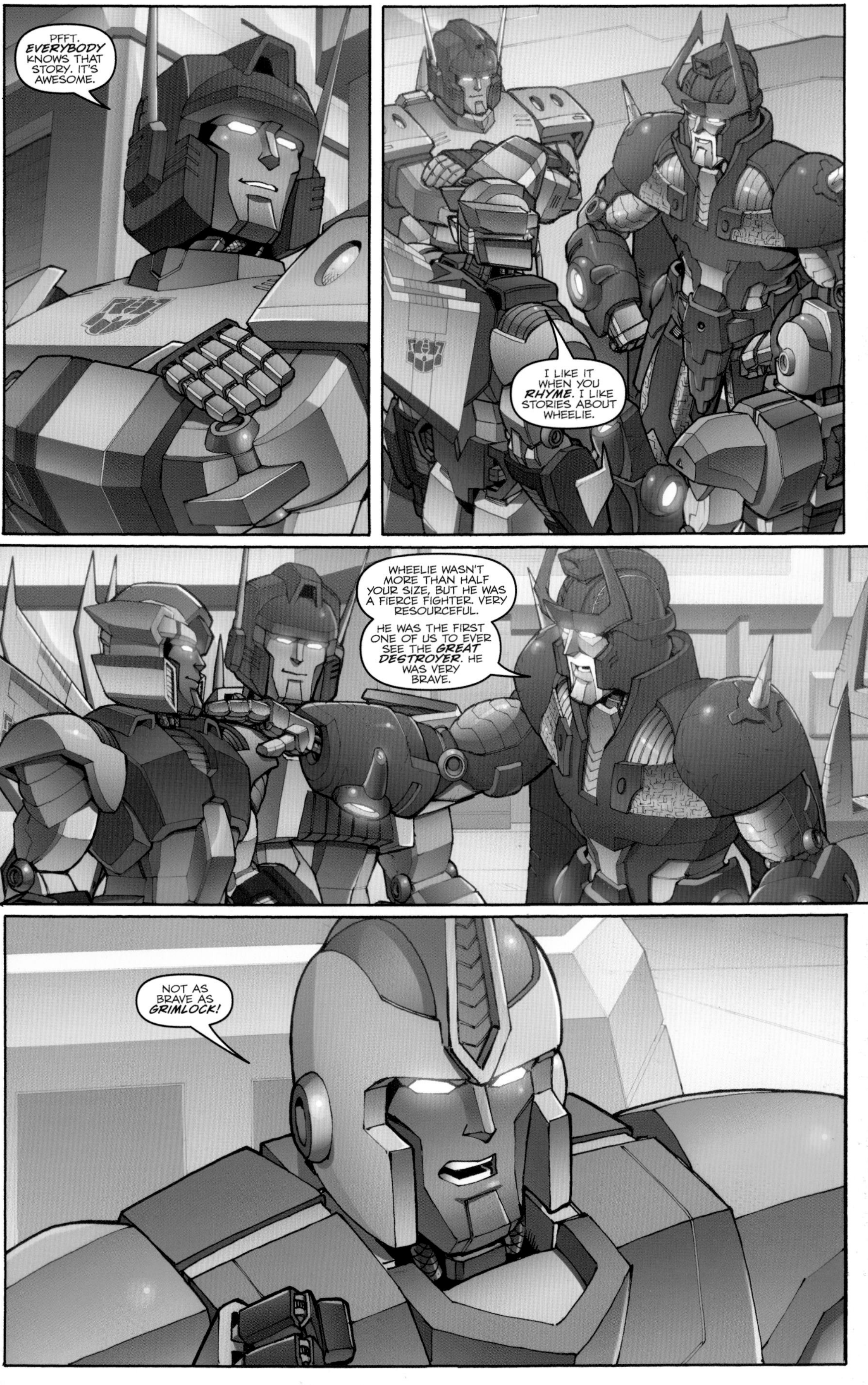
PFFT. EVERYBODY KNOWS THAT STORY. IT'S AWESOME.
I LIKE IT WHEN YOU RHYME. I LIKE STORIES ABOUT WHEELIE.
WHEELIE WASN'T MORE THAN HALF YOUR SIZE, BUT HE WAS A FIERCE FIGHTER. VERY RESOURCEFUL.
HE WAS THE FIRST ONE OF US TO EVER SEE THE GREAT DESTROYER. HE WAS VERY BRAVE.
NOT AS BRAVE AS GRIMLOCK!

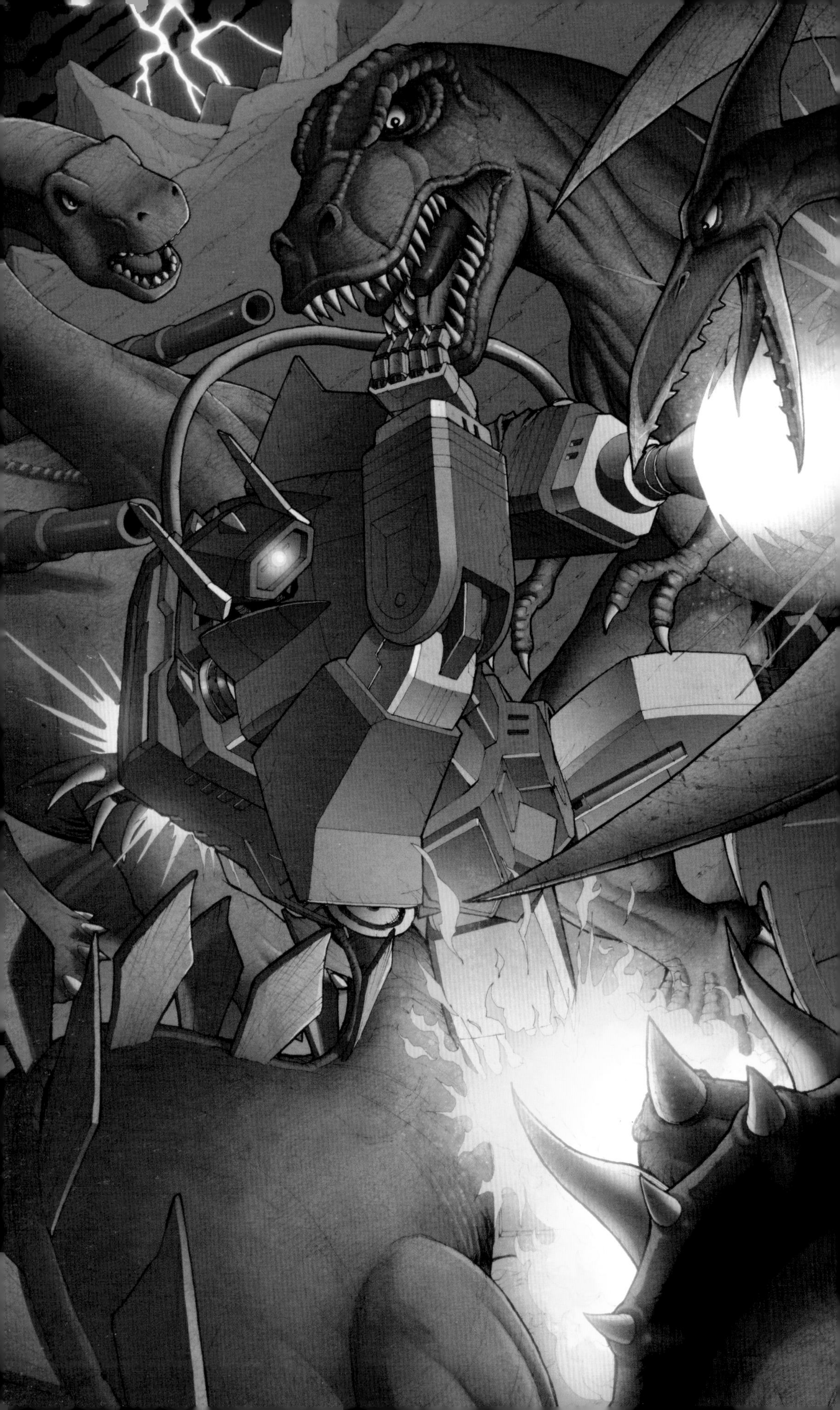

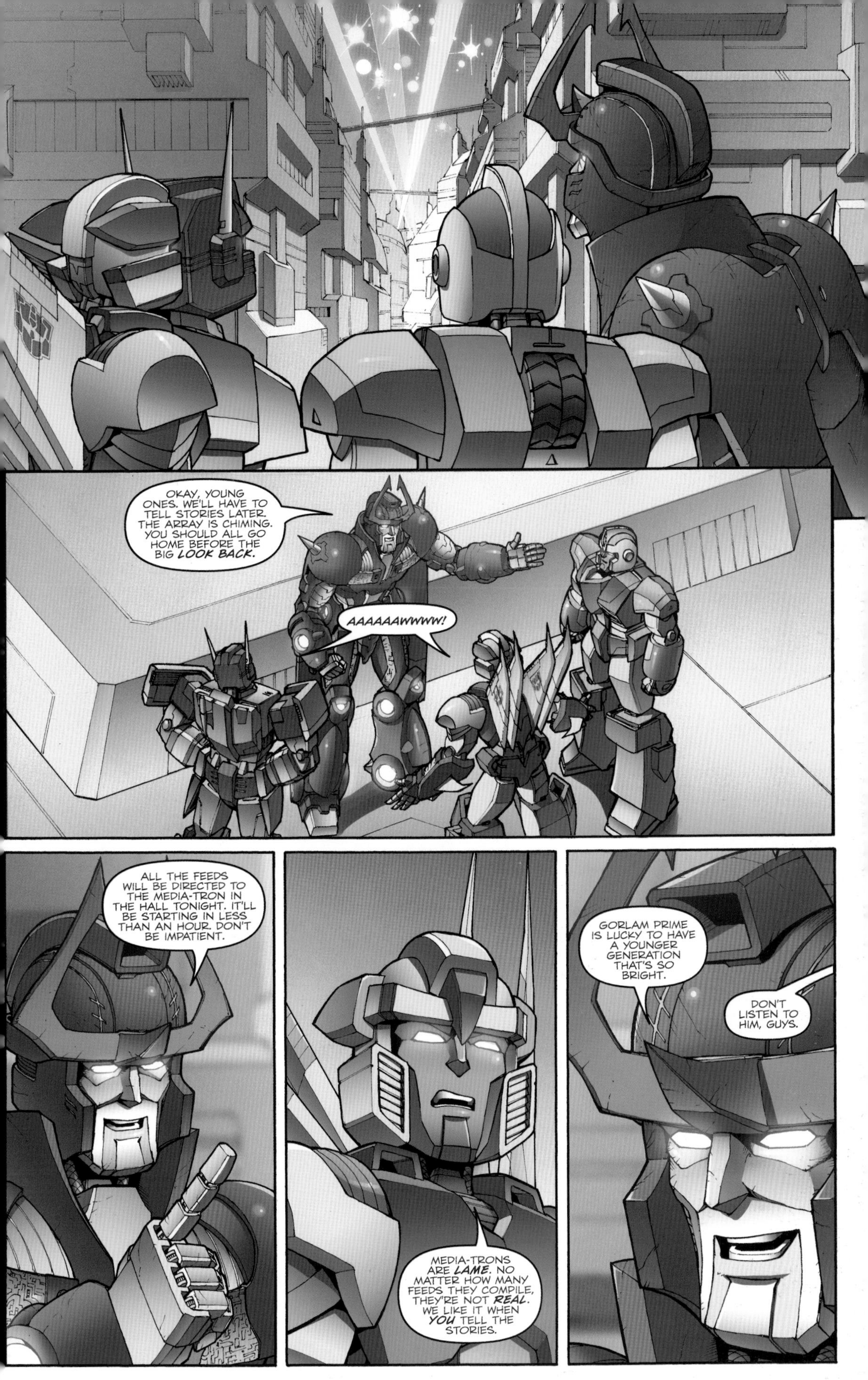
OKAY, YOUNG ONES. WE'LL HAVE TO TELL STORIES LATER. THE ARRAY IS CHIMING. YOU SHOULD ALL GO HOME BEFORE THE BIG *LOOK BACK*.
AAAAAAWWWW!
ALL THE FEEDS WILL BE DIRECTED TO THE MEDIA-TRON IN THE HALL TONIGHT. IT'LL BE STARTING IN LESS THAN AN HOUR. DON'T BE IMPATIENT.
MEDIA-TRONS ARE *LAME*. NO MATTER HOW MANY FEEDS THEY COMPILE, THEY'RE NOT *REAL*. WE LIKE IT WHEN *YOU* TELL THE STORIES.
GORLAM PRIME IS LUCKY TO HAVE A YOUNGER GENERATION THAT'S SO BRIGHT.
DON'T LISTEN TO HIM, GUYS.

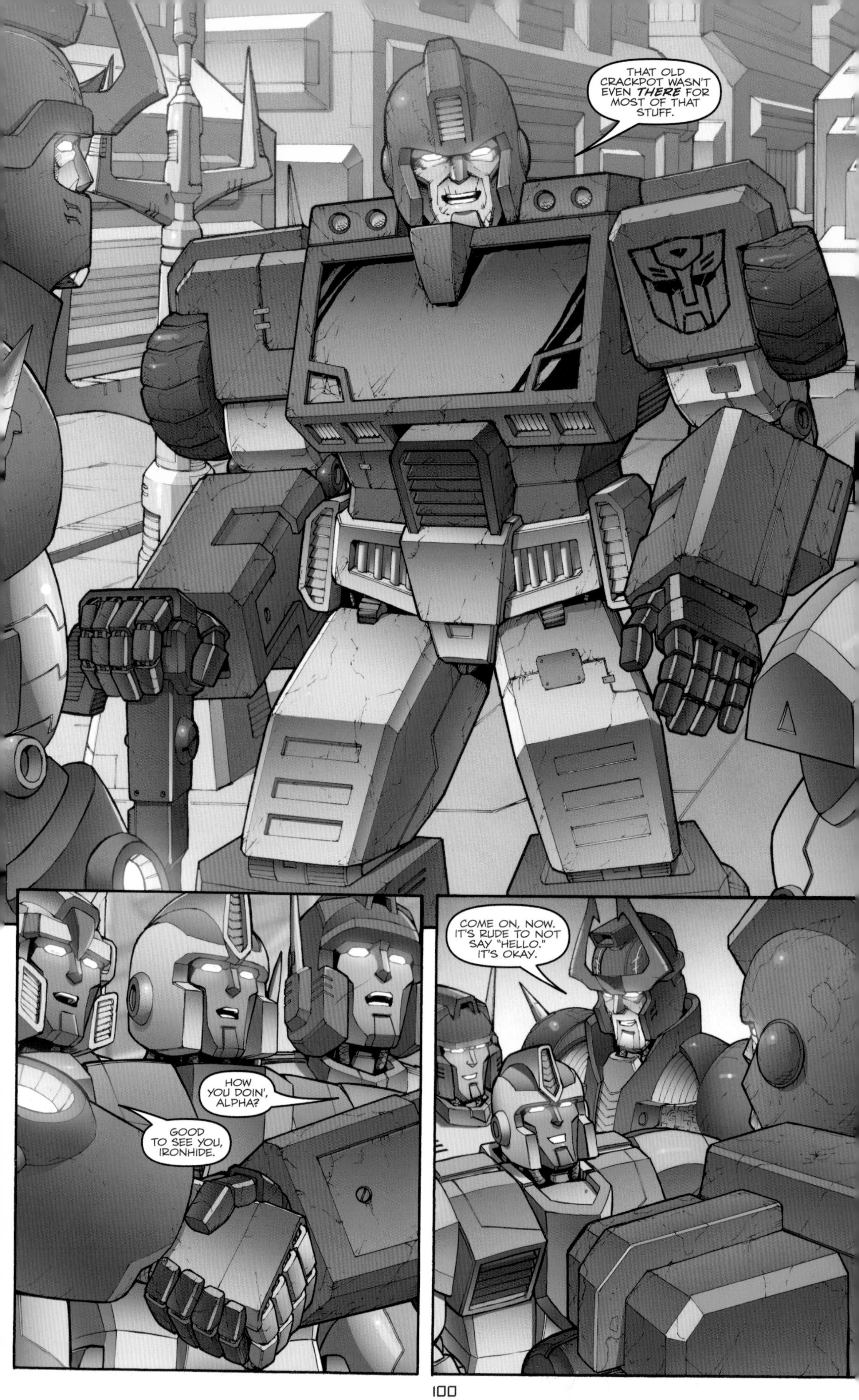

THAT OLD CRACKPOT WASN'T EVEN *THERE* FOR MOST OF THAT STUFF.
HOW YOU DOIN', ALPHA?
GOOD TO SEE YOU, IRONHIDE.
COME ON, NOW. IT'S RUDE TO NOT SAY "HELLO." IT'S OKAY.

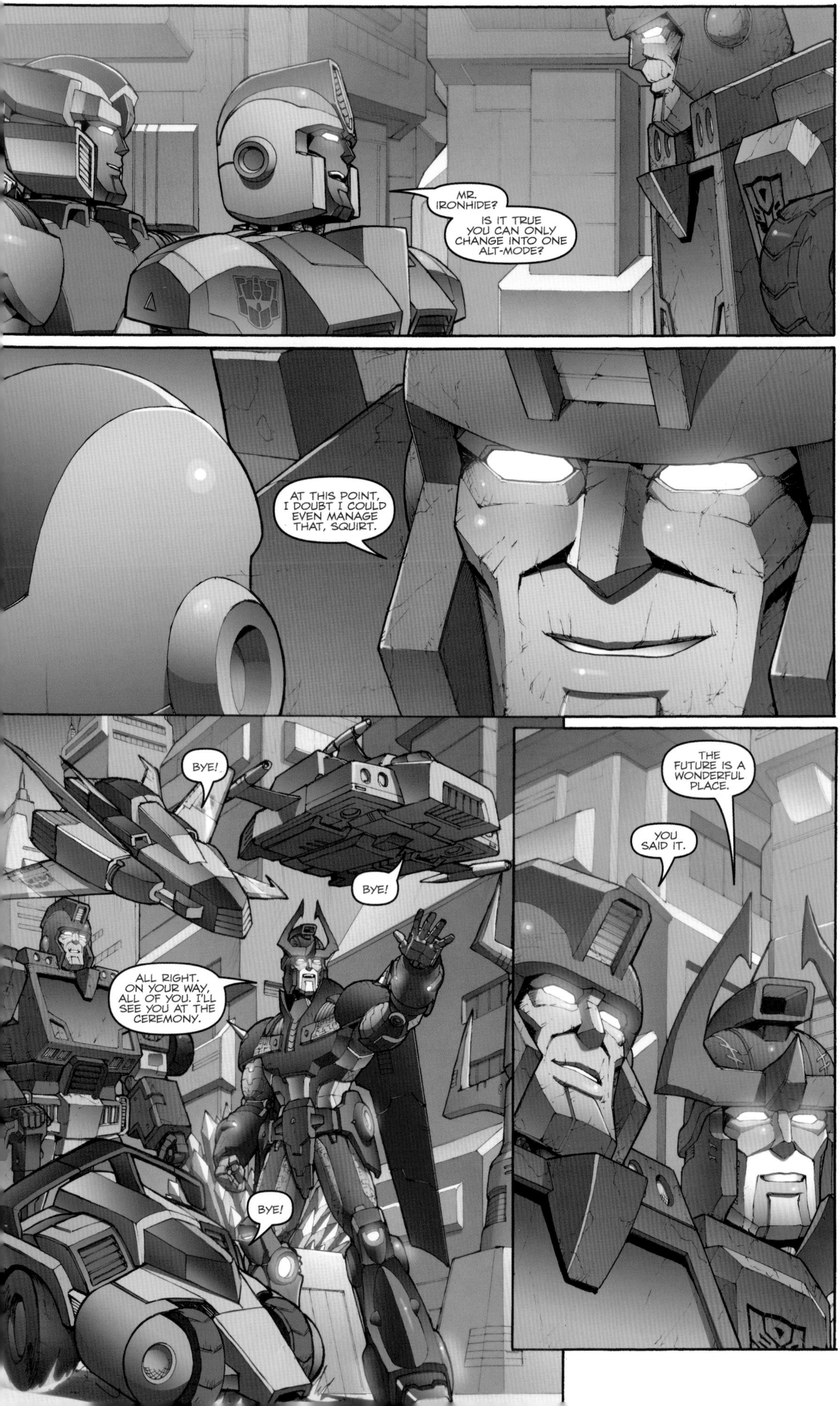
MR. IRONHIDE?
IS IT TRUE YOU CAN ONLY CHANGE INTO ONE ALT-MODE?
AT THIS POINT, I DOUBT I COULD EVEN MANAGE THAT, SQUIRT.
BYE!
BYE!
ALL RIGHT. ON YOUR WAY, ALL OF YOU. I'LL SEE YOU AT THE CEREMONY.
BYE!
THE FUTURE IS A WONDERFUL PLACE.
YOU SAID IT.

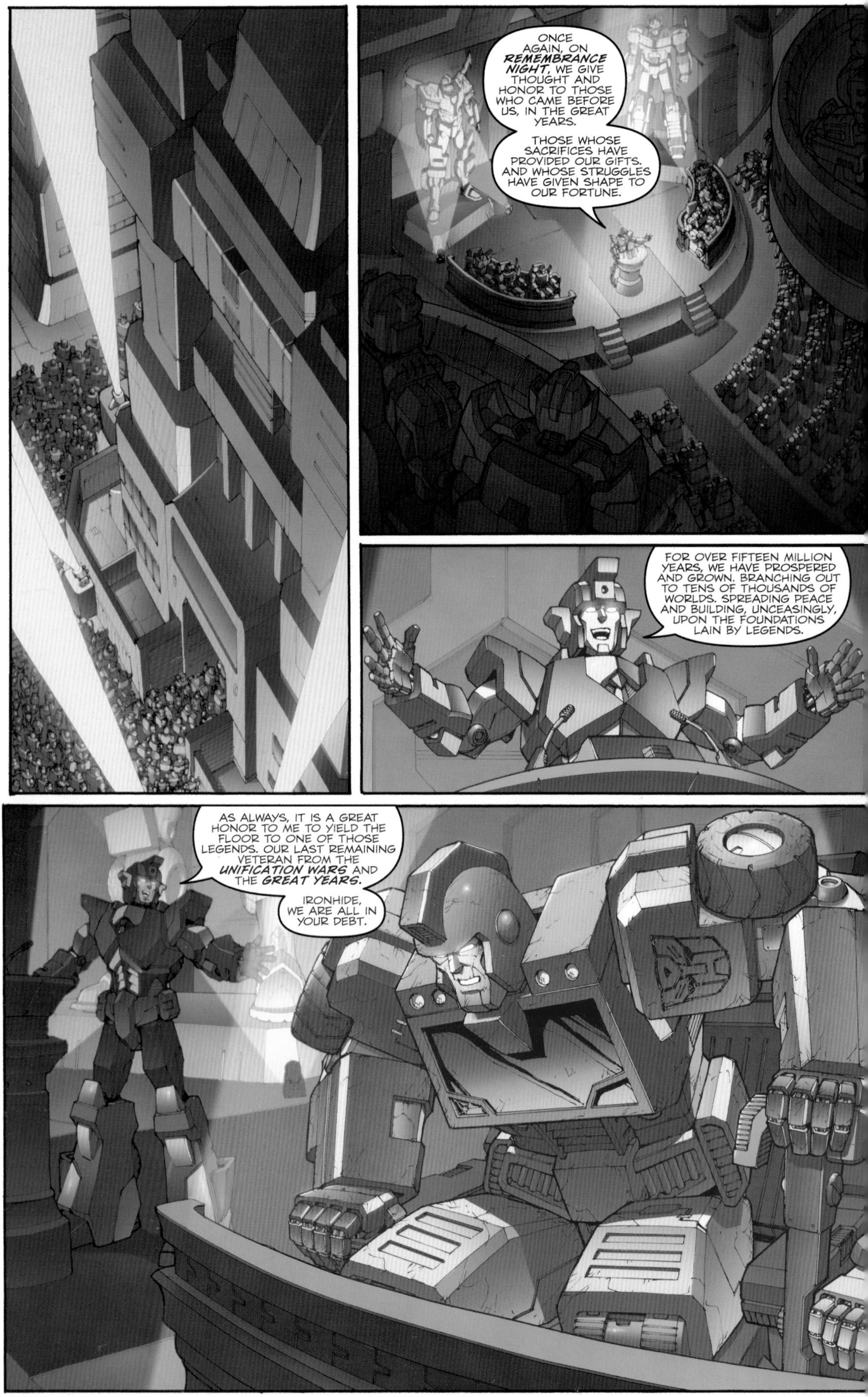
ONCE AGAIN, ON REMEMBRANCE NIGHT, WE GIVE THOUGHT AND HONOR TO THOSE WHO CAME BEFORE US, IN THE GREAT YEARS.
THOSE WHOSE SACRIFICES HAVE PROVIDED OUR GIFTS. AND WHOSE STRUGGLES HAVE GIVEN SHAPE TO OUR FORTUNE.
FOR OVER FIFTEEN MILLION YEARS, WE HAVE PROSPERED AND GROWN. BRANCHING OUT TO TENS OF THOUSANDS OF WORLDS. SPREADING PEACE AND BUILDING, UNCEASINGLY, UPON THE FOUNDATIONS LAIN BY LEGENDS.
AS ALWAYS, IT IS A GREAT HONOR TO ME TO YIELD THE FLOOR TO ONE OF THOSE LEGENDS. OUR LAST REMAINING VETERAN FROM THE UNIFICATION WARS AND THE GREAT YEARS.
IRONHIDE, WE ARE ALL IN YOUR DEBT.

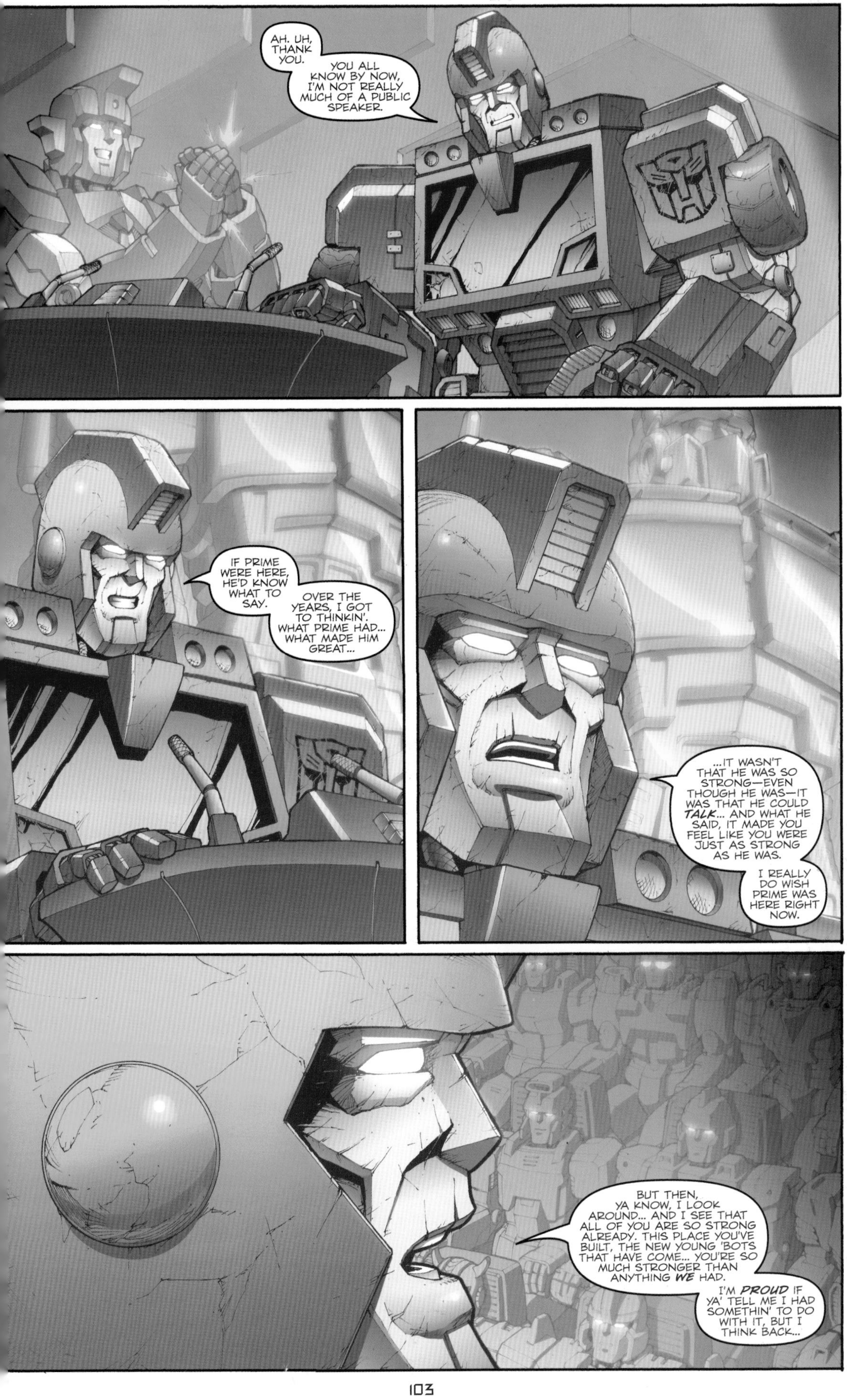
AH. UH, THANK YOU.
YOU ALL KNOW BY NOW, I'M NOT REALLY MUCH OF A PUBLIC SPEAKER.
IF PRIME WERE HERE, HE'D KNOW WHAT TO SAY.
OVER THE YEARS, I GOT TO THINKIN'. WHAT PRIME HAD... WHAT MADE HIM GREAT...
...IT WASN'T THAT HE WAS SO STRONG—EVEN THOUGH HE WAS—IT WAS THAT HE COULD TALK... AND WHAT HE SAID, IT MADE YOU FEEL LIKE YOU WERE JUST AS STRONG AS HE WAS.
I REALLY DO WISH PRIME WAS HERE RIGHT NOW.
BUT THEN, YA KNOW, I LOOK AROUND... AND I SEE THAT ALL OF YOU ARE SO STRONG ALREADY. THIS PLACE YOU'VE BUILT, THE NEW YOUNG 'BOTS THAT HAVE COME... YOU'RE SO MUCH STRONGER THAN ANYTHING WE HAD.
I'M PROUD IF YA' TELL ME I HAD SOMETHIN' TO DO WITH IT, BUT I THINK BACK...

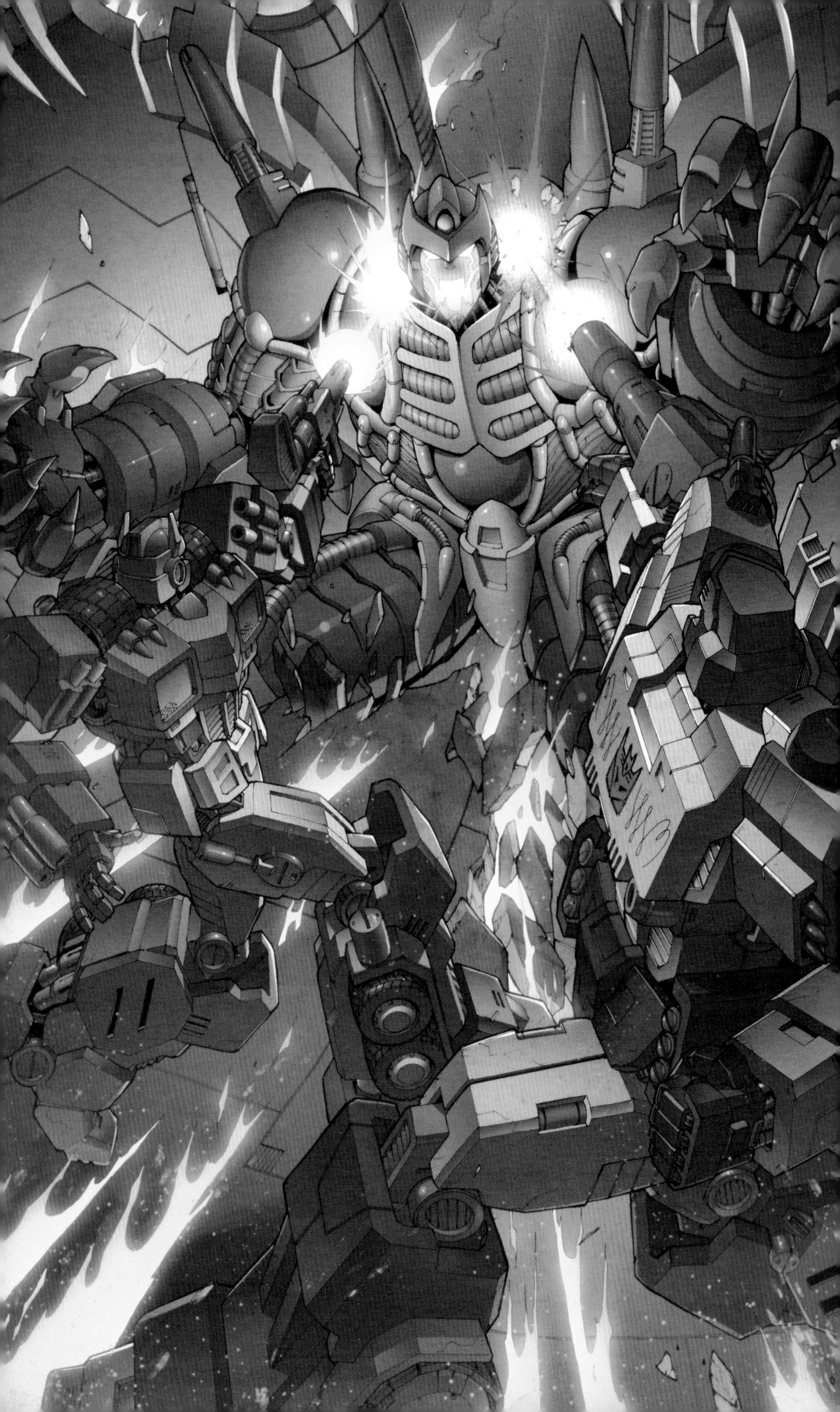

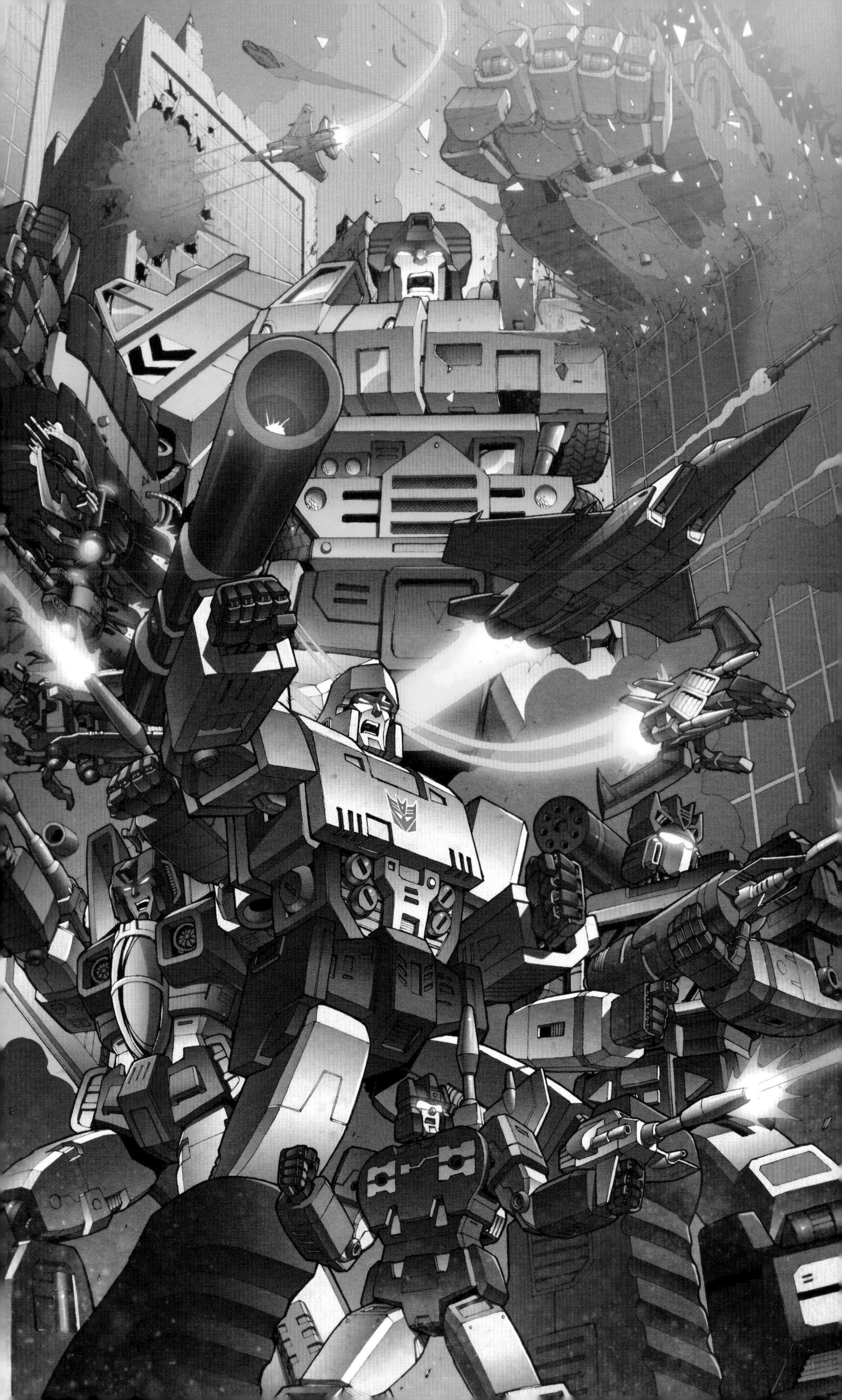

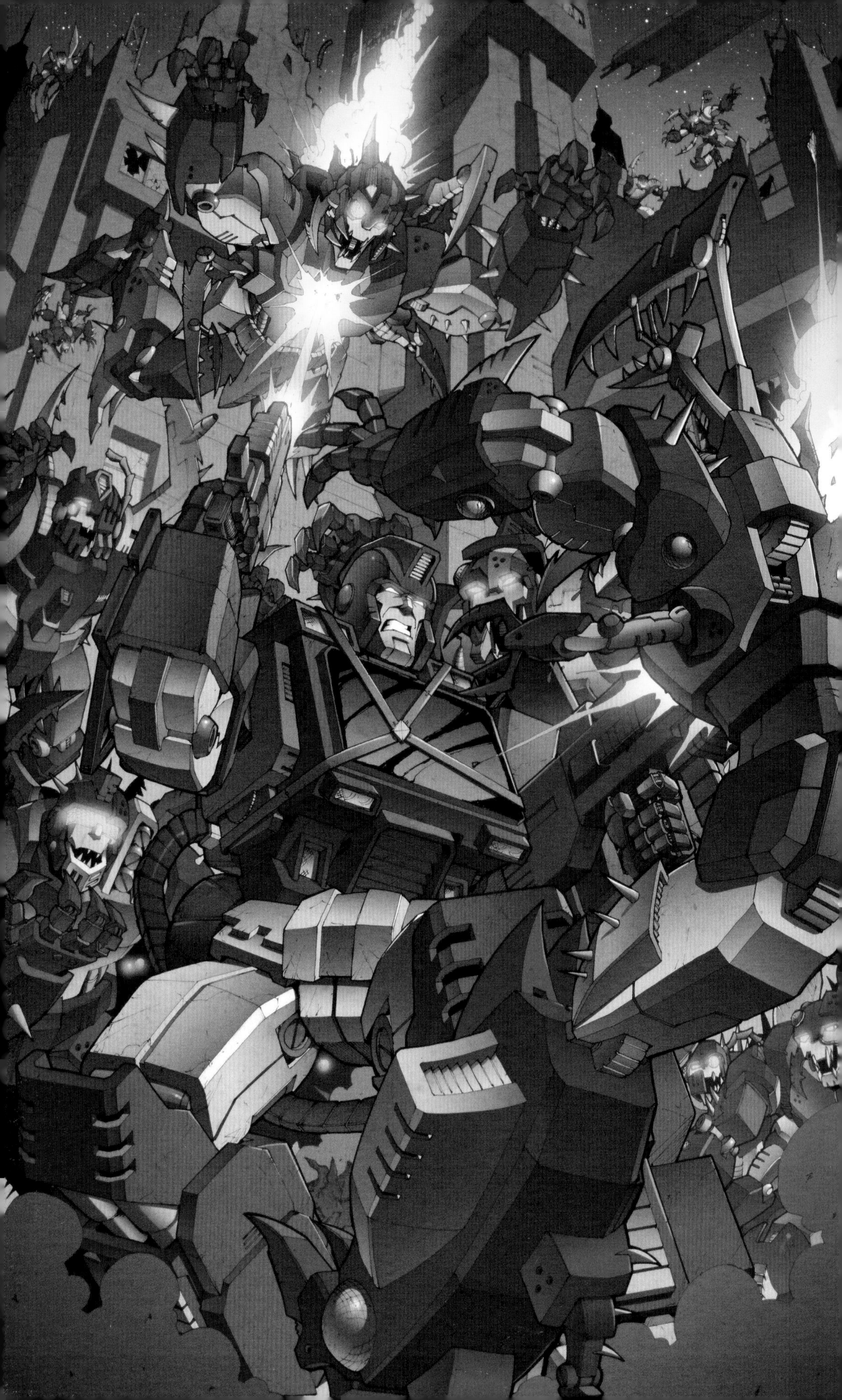

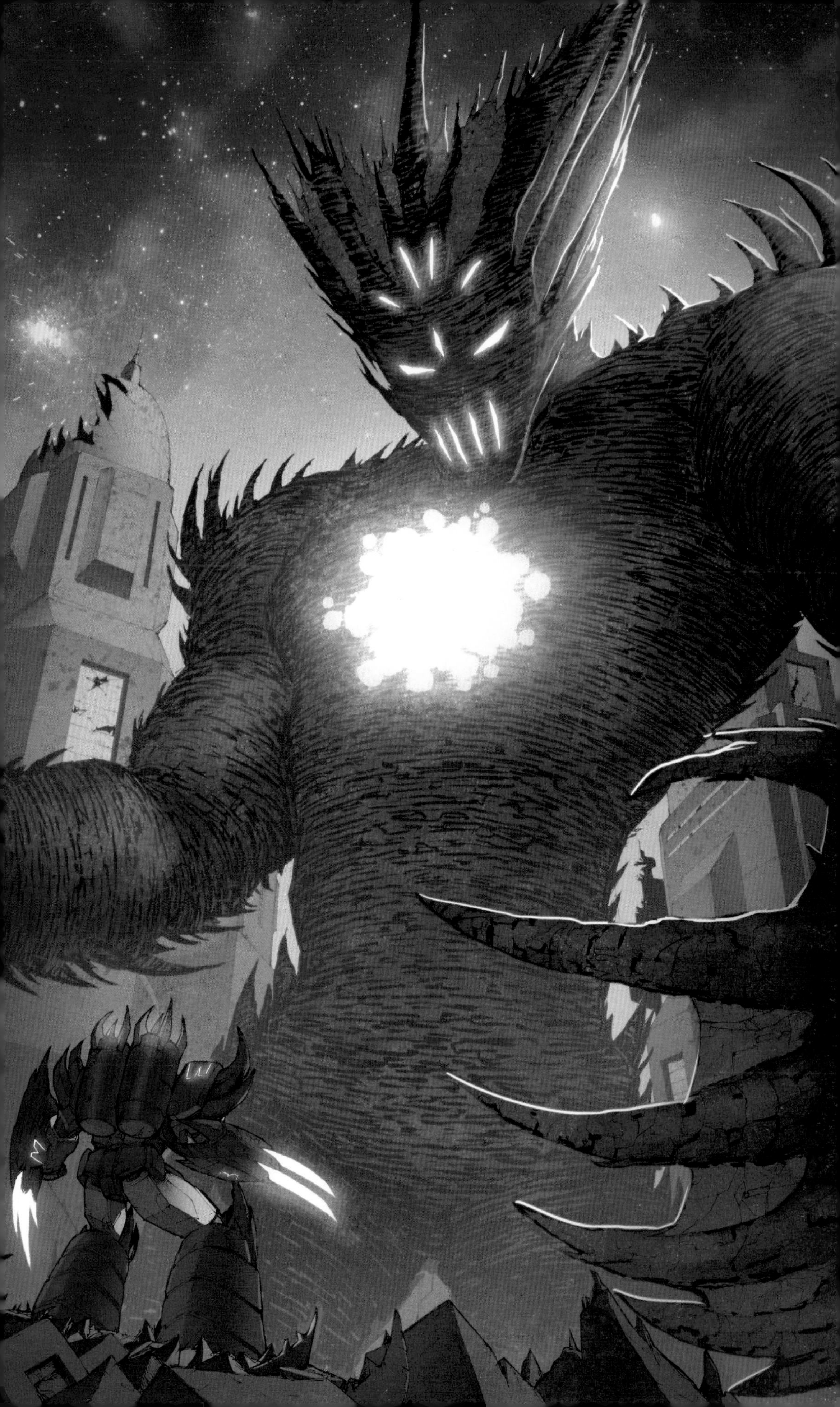

I THINK BACK AND I THINK... YOU DON'T NEED A GUY LIKE ME AROUND NOW.

YOU. THIS. *THIS* IS EVERYTHING WE WERE HOPING FOR THEN. AND I'M GLAD IT'S HERE. AND YOU DON'T NEED ME BRINGIN' IT DOWN, SO I'LL SAY GOODNIGHT.

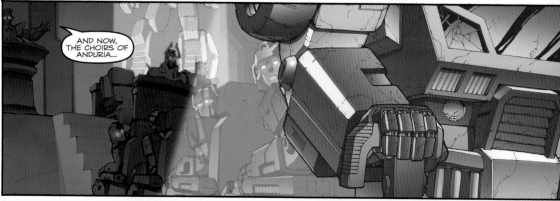

AND NOW, THE CHOIRS OF ANDURIA...

...BRINGING YOU THE BELOVED SOUNDS OF A BYGONE ERA.

YOU THINK MEGATRON'S STILL OUT THERE, DON'T YOU?

I *KNOW* HE IS. I CAN'T SHAKE IT. I PROBABLY NEVER WILL.

PRIME IS OUT THERE SOMEWHERE, TOO. TAKE COMFORT IN THAT.

BUT YOU'RE THE LAST ONE LEFT *HERE*, IRONHIDE. AND IT MEANS A LOT TO THEM THAT THEY GET TO HONOR YOU FOR EVERYTHING.

WHAT "EVERYTHING"? I DIDN'T BUILD ANY OF THIS. ALL THESE BEAUTIFUL THINGS, ALL THESE 'BOTS RUNNIN' AROUND... I DIDN'T HAVE NOTHIN' TO DO WITH THAT. IT'S BEEN MILLIONS OF YEARS, ALPHA.

HONOR ME NOTHIN'. THAT'S RIDICULOUS. ALL I EVER DID WAS PUNCH GUYS IN THE FACE.

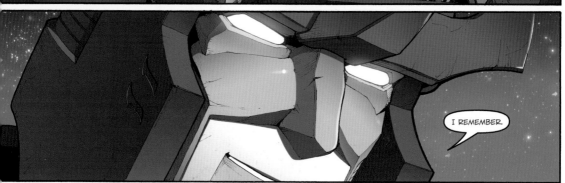

I REMEMBER.

THESE ARE THE GREAT YEARS. *ALL OF THIS.* HOW DO THEY NOT *SEE* THAT?

I THINK, MY FRIEND, THAT YOUR STORIES HELP WITH THAT. GIVE THEM *PERSPECTIVE.*

NO. THOSE OLD DAYS—MY PART IN ALL THAT STUFF—IT'S *DONE.* AND I'M DONE WITH *IT.* I'M NOT INTERESTED IN HANGIN' AROUND TO BE SOME *LIVING RELIC.* THOSE THINGS ALL HAPPENED A LONG, LONG TIME AGO, AND I DON'T HAVE ANY MORE TO SAY ABOUT THEM.

IT WAS ALL JUST A LOTTA STUPIDITY AND HEARTACHE, AND I'M GLAD MY STORY'S DONE.

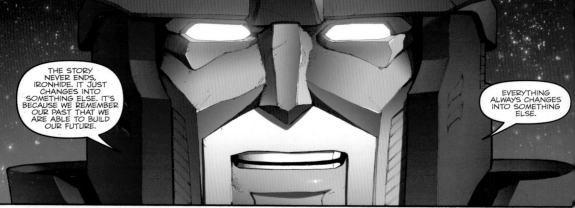

THE STORY NEVER ENDS, IRONHIDE. IT JUST CHANGES INTO SOMETHING ELSE. IT'S BECAUSE WE REMEMBER OUR PAST THAT WE ARE ABLE TO BUILD OUR FUTURE.

EVERYTHING ALWAYS CHANGES INTO SOMETHING ELSE.

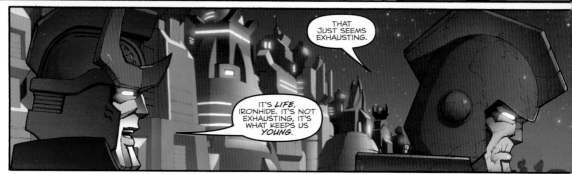

THAT JUST SEEMS EXHAUSTING.

IT'S *LIFE,* IRONHIDE. IT'S NOT EXHAUSTING, IT'S WHAT KEEPS US *YOUNG.*

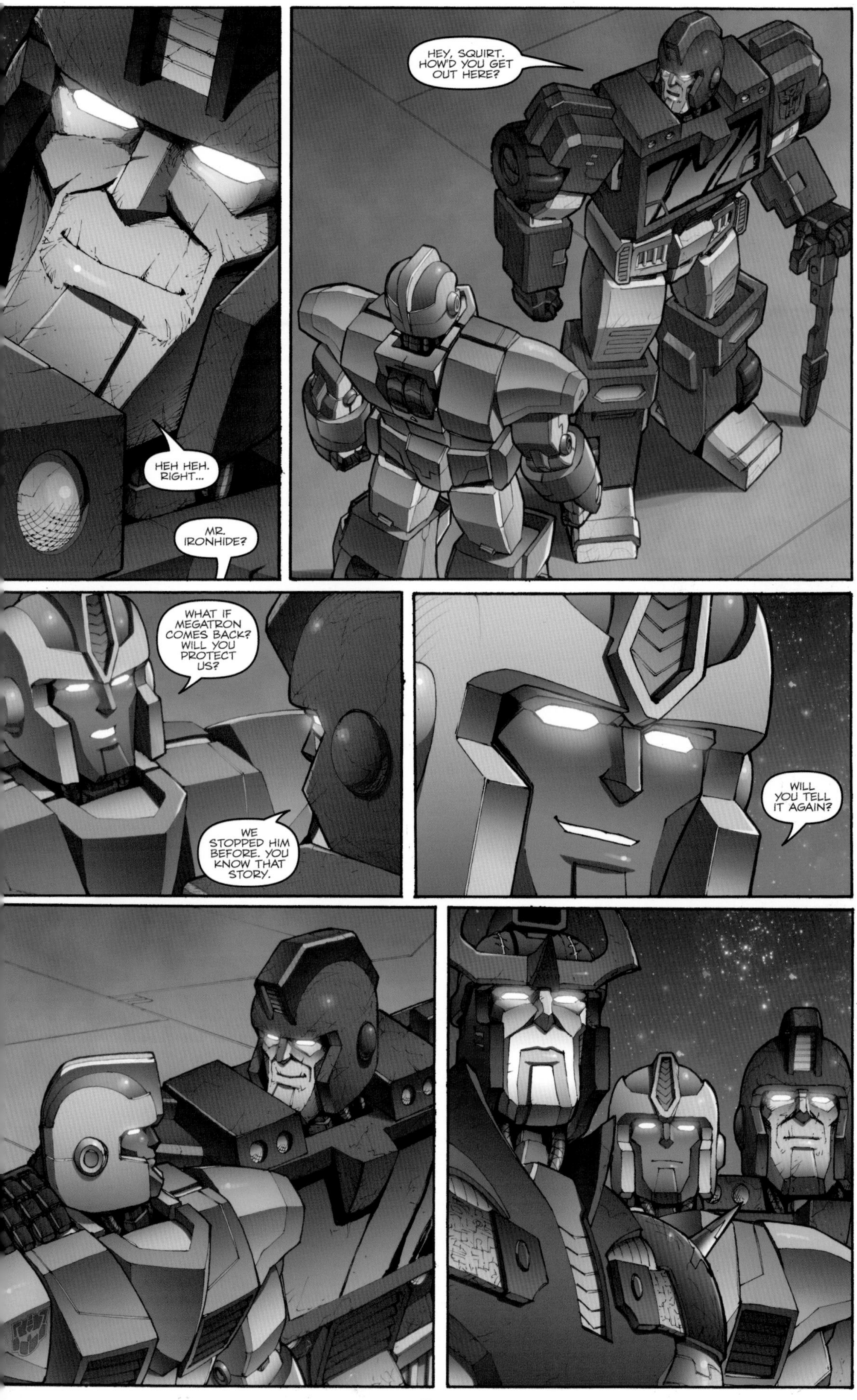
HEH HEH. RIGHT...
MR. IRONHIDE?
HEY, SQUIRT. HOW'D YOU GET OUT HERE?
WHAT IF MEGATRON COMES BACK? WILL YOU PROTECT US?
WE STOPPED HIM BEFORE. YOU KNOW THAT STORY.
WILL YOU TELL IT AGAIN?

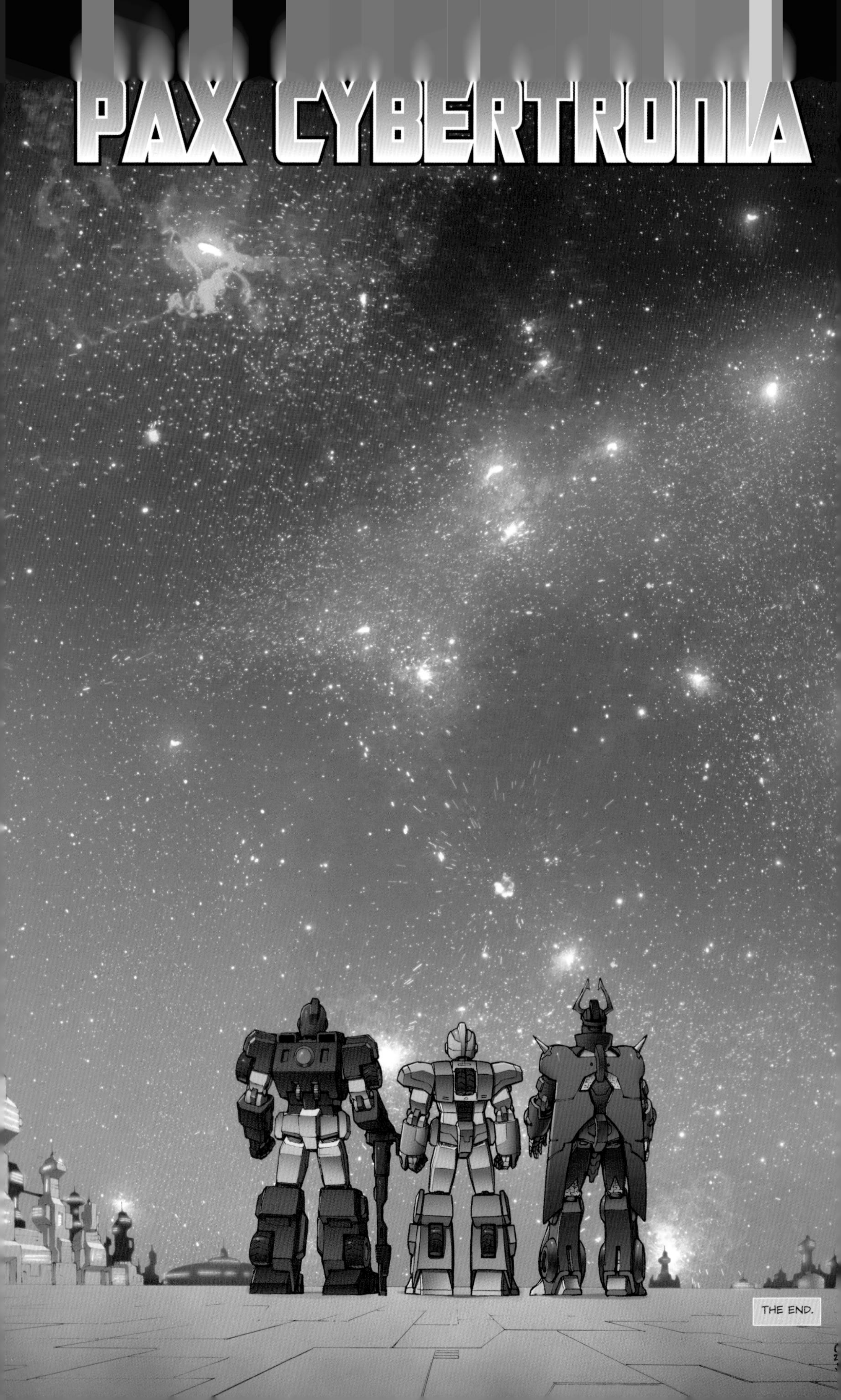
PAX CYBERTRONIA
THE END.

THE TRANSFORMERS CHAOS

VOLUME 7

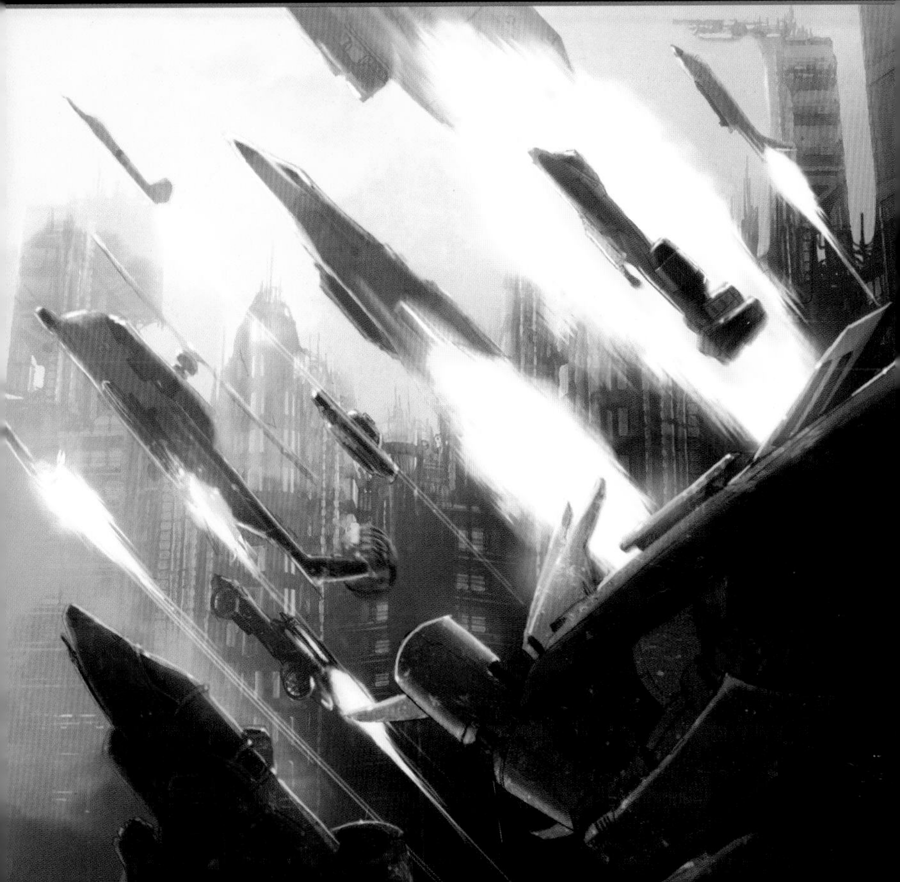

ART GALLERY

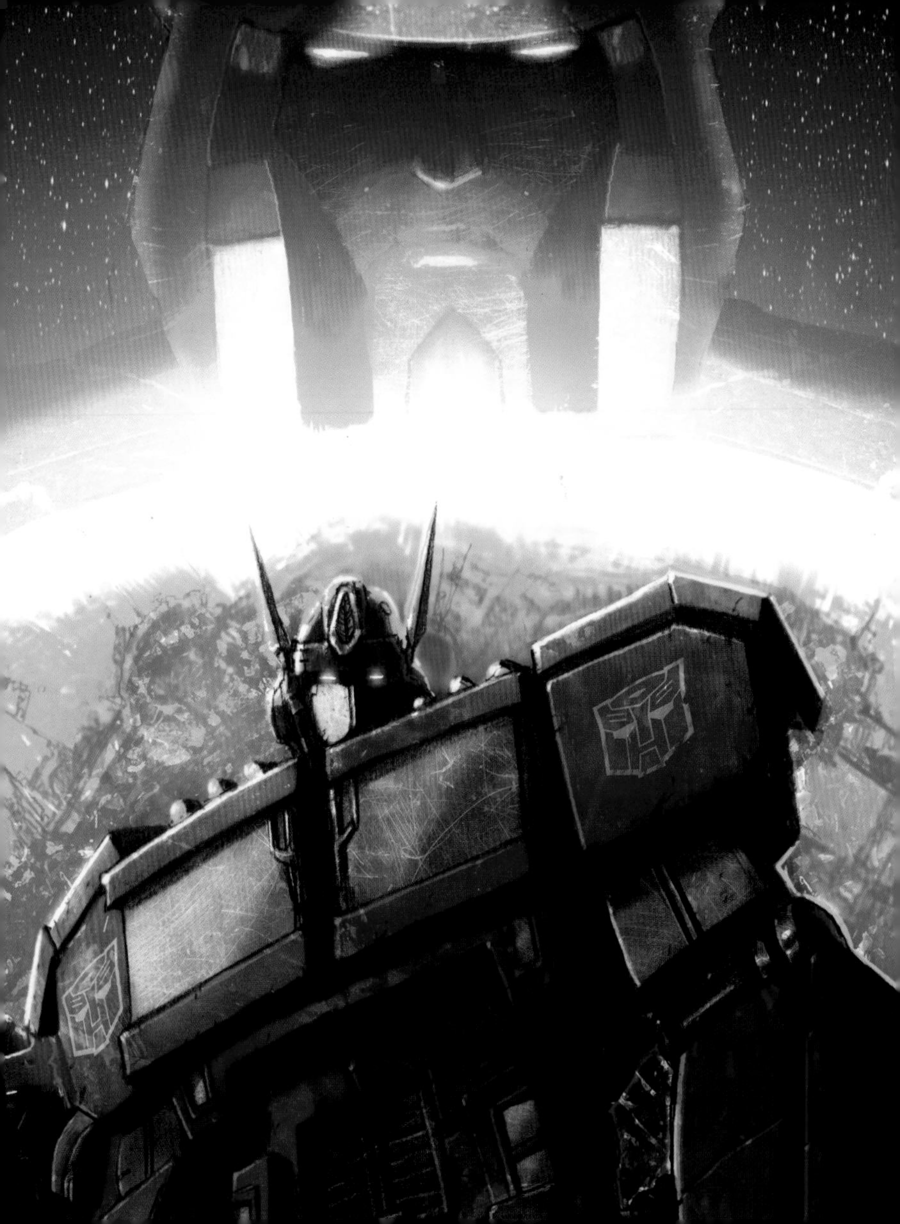

Art by
Livio Ramondelli

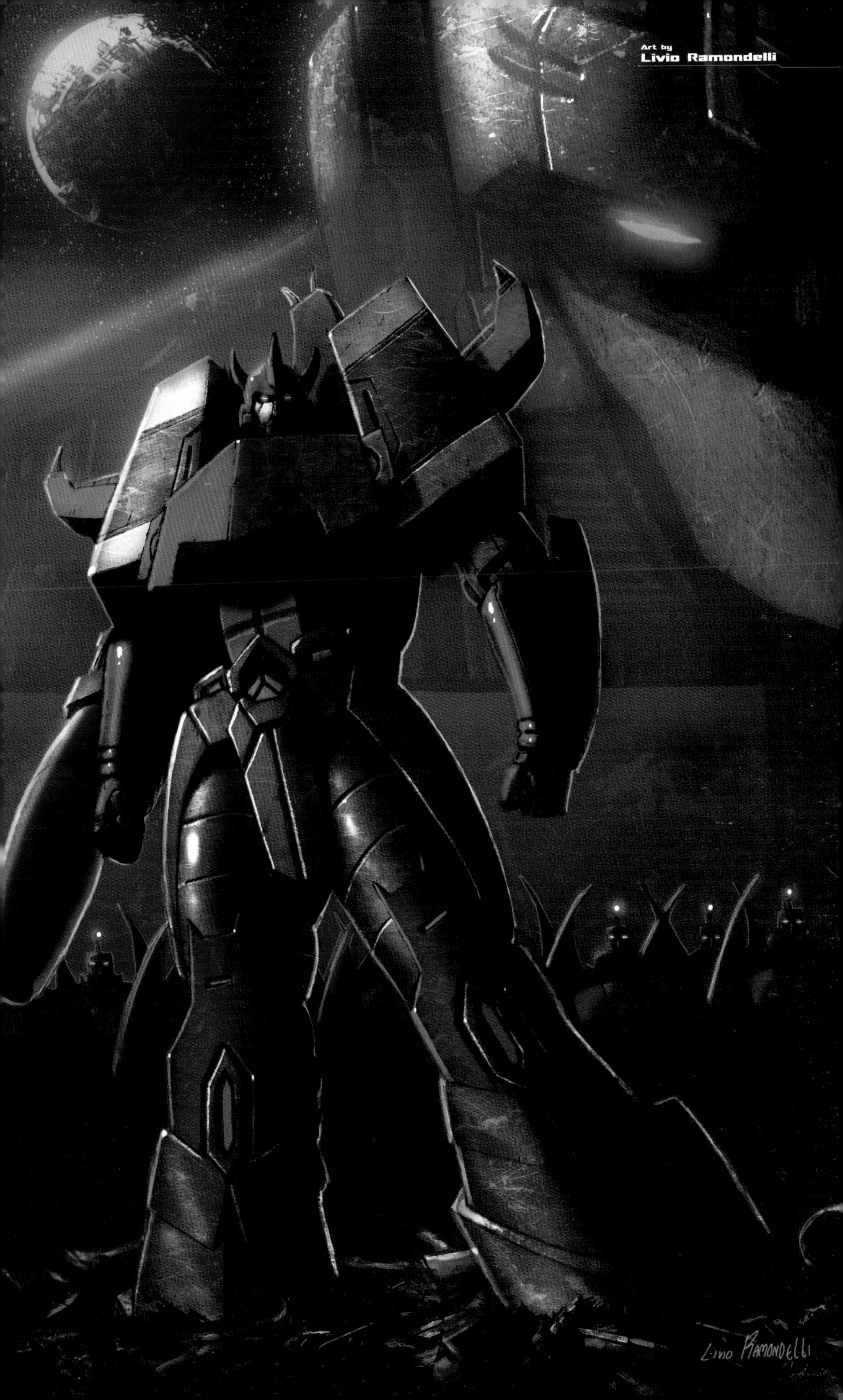
Livio Ramondelli

Art by
Livio Ramondelli

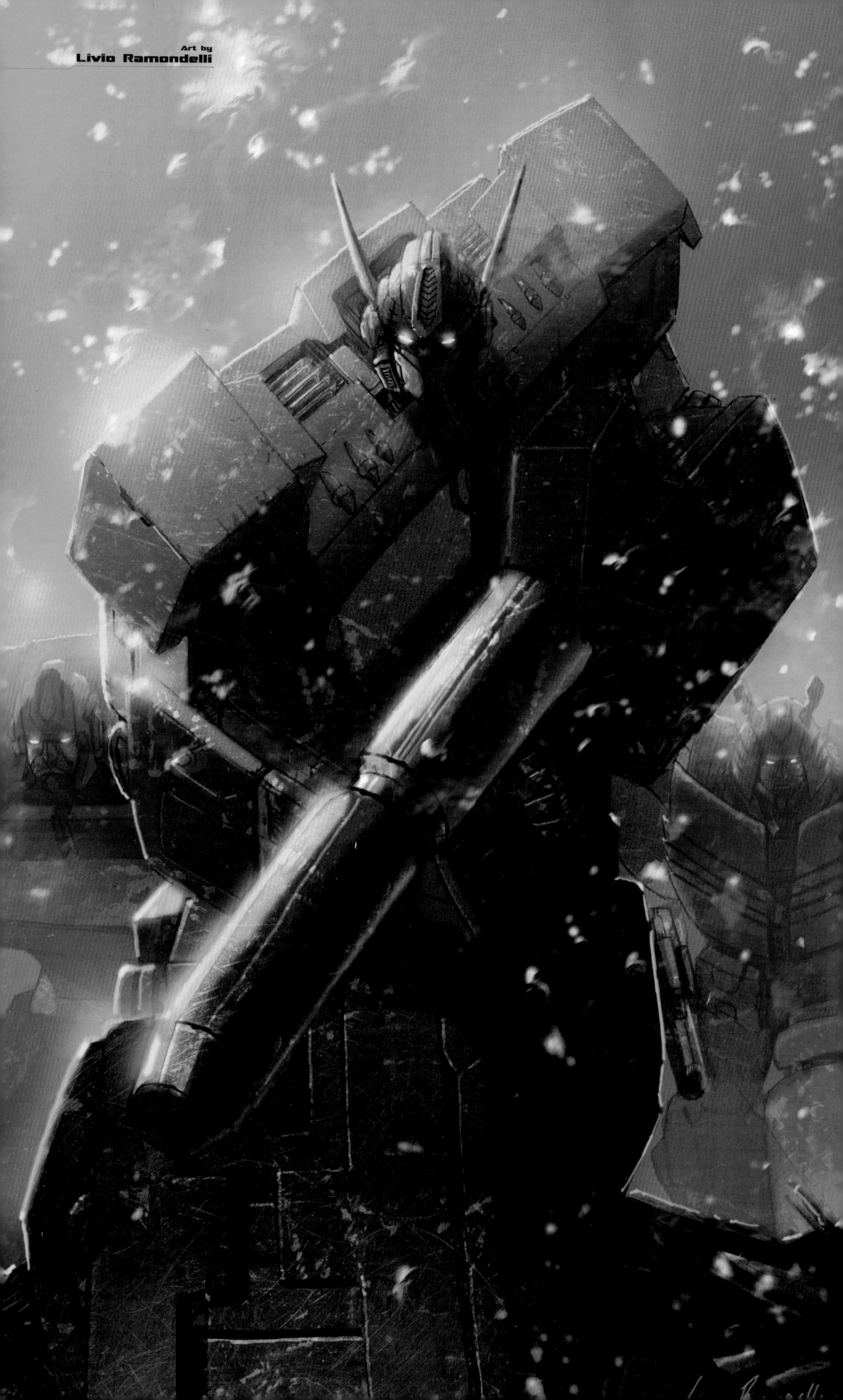

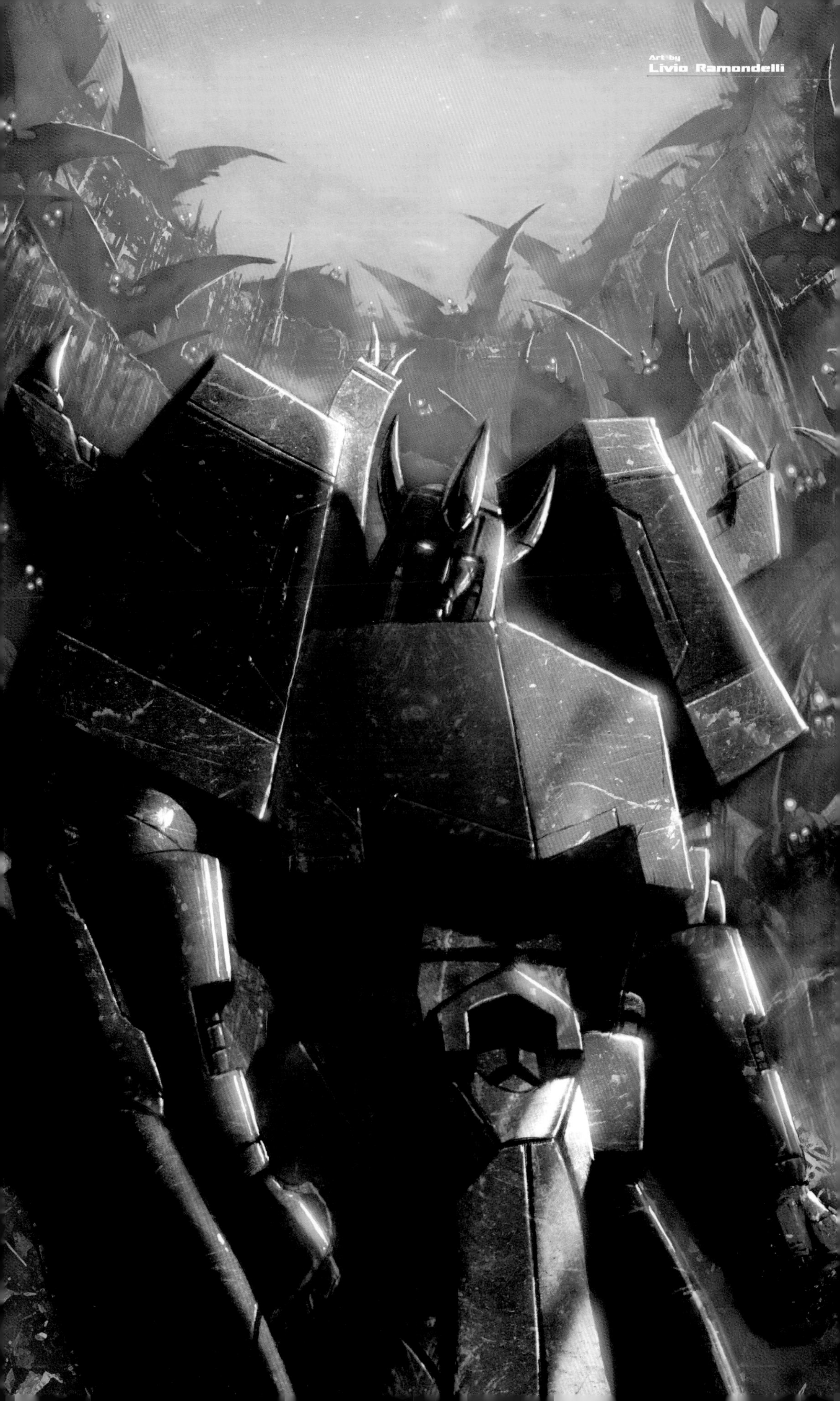
Art by
Livio Ramondelli

Art by
Livio Ramondelli

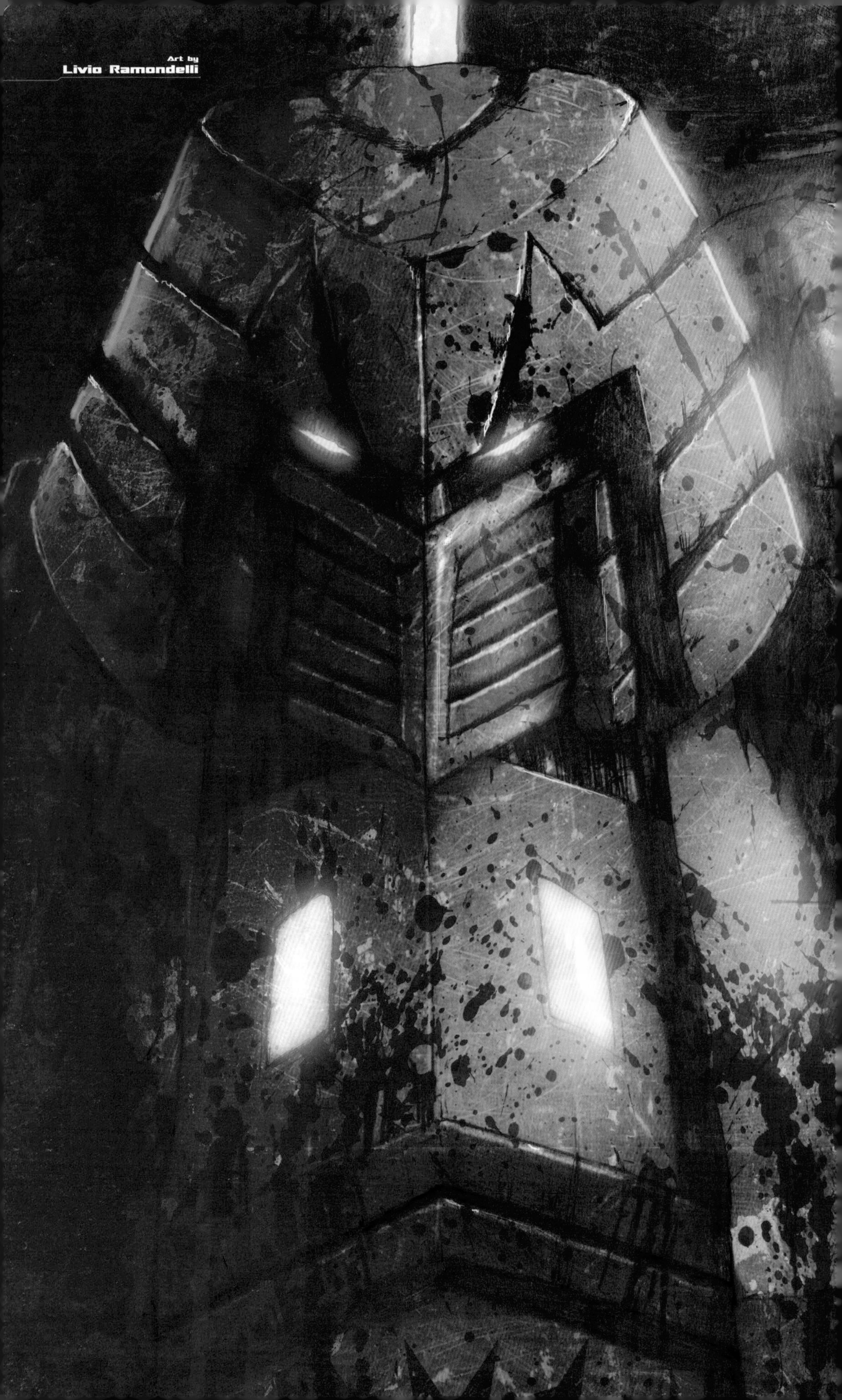

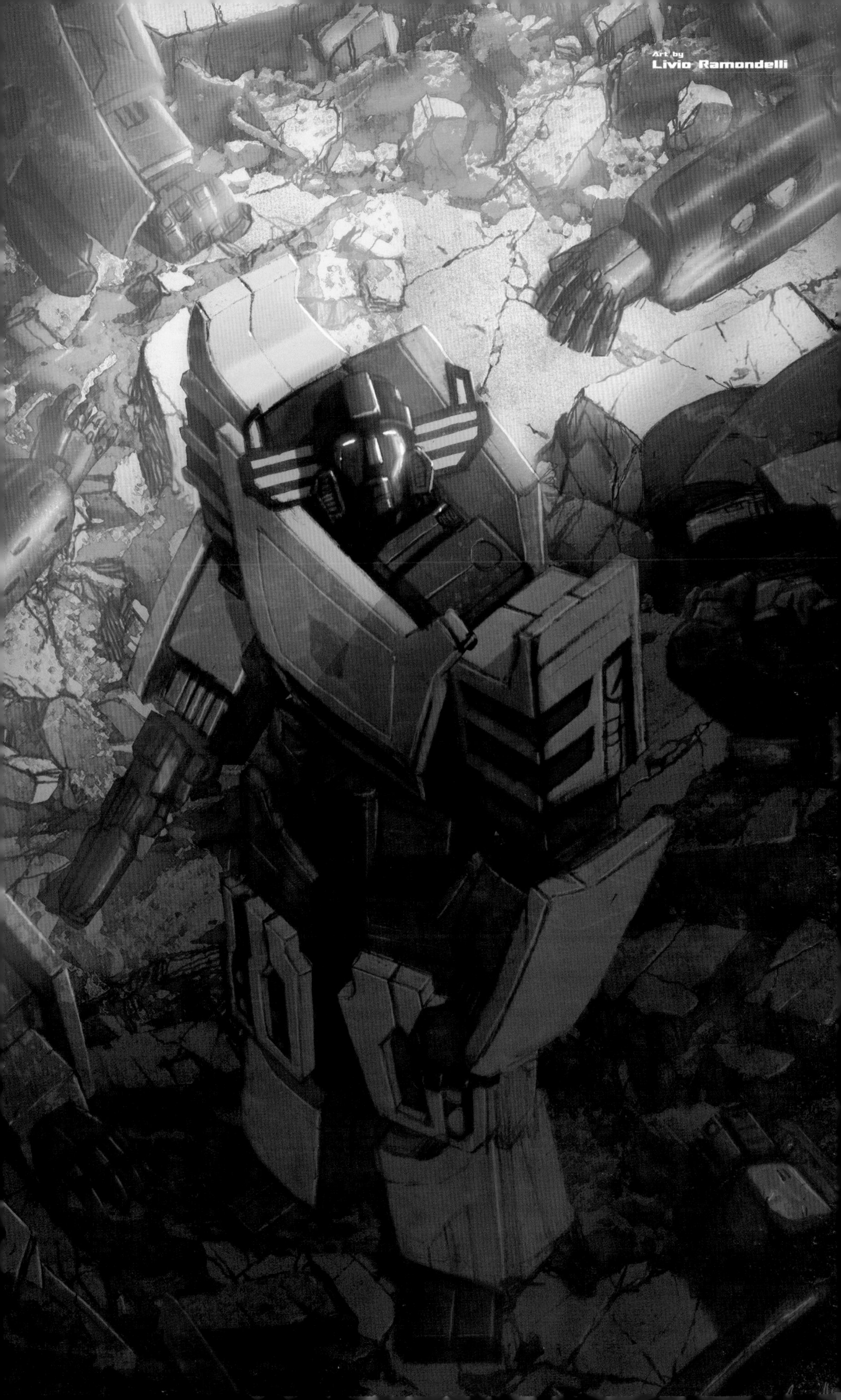
Art by
Livio Ramondelli

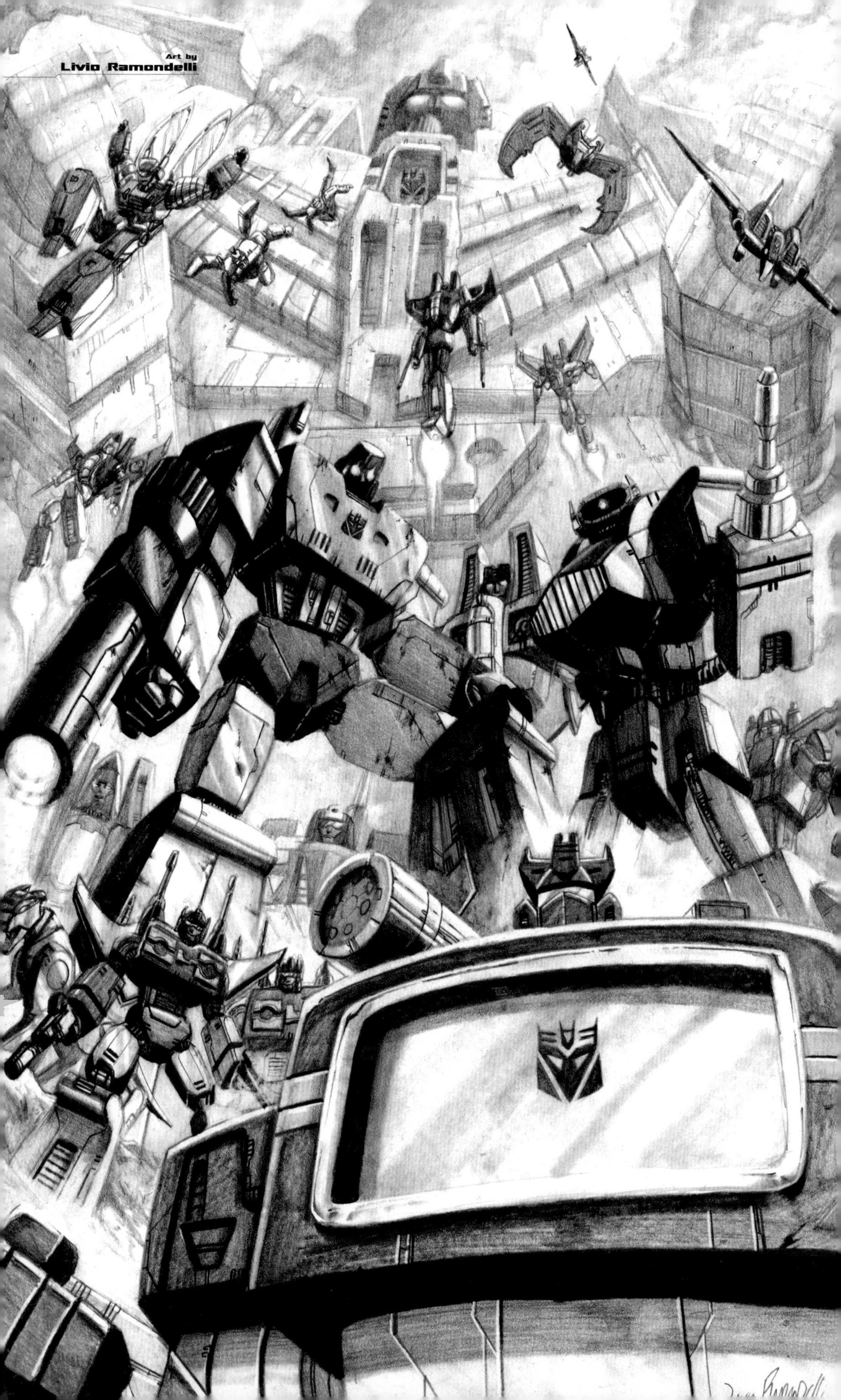
Art by
Livio Ramondelli

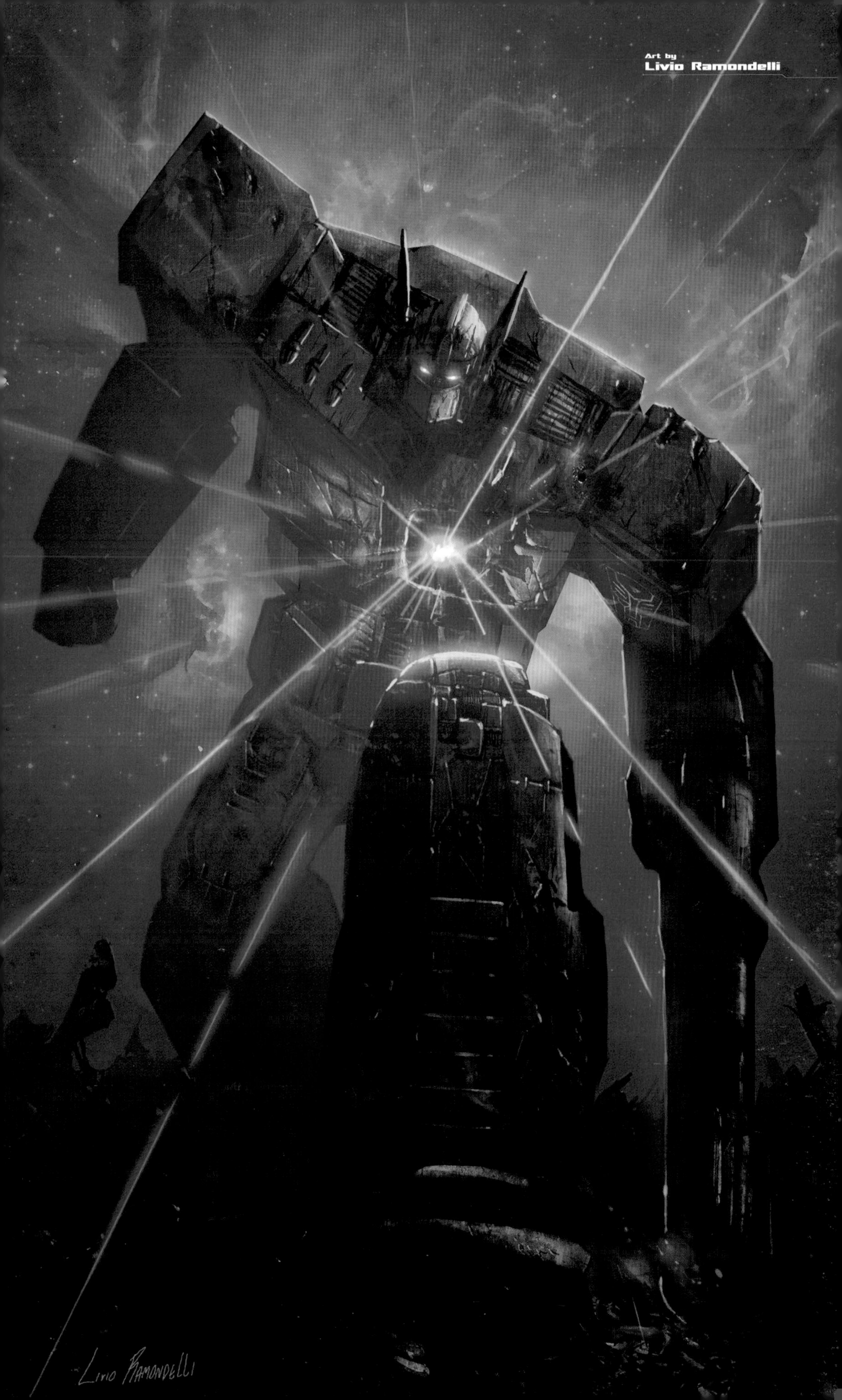
Art by
Livio Ramondelli
Livio Ramondelli

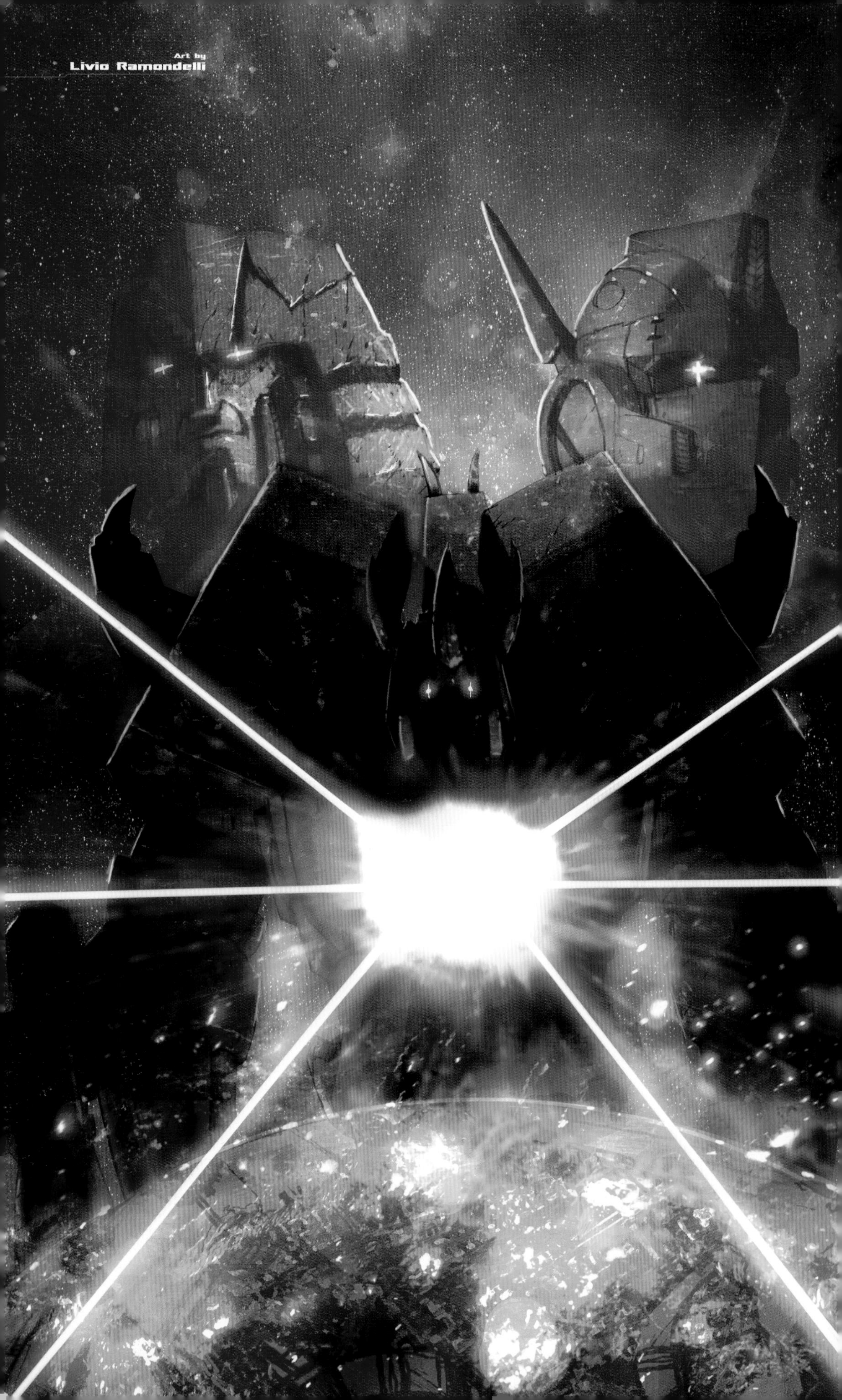
Art by
Livio Ramondelli

Photo by
Rik Alvarez

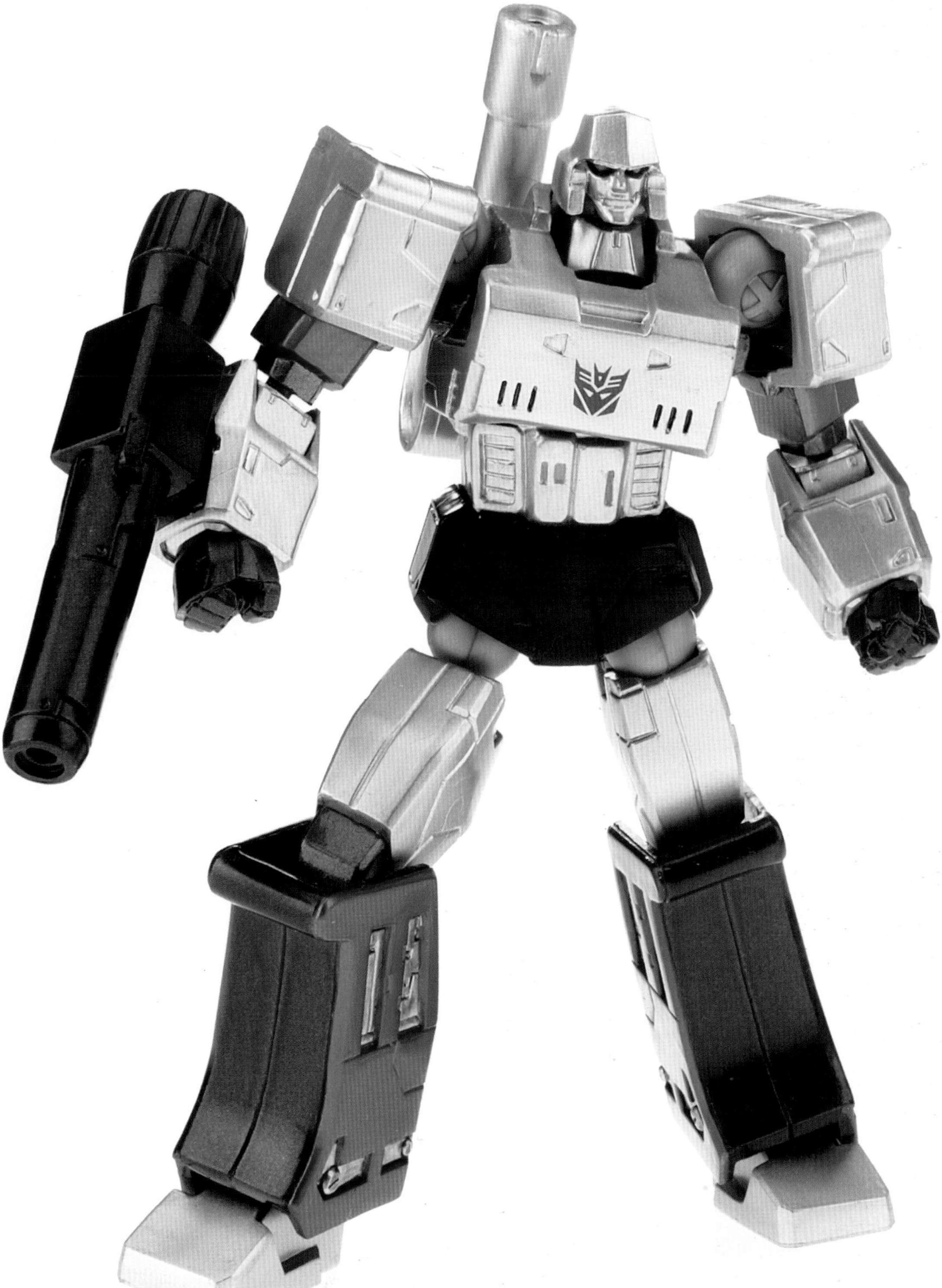

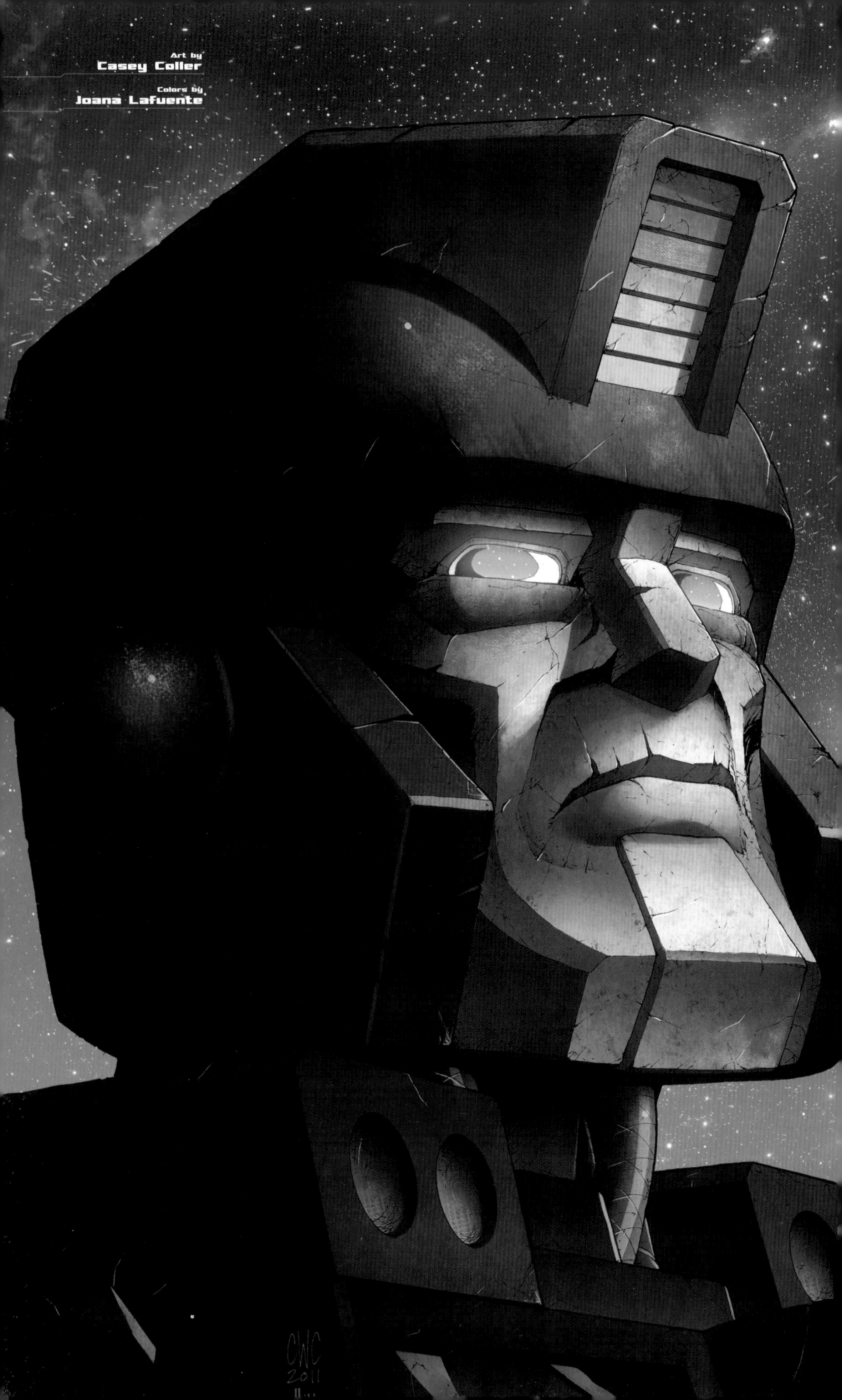
Art by
Casey Coller
Colors by
Joana Lafuente
CWC
2011

Art by
Trevor Hutchison

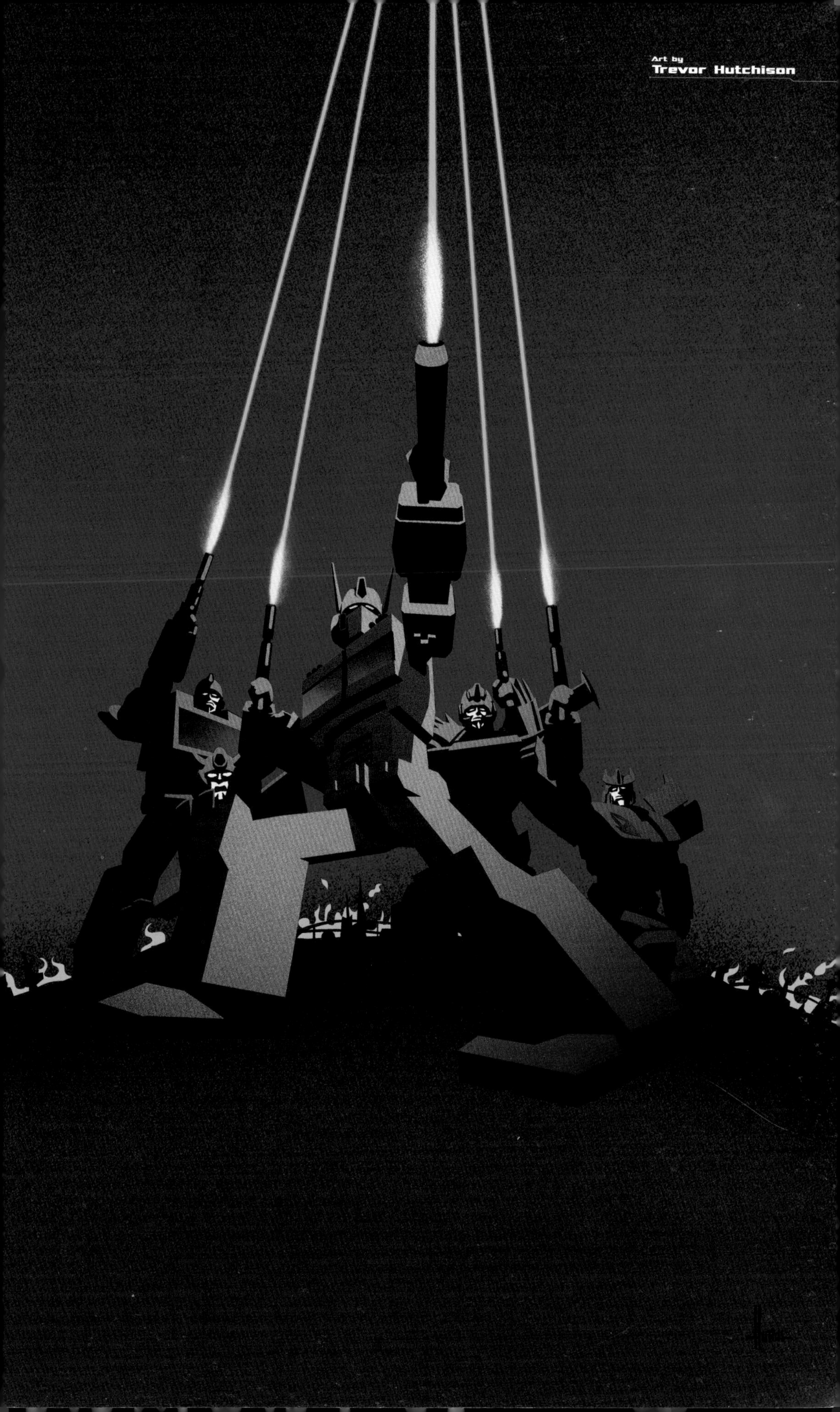

Art by
Livio Ramondelli

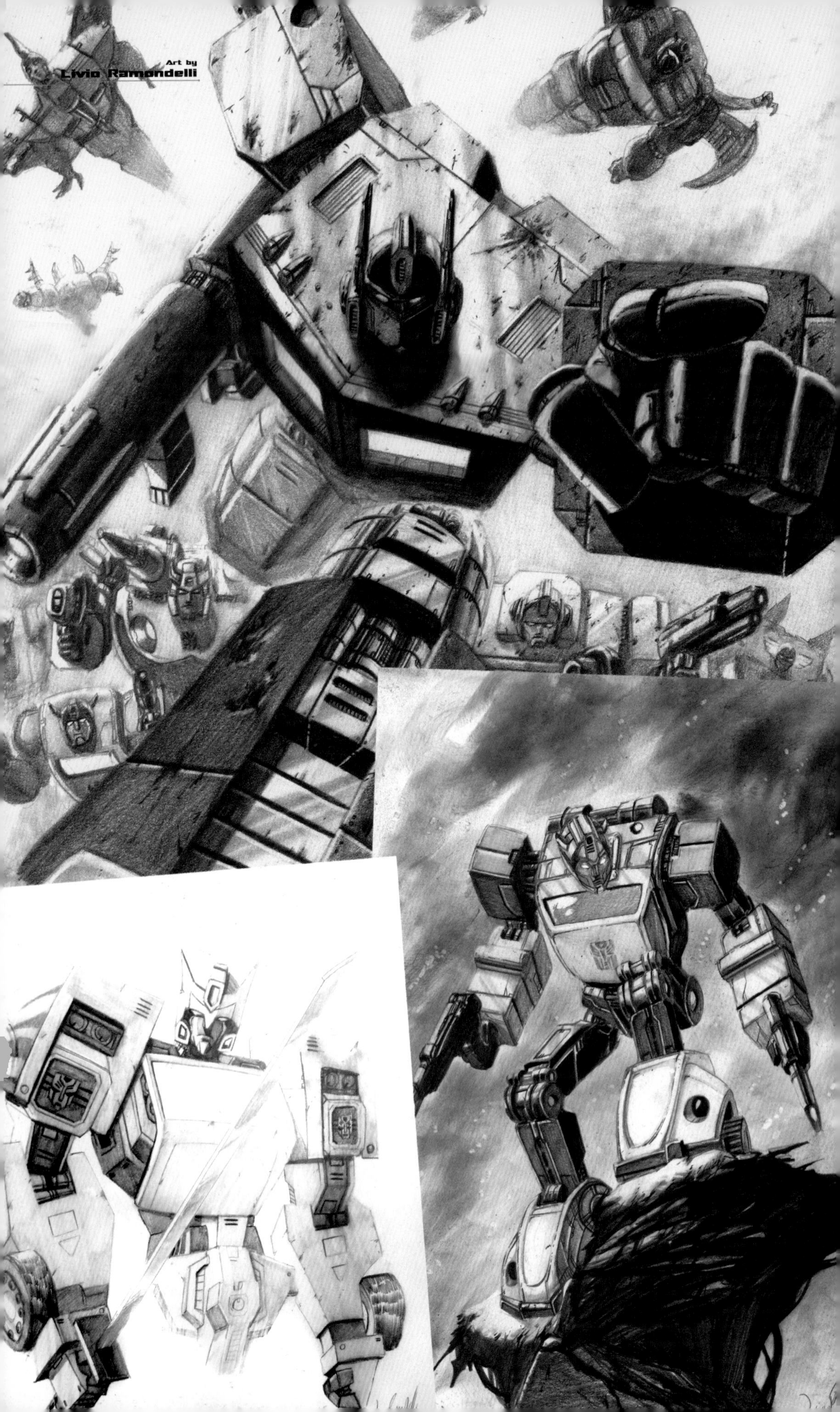

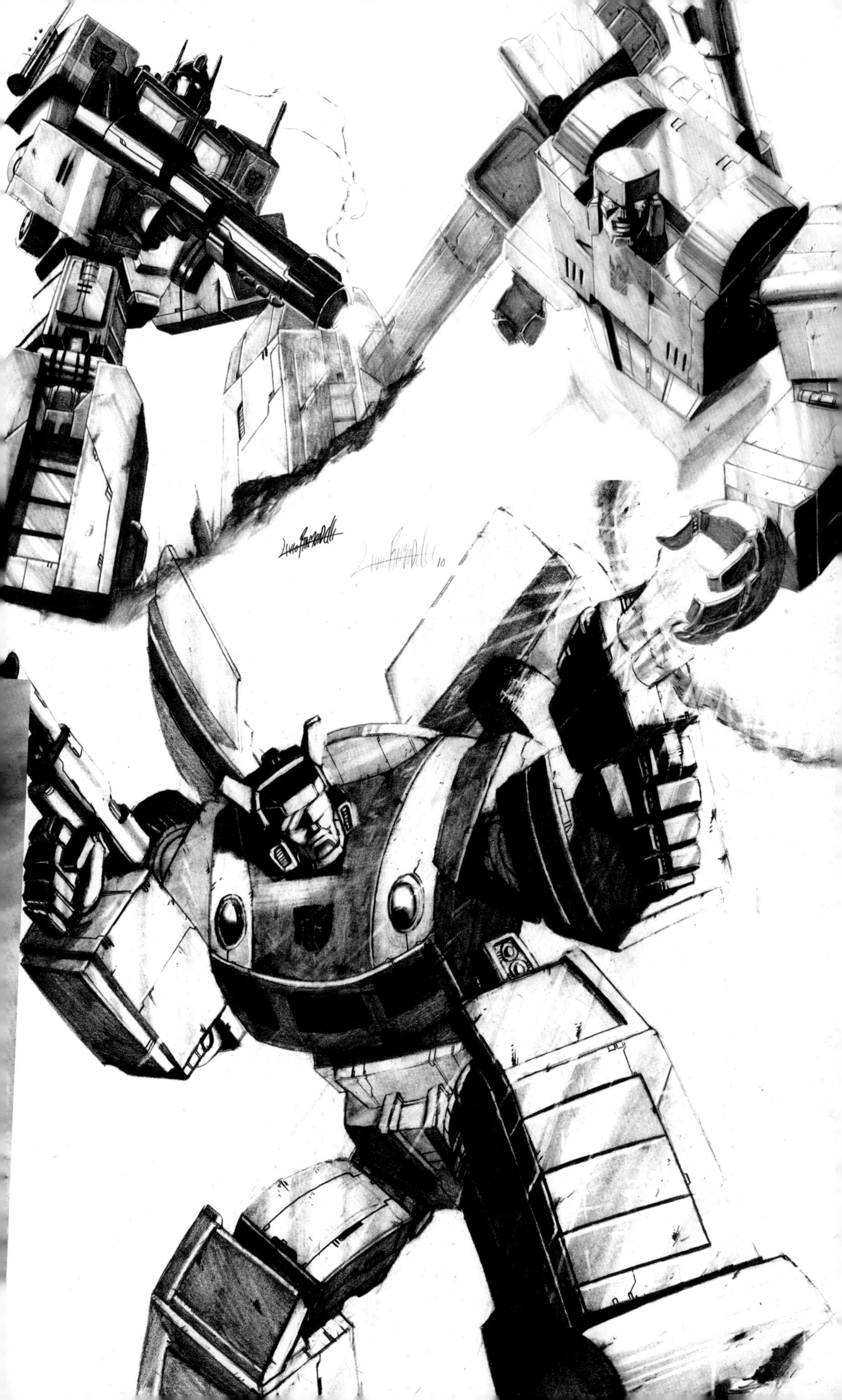

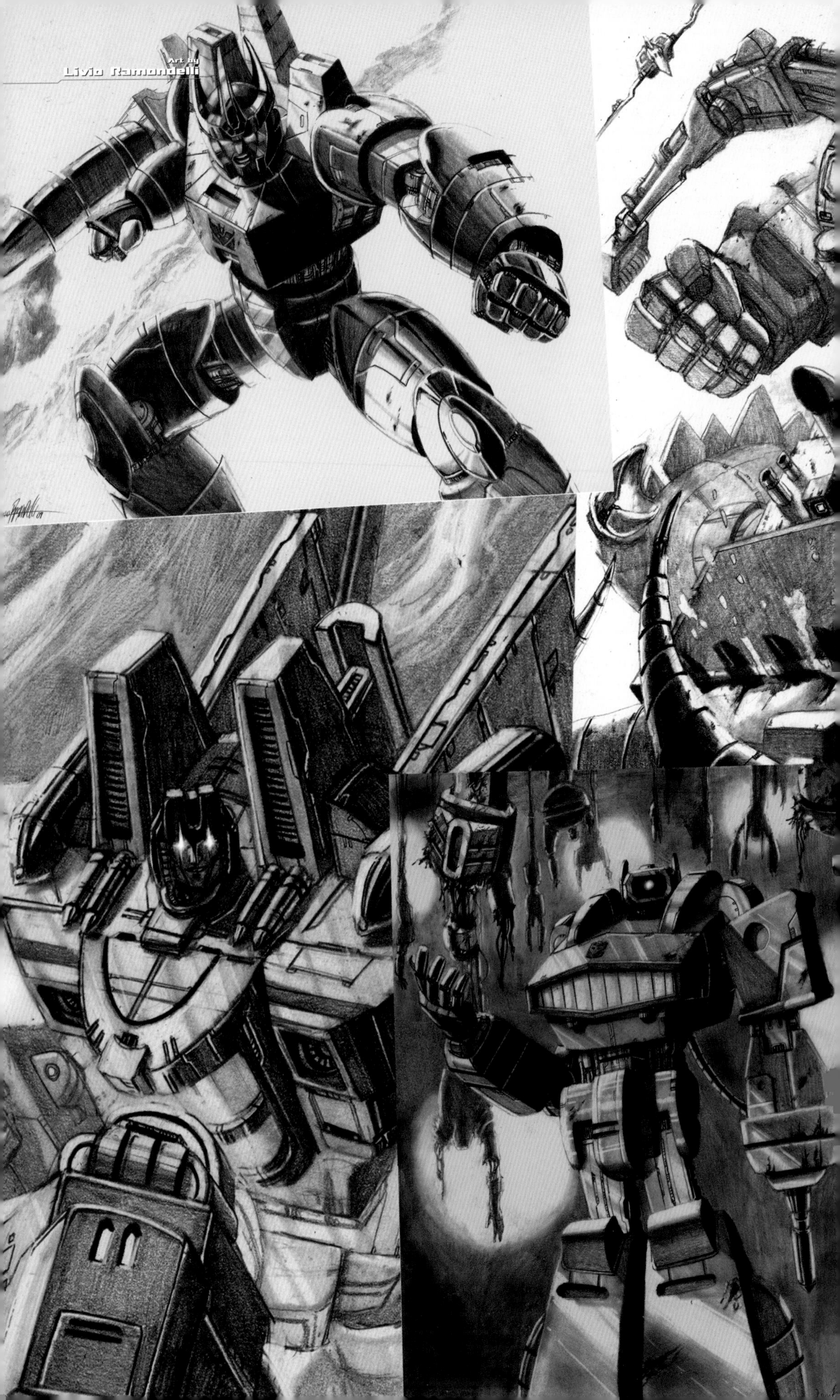
Art by
Livio Ramondelli

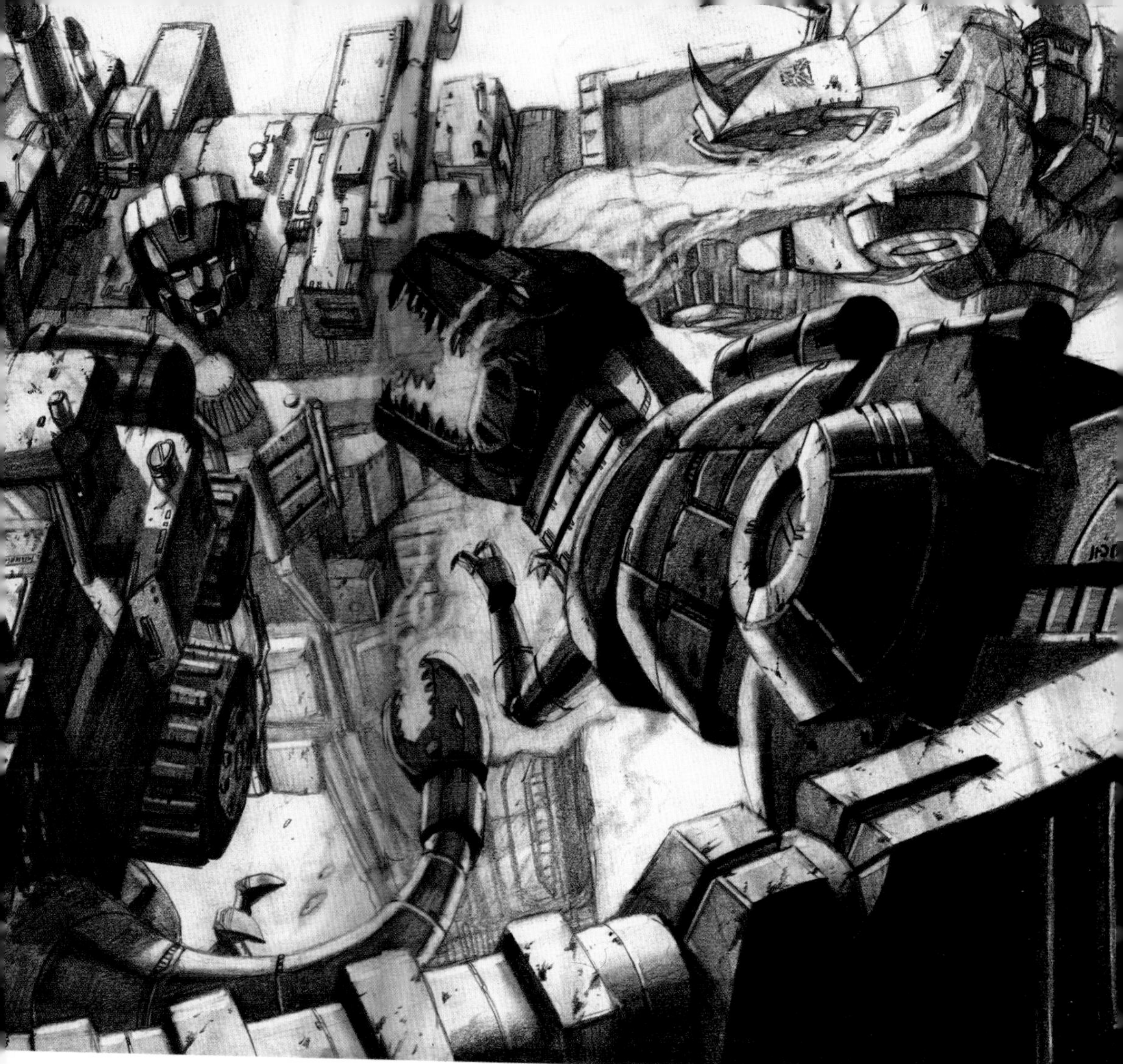

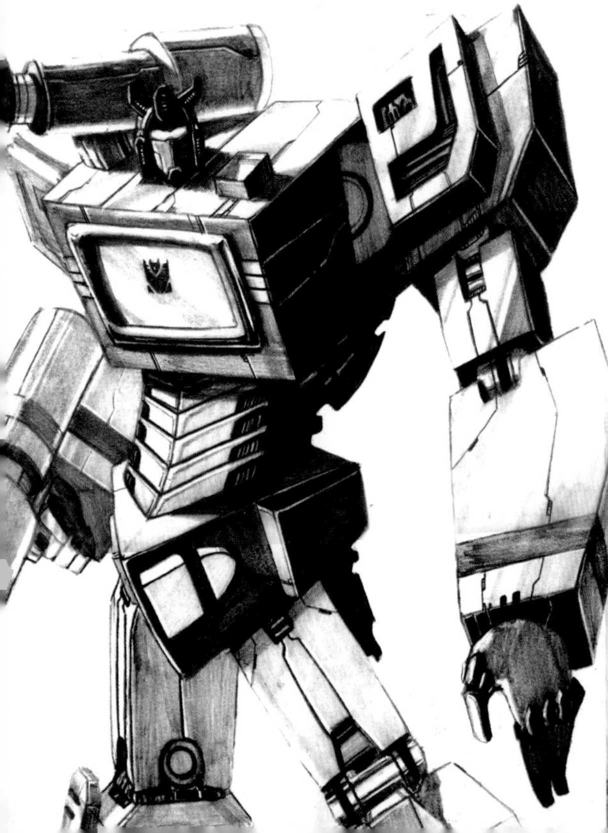

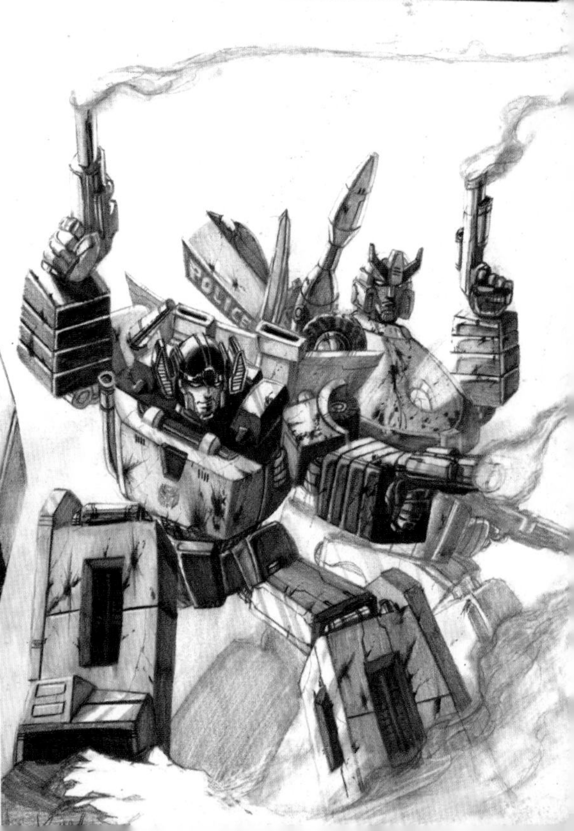
POLICE

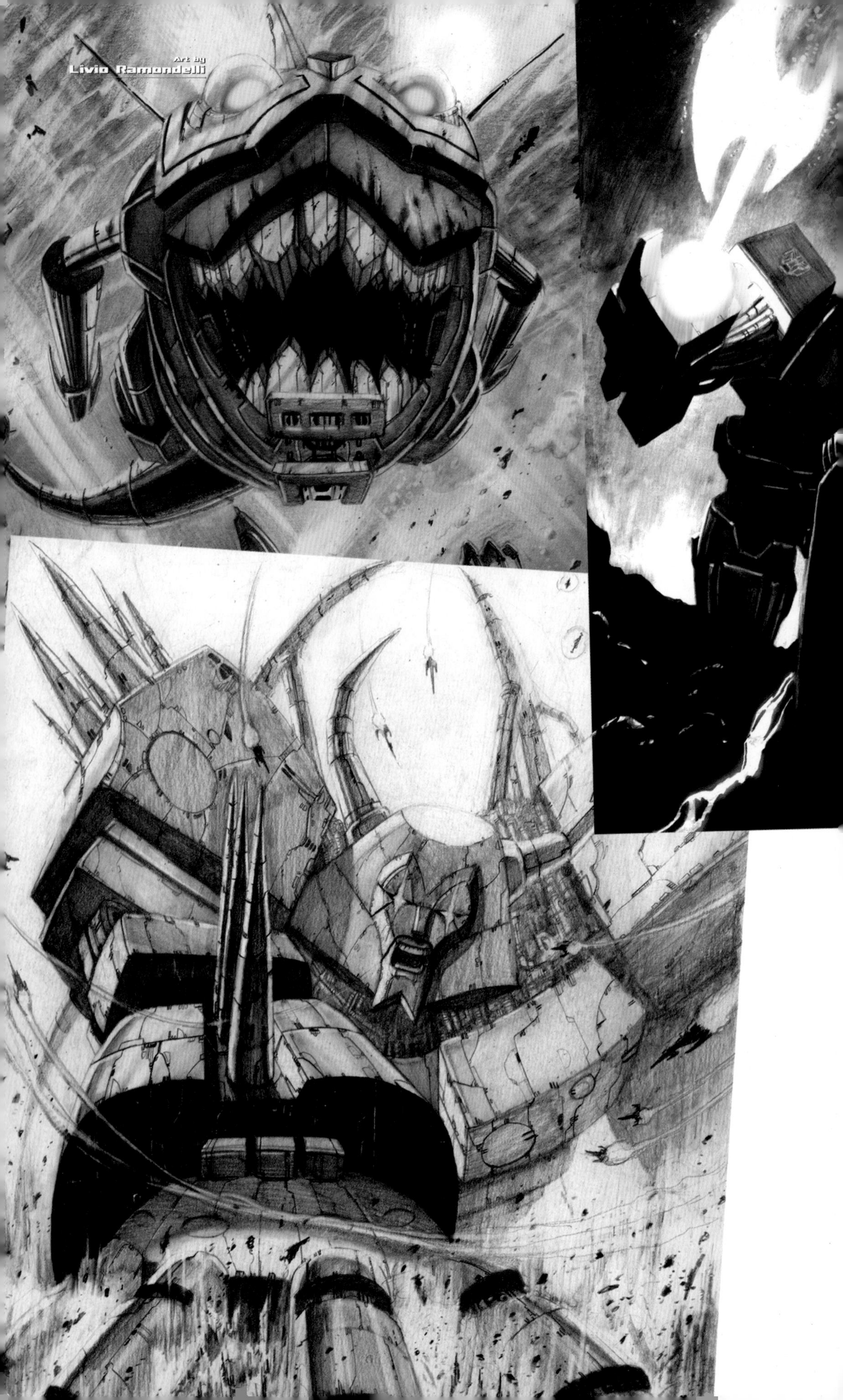
Art by
Livio Ramondelli

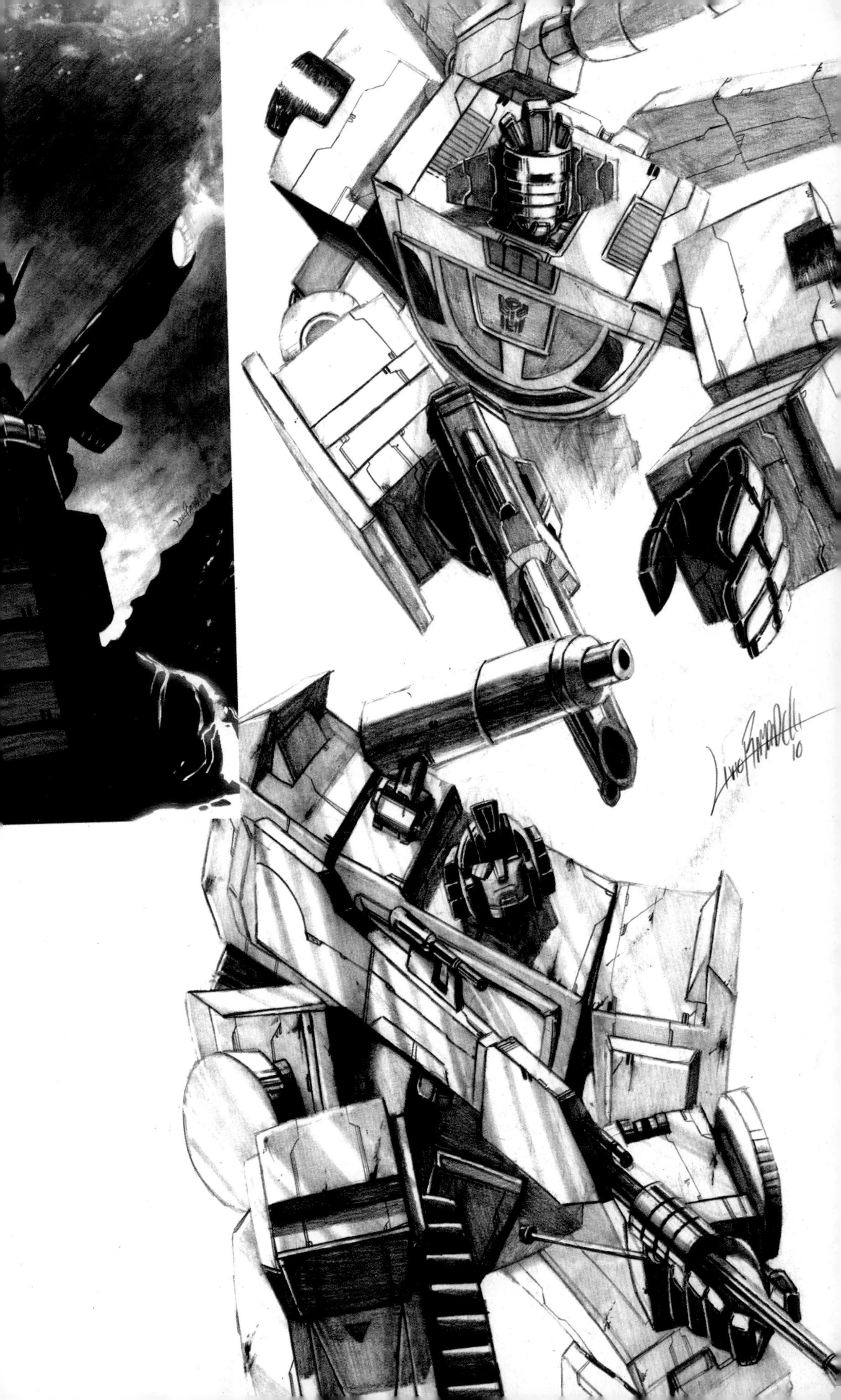

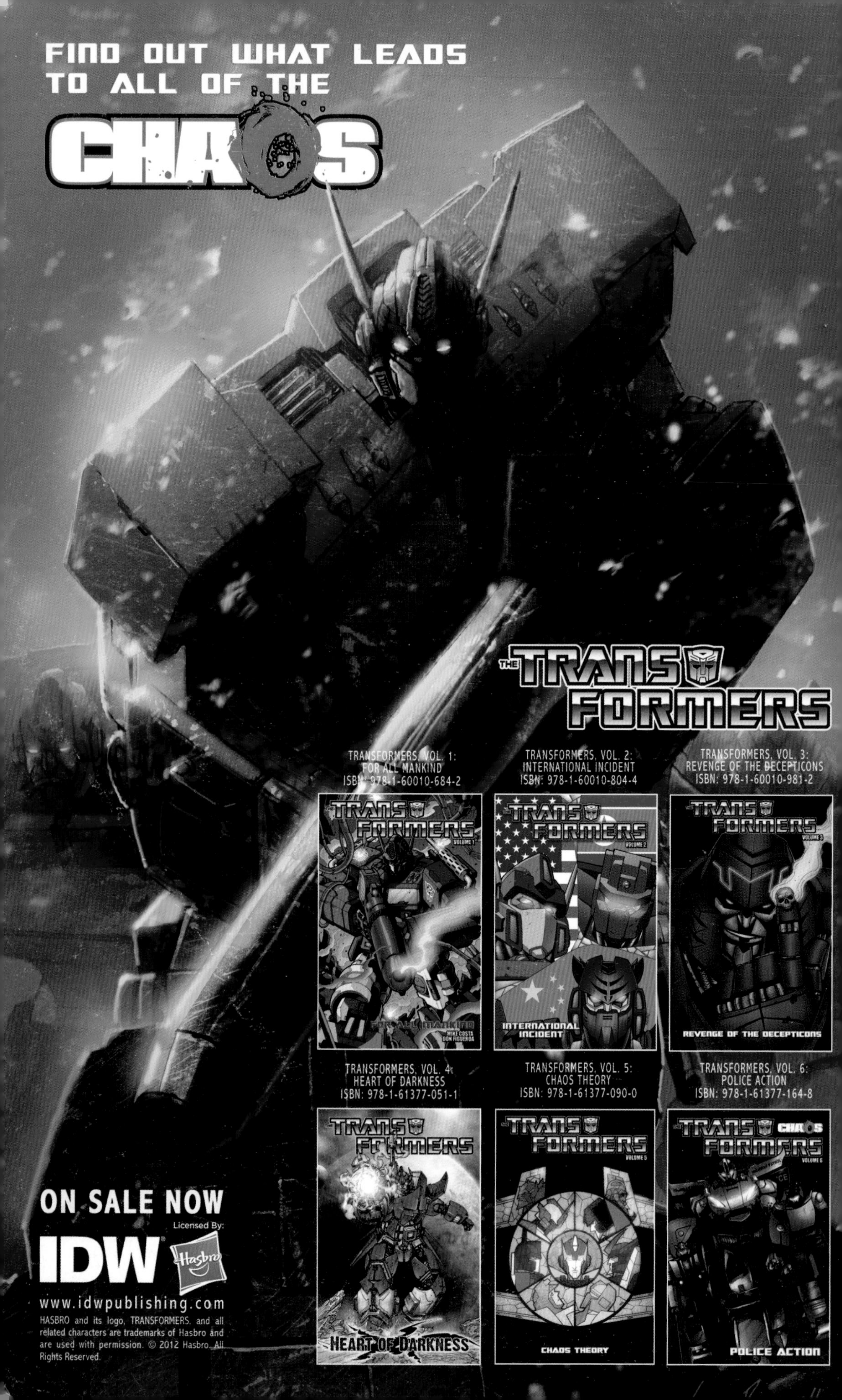
FIND OUT WHAT LEADS
TO ALL OF THE
CHAOS
THE TRANSFORMERS
TRANSFORMERS, VOL. 1:
FOR ALL MANKIND
ISBN: 978-1-60010-684-2
TRANSFORMERS, VOL. 2:
INTERNATIONAL INCIDENT
ISBN: 978-1-60010-804-4
TRANSFORMERS, VOL. 3:
REVENGE OF THE DECEPTICONS
ISBN: 978-1-60010-981-2
TRANSFORMERS, VOL. 4:
HEART OF DARKNESS
ISBN: 978-1-61377-051-1
TRANSFORMERS, VOL. 5:
CHAOS THEORY
ISBN: 978-1-61377-090-0
TRANSFORMERS, VOL. 6:
POLICE ACTION
ISBN: 978-1-61377-164-8
ON SALE NOW
Licensed By:
IDW
Hasbro
www.idwpublishing.com
HASBRO and its logo, TRANSFORMERS, and all related characters are trademarks of Hasbro and are used with permission. © 2012 Hasbro. All Rights Reserved.